UNPACKED

A volume in the series

Histories and Cultures of Tourism

Edited by Eric G. E. Zuelow

A list of titles in this series is available at cornellpress.cornell.edu.

UNPACKED

A HISTORY OF CARIBBEAN TOURISM

BLAKE C. SCOTT

FOREWORD BY ERIC G. E. ZUELOW

CORNELL UNIVERSITY PRESS
Ithaca and London

First published 2022 by Cornell University Press

Librarians: A CIP catalog record for this book is available from the Library of Congress.

ISBN 978-1-501-76640-4 (hardcover)
ISBN 978-1-501-76642-8 (paperback)
ISBN 978-1-501-76643-5 (pdf)
ISBN 978-1-501-76641-1 (epub)

Contents

ILLUSTRATIONS

FOREWORD

Until recently most tourism historians told a story about the evolution of their subject that is defined by democratization. It started with the Grand Tour in Europe when a very small and overwhelmingly elite pastime emerged in which the überwealthy virtually competed with one another to see how much they could spend.[1] Only a few women took the trip, but when they did, the journey offered escape. It offered liberation.[2] With the development of steamboats and railways, as well as shorter work weeks, more and more people sought relaxation, education, and fun through travel.[3] Workers went to the seaside to frolic.[4] Women embarked in large numbers on Cook's Tours.[5] The middle classes headed off to the countryside and then farther afield, anxious to improve themselves. Historical sites and places of natural beauty emerged as secular pilgrimage destinations, places at which to celebrate the nation.[6] By the twentieth century, ideologically driven governments recognized the power of tourism, using it to sell their respective worldviews while gaining followers.[7] Automobiles made it possible for virtually everybody to break from the beaten track (or, at least, to explore it more efficiently and cheaply). After World War II, rapidly improving living standards created mass tourism and more niche travel experiences than you could shake a sun hat at.[8] Soon, everybody was traveling. We were all tourists.

Except, of course, we weren't. Tourism is fundamentally a service industry, yet historians know little about tourism labor. It is not usually well-paid work. Local communities, many inhabited by people of color, tend to benefit little; the big money flows through the hands of poor workers who cannot afford vacations and into the coffers of massive multinational corporations managed by whites.[9] We know very little about this side of the story.

Likewise, leisure travel is premised upon escape from the everyday. It celebrates the exotic. Tourists are encouraged to gaze at locals. They often imagine happy primitives, noble savages living as they have always done. The existence of so-called human safaris is only the most visible and crass manifestation of this practice.[10]

We probably shouldn't be surprised. Tourism spread out of Europe along the vectors of empire. The tourist gaze worked well alongside the stories that at least some imperialists told themselves about the places and people they colonized. The locals were childlike, unsophisticated, effeminate. They needed instruction and improvement.[11] Leisure travelers could not conceive of any reason to challenge this accepted wisdom. Tourists don't often ask a lot of difficult questions. While the promise of education might be part of the appeal of tourism, most travelers do not get a lot of breadth and depth of learning.

Unpacked: A History of Caribbean Tourism represents a vital corrective and a challenge to the narrative of democratization. From the start, Blake C. Scott pulls no punches: "If you are looking for a fun-filled guide to leisure, then read no further and return this book to the shelf. What follows may be disturbing and ruin your vacation." He's only partly right. The content *is* often upsetting, but the stories that he tells are so engagingly rendered, the characters so interesting, and the material so important that this book is a pleasure to read. In fact, it is difficult to put down. What is more, positive change is only possible if we recognize the problem. This book does a beautiful job of showing what it is and how it came to be.

Scott's secret is that he never loses sight of the fact that the story of Caribbean tourism is ultimately a *human* one that is born of *human* decisions, a story of politics as much as society and culture. The "hegemonic identity of a tourist—historically white, affluent, from the United States, Canada, or Europe," Scott writes,

> has depended on profound social shifts in the twentieth century, including understandings of tropical disease and health, transportation technology, and infrastructure, US foreign policy, racialized immigration restrictions, visions of development and nature, and traveler imaginations of abroad and home. But the only way to see all of these elements coming together in one's life and a society's way of being is through the study of lived experience. People carried tourism's history within.

The narrative of tourism is not one of haves and have-nots by happenstance. It was built that way. Developers and promoters made conscious decisions. Inequality, all-too-frequently defined by racial ideas about who is "desirable" and who isn't, is part of the original sin of modern leisure travel.

Given its complexity, detailing the story of tourism is daunting. Scott's strategy is to present a series of short accounts addressing issues such as American imperialism, political decision-making, scientific study and adventure, travel writing, and the often violent story of decolonization. To this end, he merges careful archival research, literary breadth, family history ("I am, like so many, a product of tourism's history"), and even participant observation. It is a successful approach. We ultimately discover that the "Caribbean's history is . . . defined by its *routes* as much as by its historical *roots*."

Scott begins his narrative with the construction of the Panama Canal (1904–14) and the "transformation" of the Caribbean from "disease to desire." In so doing, he demonstrates that US expansion and Caribbean tourism were intimately connected. The canal did not simply represent a "big ditch"—it also symbolized a successful effort to vanquish "a wicked dragon that exhaled poison with every breath," resulting in the death of countless travelers and visitors who "withered away and died as soon as they put foot upon the shore." Once this was done, the canal's infrastructure made it easy for tourists to arrive, and the ability to control disease made it safe for them to do so, repackaging the Caribbean "as a health resort." To tell this story, Scott introduces us to young men keen to earn money and to have adventures, military doctors impatient to defeat mosquito-borne illness, and politicians anxious to promote patriotic feelings that grew from pride in both engineering and medical advances. We meet black Caribbean migrants looking for a brighter future. And we learn about the prevalence of racist views that were exported from the Jim Crow United States to Panama and other Caribbean countries and that soon governed the racial hierarchy of labor in the area. White Americans ran the construction effort; black people "were relegated to positions of dangerous and difficult work." It was a structure that soon came to define the tourism economy as well: white Americans and Europeans were welcome, while black and brown people served them. At the same time, the imperialist infrastructure that made the canal project was also repurposed. Now it constituted the building blocks of leisure time.

With the canal in place and ever-greater numbers traveling to Florida, Cuba, and Panama, political leaders in the circum-Caribbean such as President Belisario Porras, "the architect of Panama's modernization," pushed to expand the travel business. Scott shows how Porras, a Panamanian nationalist with strong anti-imperialist credentials, came to see tourism as the way forward. American imperialism might be bad on the face of it, but Americans had brought better sanitation and improved transportation, so now it was time to capitalize by attracting gringos. As Scott puts it, "tourism appeared to be a potential middle ground between foreign domination and nationalist desires to guide the economy." A National Exposition and other promotional activities, along with investment in leisure infrastructure, followed.

Yet if Porras and other leaders saw tourism as the way forward, they also internalized the notion that it was the "white race," and not dark-skinned residents, who should carry it out because "the actual population of our Republic . . . [is] . . . insufficient to carry out her development." Whites needed to be attracted as residents and visitors, while people of "low social efficiency" could not be expected to contribute more than their blood and sweat. At best, these people were suited to be service staff, and they were even actively barred from tourist areas and casinos unless they had a tray of drinks in hand and the correct uniform on their backs. Such segregation was not unique to Panama: "While Caribbean and Latin American elites created extremely liberal and generous incentives for white people of European descent to visit and invest, they intensely discriminated against nonwhite travelers and migrants." They carefully defined who could be a guest and who could not. Race and nationality were the determining factors. Not surprisingly early tourism promotional materials often omitted "Afro-Caribbean elements of national life."

The evolution of sea and (especially) air travel represented another revolution, warping earlier notions of time and space. But it did little to erase the racial divisions fast becoming enshrined in the travel business. Indeed, new modes of mobility "accentuated rather than decreased social inequalities." Where ships and planes came and went generated a flyover culture. Smaller ports of call were bypassed. Places not of interest to affluent travelers were skipped over and disconnected from elsewhere. Wealth was ever more concentrated in fewer and fewer places. Those not on the route grew increasingly isolated.

There were other factors mediating travel and further ingraining the desire for Caribbean holidays. Scientists and naturalists alike reported on their trips to the tropics, creating a popular image of the rugged explorer, an "Indiana Jones or Roosevelt-type" individual. The tourism industry moved to capitalize. Scott sums up the result: "Adventure had reached a ubiquitous role in popular culture in the twentieth century." But just as imperial regimes—the British Raj, for example—strictly limited hunting to whites while allowing South Asians only to be guides or to flush tigers out into the open for shooting,[12] so research and adventure experiences in the Caribbean were usually limited to white males. People of color could play a service role, but otherwise they were deemed unsuitable. This legacy was passed on to tourism, which

> carried the historical baggage of privileged and exclusionary practices of colonial explorer culture. . . . Modern tourism has mimicked and packaged this type of social and naturalized order for mass consumption, where tourists can imagine themselves as explorers of undiscovered nature, while guides, trail cutters, maids, drivers, and a whole

host of servants labored in the shadows to produce the sensation of discovery.

Authors, including figures such as Ernest Hemingway, added another role that white tourists could attempt to inhabit: the "writer's lifestyle." They fueled a desire to go abroad in search of experience and the usually unrealized dream of making a living through itinerancy and prose. They functioned as mediators, selling self-exile while depending on the very forces they claimed to reject—technology and political and economic power—in order to make their escapes possible. At the same time, they presented perceptions of racial difference and pleasure-seeking to wide readerships. Hemingway, for example, "employed racist and racial privilege in his stories." His leading characters, "almost always white men," face down danger while embodying "something special" and worth aspiring to. Meanwhile, people of color "were depicted in servile positions." In the end, the early Caribbean tourism industry emerged as a "white man's fantasy," and authors sold it to a wide readership. That legacy still matters.

Given this background, it should be no surprise that tourist infrastructure, and especially prominent hotels, often provided tantalizing targets for "the cross-cultural clash at the heart of decolonization." As Scott carefully details, the Hotel Tivoli, a popular American-owned destination for American and European tourists in Panama City, was attacked in early 1964, including an effort by two young Panamanians to bomb the hotel from the air as part of a popular uprising against the US presence in the area. Their effort failed but was part of larger three-day assault complete with bullets, rocks, and an attempt to set it on fire.

The hotel, which opened in 1906, hosted white guests served by black waiters. This arrangement did not bother the visitors. For Panamanians, however, the lavish hotel represented a shocking opposite to a daily life defined by struggle. They could not enjoy the Tivoli, a potent symbol of the racism that was everywhere; they were banned from staying there. They also lacked adequate health care or public education through high school. Americans enjoyed "the best of conditions—swimming pools, tennis courts, gardens"—while locals lived in "dilapidated shacks." Scott makes clear that the Tivoli is but one example of such backlash. Fidel Castro quickly turned the Havana Hilton hotel into his headquarters, naming the building "Free Havana." Shepheard's Hotel in Egypt suffered a similar fate, symbolizing the "end of British decadence." Now these sites stood for something different from the decades of foreign consumption and excess. They represented a population that simply wasn't going to take it anymore.

Such violence did little to eliminate the now fully enshrined racial dynamic or to erase tourism practices that embodied it. As nationalist governments took root in the wake of decolonization, they adopted tourism as a promising economic engine. The inequalities that defined the practice from the beginning remained. As *Unpacked* makes abundantly clear, tourism is ultimately a product of empire, but tourists "have seemingly forgotten this process of historical assemblage." "Tourists do not need to know where their ideas and behavior come from in order to be influenced by them."

Seen from this vantage point, the story of tourism is anything but a story of democratization. Most of the world was excluded from the start. We certainly can hope for something better. As this book enters production, tourists are once again boarding airplanes and cruise ships following COVID-19 lockdowns. As they do this, columnists and commentators point to environmental and class-related problems with the industry. They note that locals have been pushed out of the old city of Venice, unable to afford to live there. They draw attention to the problem of overtourism in many sensitive historic and natural environments. They worry about the low salaries associated with most tourism labor. They wonder if the relaunch of tourism might promise the possibility of a reset. Perhaps a new tourism could emerge from the pandemic, a leisure travel premised on sustainability, social responsibility, mutual understanding, and greater economic fairness.[13]

Maybe. The trick is to know where the tourism we've known came from and why, to recognize its many failings, and to reflect on the discourses and behaviors that have defined it since inception. We cannot do any of those things, however, until we recognize its complexity. This book represents a vital step in that direction. While the story it tells may not be immediately heartwarming, we should *not* put it back on the shelf for that. Quite the opposite. The rewards for reading it are just too many and too great. Who knows? Perhaps we might one day be able to fairly tell a story of democratization that is actually realized.

Eric G. E. Zuelow

PREFACE:
THE PROBLEM OF MOBILITY

If you are looking for a fun-filled guide to leisure, then read no further and return this book to the shelf. What follows may be disturbing and ruin your vacation. Facts sometimes have that effect.

In the spring of 2020, as cities shut down and national borders closed to stop the spread of the novel coronavirus (COVID-19), it became clear that travel for work, for pleasure, or for necessity was the key human vector for the emerging pandemic. Tourists were told to go home. Migrants were forced to flee or were stuck on the border. Transportation networks from airplanes to cruise ships to trains closed their routes. It was a global shutdown. But despite what politicians and health authorities claimed, we were not all "in the same boat." As global cities such as New York and Tokyo went into quarantine, the richest neighborhoods quickly emptied as residents fled to second homes and vacation rentals, while the poor and struggling classes were stuck, immobile, for months.[1]

The spread of COVID-19 was another reminder of a profound and global predicament: the problem of mobility. As the sociologist and mobilities scholar Mimi Sheller summed up the situation, "all around the world people and governments are grappling with a series of crises related to how we move."[2] Whether a pandemic, a hurricane, or its seeming opposite—a vacation—the issue of mobility remains a central concern for the human experience. The historian and Caribbean scholar C. L. R. James articulated this modern problem in his 1963 memoir, explaining, "Time would pass, old empires would fall and new ones take their place, the relations of countries and the relations of classes had to change, before I discovered that it is not quality of goods and utility that matter, but movement; not where you are or what you have, but where you have come from, where you are going and the rate at which you are getting there."[3] In short, some people can travel, be socially mobile, and change their reality, and some cannot. On the extremes, some people are able to leave home for pleasure and in luxury, while others never get the chance to leave or, worse, are forced to travel to survive, to escape persecution and poverty.

The roots of this problem are historically deep, but its sustaining ideas and social practices—the freedom of movement or lack thereof—have taken on renewed power in our globalized era.

There are of course many ways to examine the problem of mobility, but as I argue in this book, the history of tourism offers a necessary and illuminating perspective on this now taken-for-granted aspect of modern life. Tourism embodies mobile haves and have-nots. According to the United Nations, the tourism industry also accounts for one out of every ten jobs in the world.[4] The industry is one of the world's largest and most lucrative economic activities. Nearly everyone, it seems, has dreamed of a vacation. But in practice, leisure travel remains an exclusive and elite form of mobility. Parallel to mass tourism in the early twenty-first century, the world has also experienced one of the worst migratory crises in history. Millions of immigrants, fleeing violence, poverty, and environmental disaster, have been turned away at border after border. Meanwhile, privileged tourists have traveled southward visiting luxurious resorts.

In the center of the Americas—the Caribbean—hundreds of millions of tourists have gone on vacation, while countless Mexicans, Cubans, Haitians, Jamaicans, and Central Americans from those same destinations have searched for a clandestine way to cross the border into the United States. On average, it costs a tourist $1,500 to take a luxury Caribbean cruise crossing multiple national borders, with few questions ever asked by the authorities. In contrast, an undocumented migrant from Central America seeking a better life may pay upward of $10,000 to be hidden in trucks and safe houses, abused by smugglers, and demonized by politicians.[5] Something obviously is wrong. Some travelers are welcomed (red carpets rolled out, lobsters buttered, best wine served), while others are treated as unwanted refugees, hunted and locked up in prisons, separated from their children and deported south. Some people have been deemed "desirable" travelers and others as illegal "undesirables." Where in the world did these boundaries of mobility and immobility come from?

Unpacked examines this paradox of mobility by examining the history of tourism in the Caribbean. One might ask, however, why focus on the Caribbean region when so many communities around the world are impacted by these mobile/immobile issues? First, the Caribbean is one of the most tourism-dependent regions in the world. Second, the region is essential for understanding the history of globalization. The circum-Caribbean, a region stretching from Florida to the Antilles to Central America and northern South America, was the first truly global crossroads in the modern world. Analyzing the history of one of the most international industries from the perspective of the Caribbean reveals historical connections between tourism and the history of other political, cultural, economic, and environmental forms of interconnection known broadly today as globalization. The history of Caribbean tourism is a bellwether for a global phenomenon of mobility / immobility.

Tourism is also a form of travel I know, and I imagine many readers will know, from personal experience. Many of us have felt tourism's impact from both sides, traveling as tourists but also coming from communities that have consistently been *touristed* upon. Growing up in central Florida, in a small community neighboring Orlando, I can never forget the image of a disembarking tourist, nor can I forget the intimate proximity of travel inequities. My home state is a destination for retirees and tourists, with money to spend. But the peninsula has also been the destination for migrants and refugees from the Global South. In Orlando, on one side of International Drive, there are tourist attractions and luxurious hotels; on the other, there are rundown apartment complexes and crowded homes of undocumented workers who make the tourist machine operate and who, with their low wages, have kept the vacation dream affordable. This entangled relationship between visible leisure and often invisible labor is socially revealing yet mostly ignored by the traveling public.

Local people, born and raised in vacation towns, have also joined the global tourist economy, serving drinks, food, and entertainment. For a smile and a fun experience, they may earn more than working in a field related to a university degree. In the city where I now live, Charleston, South Carolina, over seven million tourists annually visited in 2018 and 2019. A historically southern, racially fraught, military-industrial port town, Charleston has come to depend on international tourism for its economy and arguably its identity. For many of my neighbors and young people contemplating their future, the quick money to be made in a bar or hotel on King Street has become enticing. However, to be in service of someone else's vacation every day, year after year, can be taxing on one's body and soul. As the global crisis of spring 2020 reminds us, tourist dollars can also disappear as fast as they arrived, leaving businesses and service workers stranded and unable to pay their bills.[6] The golden tourist eggs all cracked.

Anthropologists, sociologists, journalists, and social critics have tried to make sense of the tourist cultures shaping communities in the US South, the Caribbean islands, and throughout the world of sunny and tropical destinations. These studies, though, more often focus on the present, describing contemporary effects. But I want to understand—and I hope you do too—how and why did it ever begin? One cannot assume that it was always this way or that it had to be. How does a community become a tourist destination? What does the history of tourism in the Caribbean tell us about the region and its position in the world? What can history reveal about ongoing experiences of mobility and immobility, of disparate identities of tourists and migrants, of desirable and undesirable travelers?

Through the power of storytelling, closely following and analyzing the experiences of an earlier generation of travelers, one can begin to understand some of the historical *roots* and transnational *routes* that shaped tourism and mobility in the modern era. Beginnings matter. Social and economic patterns formed over a century ago have become the guiding principles and practices of today's tourist culture. We are all, for better and for worse, living the effects of a vacation fantasy.

Acknowledgments

Books like this one depend on a village to raise them. In this case, the community is dispersed across the mainland United States and the Caribbean. I have many people to thank. At the College of Charleston, my colleagues Lisa Pinley Covert, Sandra Slater, Mary Jo Fairchild, Jacob Steere Williams, Malte Pehl, Sarah Wuigk, Andrew Alwine, Robert Sapp, Kristen McLean, Beatriz Maldonado-Bird, Max Kovalov, Doug Friedman, Brumby McLeod, Amy Malek, and Hollis France have created a supportive and inspiring community to share and refine ideas. The Fulbright Program, the Smithsonian Institution, the Virginia Wellington Cabot Foundation, the University of Texas at Austin, and the School of Languages, Cultures, and World Affairs at the College of Charleston have also offered generous support and given me the time and space to think and write.

I am especially grateful to Frank A. Guridy, who offered invaluable advice in the earliest stages of this project while I was a doctoral student at UT-Austin. Virginia Garrard-Burnett and Mark Lawrence also created a thoughtful network of knowledge and accountability for creatively researching US–Latin American relations. While I was at the Smithsonian, Pamela Henson pushed me to dig deeper into the archives and my own assumptions of what it meant to be a fellow traveler. Jeffrey Stine and Marcel LaFollette also offered kind words and useful reading recommendations during my time there.

At Cornell University Press, everyone has been kind, professional, and on time, despite the difficult pandemic conditions. I would like to thank in particular my editors at the press, Emily Andrew, Bethany Wasik, Eric Zuelow, and Don McKeon, for their insights and dedication to this project. Along the long journey to production, fragments of the general argument (in its earliest iteration) appeared as "From Disease to Desire: The Rise of Tourism at the Panama Canal," *Environmental History* 21, no. 2 (April 2016): 270–77, along with variants of chapters 3 and 6 as "Changing Caribbean Routes: The Rise of International Air Travel," in *The Business of Leisure: Tourism History in Latin America and the Caribbean*, edited by Andrew Grant Wood (Lincoln: University of Nebraska Press, 2021), and "Revolution at the Hotel: Panama and Luxury Travel in the Age of Decolonisation," *Journal of Tourism History* 10, no. 2 (June 2018): 146–64. I appreciate the chance to work through my research ideas in those earlier versions, and the opportunity to combine, add, and reassemble them into a unique monograph.

Over the years, much of the research for this book took place in Panama. The isthmus has been an insightful place to think about interconnections and the movement of people, ideas, and goods across the Caribbean. I first visited Panama, now decades ago, as an undergraduate student when Lucas Castrellón invited a group of college friends to meet his family. Our undergrad alma mater, Florida State University, has been a popular university for Panamanians looking to study in the United States. During our conversations, Lucas and his family taught me more about Panama and US-Panamanian relations than I could ever learn in books. I thank them for their friendship and historical insights. In Panama, I'd also like to thank in particular Noris Herrera, Michael Brown, Orlando Savage, Jesús David Blanco, Diana Moschos, and the students at Cambio Creativo, a youth educational program in Colón. As a volunteer at Cambio Creativo for several years, I learned from fellow teachers and organizers Rose Cromwell, Kumi James, Martin Danyluk, Maya deVries, and Susan Brewer. Carrying out archival research in Panama, I also met inspiring colleagues: Ashley Carse, Marixa Lasso, Megan Raby, Ezer Vierba, Christine Keiner, Matt Scalena, Katherine Zien, Jeff Parker, Stanley Heckadon-Moreno, Patricia Pizzurno and Francisco Herrera.

Traveling the route of my research, I journeyed from Panama to Jamaica and Cuba, where I also completed archival research and relied on the support of colleagues on those islands. In Kingston, I'd like to thank Courtney Minors and his brother for going beyond the hospitality of renting a room. In Havana, Julia Grecia Portela Ponce de León and her son Marcel also opened their home, gave me access to their extensive library, and treated me as if I were part of the family. At the National Library of Cuba, Rey Salermo shared insights on Cuban literature and culture. Fellow researchers Takkara Brunson, Joseph Gonzalez, and Fidel Luis Acosta also offered guidance and companionship.

Consulting archives and libraries across the Americas—from New York to DC to Miami, Havana, Kingston, and Panama City—introduced me to an array of source materials and experiences: memoirs, interviews, personal papers, government reports and correspondence, travelogues, and newspapers, among others. Deciding what to include and exclude in this story was often a difficult decision. A book that attempts to account for a history crisscrossing national borders inevitably needs help from other researchers. My research interweaves both original research and secondary sources to tell a larger story. To all the historians and archivists who shared their work, I will be eternally grateful.

When I began to formulate this project, back at UT-Austin, a diverse and inspiring community of colleagues and friends also influenced my thinking. The PhD program in Latin American and Caribbean history felt collegial and at times familial. For the warm feelings I carried with me out of Texas, I am grateful to Franz Hensel-Riveros, Maria José Afanador, Alex Ferrell, Andres Lombana Bermudez, Brian Stauffer, Manuel Salas, Rudy Dunlap, Eva Hershaw, Pamela Neumann, Cristina Metz, Eyal Weinberg, Mary Pauline Lowry, Kieran Fitzgerald, Juan Sequeda, Juan Camilo Agudelo, José Barragán, Matt Gildner, and Mónica Alexandra Jiménez.

Before I moved west, Austin was already in my imagination. During my time at the University of Georgia as an MA student, Pamela Voekel had encouraged me to apply to her alma mater in Texas. Pamela has been an inspiring example of how to be a critical and engaged scholar. I have carried her lessons with me ever since. In Athens, Paul Sutter, Reinaldo Román, and Bethany Moreton also encouraged me to critically deconstruct the past. My colleagues from UGA's graduate program—Levi Van Sant, La Shonda Mims, and Tore Olson —reminded me that the key to learning is to appreciate and listen to those around you.

Growing up in Florida was also a source of early research ideas. While an undergraduate student at the state university, trying to make sense of U.S. foreign policy in the midst of another war, I met a professor who helped me understand its long history. Matt Childs, another UT-alum, gave me needed academic direction. His insights, his reading recommendations, and his sense of care for students guided me to graduate studies in Latin American and Caribbean history. Through the study of history, I began to find answers for the news I watched and read about between 2001 and 2005. US foreign policy and war in the Middle East have a history, I realized, closer to home in the Caribbean. For those transformative years in Tallahassee, I'd also like to thank Joseph Saunders and Chad Carter for the conversations and travels we shared.

In the beginning and the end, I am grateful for my family. Back in Winter Park, Florida, my parents encouraged and supported my curiosity to learn and critically imagine. My grandmother, Cornelia, aka "Moe," was also there for every step of my education. Born in 1913 to Italian immigrants, Moe was my first history teacher, telling stories about her childhood, the Great

Depression, World War II, and the trials and joys of living in Florida before Disney World. This book is written in her honor and in memory of the lessons she shared with me, our family, and the generations of students she influenced as a teacher.

Introduction

Growing up in Florida's Vacationland

> It seems to me that certain basic, general elements of our modern-day educated society shine through, as it were, in the picture of this nice little family, oh, not all the elements, and they shine only microscopically, "like to the sun in a small water-drop," yet something has been reflected, something has betrayed itself.
>
> —Fyodor Dostoevsky, *The Brothers Karamazov*

In 1968, after half a century in the American Midwest, my grandparents retired to Florida. It was their dream to live year-round in the Florida Keys, what folks at the time called the "American Caribbean." After World War II, they had begun to drive down each winter from Illinois with their three young children and rent a house near the water. In retirement, Cornelia and Howard Scott planned to return permanently to claim their own piece of "paradise." "We loved it," my grandmother remembered. "We would have people come down, and they would stay for weeks!" While Grandpa Howard golfed, played poker, drank, and fished with his buddies, Grandma tended the house and garden and entertained guests.[1] It was a vacation fantasy, rooted in history, that would have a long-term impact on our family. Their decision to move south, in fact, sparked a small migration. Soon the next generation was living in Florida as well and raising their own families in the "Sunshine State."[2] From tourists and retirees, we became Floridians, residents of vacationland.

"My folks are sixty," the comedian Jerry Seinfeld liked to joke. "They're moving to Florida. They don't want to go. But's that's the law!"[3] Seinfeld was on to something. It seems obvious and sometimes funny that "old folks" would vacation and retire to Florida and to other sunny destinations. It was a common American dream in the twentieth century, and it still is. Hotels,

1

restaurants and bars, beverage distributors, airlines, tour companies, and local and national governments have reified images of tropical vacationing. On US Route 1, the old highway running down Florida's east coast all the way to Key West, travelers pass an abundance of hotels and attractions with images of wavy palm trees and clichéd names like "Caribbean Dream" and "Tropical Inn." As tourism operators big and small, including Costco, tell customers, "idyllic beaches, sapphire seas and swashbuckling tales make the Caribbean a warm-weather wonderland." This promise of pleasure and escape into sunshine and warm weather has materialized into a lucrative industry and also a set of social practices affecting both tourists and those visited.[4]

Where, though, did this desire for tropical leisure come from? What happened to communities and social relations when millions of people embraced this mobile mode of living? These questions extend across national borders and across the Caribbean. They are not just about Florida or grandparents. The rise of tourism has profoundly reshaped the economies, cultures, and ecologies of communities across the circum-Caribbean and around the world. Yet few visitors, and in fact few locals, ever ask: how did this tourist way of life become so culturally pervasive?

This book denaturalizes the dream and experience of a Caribbean vacation. It documents how tourism was a historical creation, not the result of inevitable or timeless forces. It asks all of us—tourists and locals—to question taken-for-granted desirability and examine its origins. More specifically, the book sheds new light on the Caribbean's historical relationship with the United States, proving that imperial expansion in the early twentieth century was a key catalyst in the region's development of tourism. Critics of the industry have argued that modern tourism is a form of neocolonialism.[5] But rarely in these critiques do we learn about the cause-and-effect chain of historical connections linking the Caribbean's colonial past to the present. *Unpacked* documents those very real and historically grounded linkages. After indigenous communities and landscapes in the American South and Florida were conquered by the US military and white settler colonialism, soldiers and colonial administrators continued farther south into the Caribbean basin of Latin America.

Tourism development in the Caribbean followed a pattern, from conquest to playground, from Florida to Cuba all the way to Panama. Scholars, however, have tended to focus on tourism's history in one particular nation or community, especially after World War II, and in the process have overlooked earlier geographic and cultural connections stretching across the region.[6] Tourism in the circum-Caribbean began as a maritime route dependent on imperial and commercial expansion emanating from the United States, calling on various ports of call. The industry relied on shipping and its transnational routes. To visit Havana as a tourist, for instance, involved visiting other sea-ports, such as Key West and, farther south, Colón in Panama. The history of tourism in one particular destination cannot be understood in geographic or analytical isolation. By unearthing this forgotten transnational history, it becomes clear there is not a US history and a Caribbean history of tourism but an interdependent one.

Although the contemporary tourism industry evokes romantic visions of the Caribbean's past, industry boosters and consumers are seemingly unaware of the long arc of power, violence, and social and environmental transformation that made the industry possible. In dialogue with scholars already versed in tourism's history, this book provides a new layer of con-text showing that Caribbean tourism began decades before the post–World War II economic boom traditionally studied.[7] Tourist perceptions and experi-ences of the Caribbean had actually begun to shift in the first decade of the twentieth century, from imagining a dangerous and diseased crossroads to seeing the region as a desirable destination associated with comfort and lux-ury. US imperial expansion to Cuba and Panama, and the subsequent need to limit the spread of yellow fever and malaria, precipitated this new era of leisure travel. It was at that point, at the turn of the twentieth century, that the Caribbean became a conquered "paradise" reimagined and increasingly accessible to tourism. Drawing on research from archival materials from the United States and Caribbean nations such as Cuba, Jamaica, and Panama, *Unpacked* examines the multifaceted ways that imperialism and visions of the frontier, capitalism, science and technology, environmental change, literary imaginations, and political power struggles converged to remake the Carib-bean into a modern vacation.[8]

Islands and peninsulas, contrary to timeless-looking brochures, did not rise out of the sea to bless eager visitors in search of paradise. Before the time of tourists and retirees, diverse Native American communities, Euro-pean conquistadores and pirates, settlers and frontiersmen, and slaves and planters also traveled and occupied the Caribbean region. Early European and Euro-American travelers, like their tourist descendants, imagined the Caribbean, and the tropics more generally, as an escape from the confines of modern civilization. The past and present are more connected than most people realize. As the environmental historian Richard Grove described it, the tropical environment as early as the 1600s became "the symbolic location for the idealized landscapes and aspirations of the Western imagination."[9] This cultural desire—a longing—for the Caribbean remains embedded in hegemonic visions of leisure.

Tourism in the Caribbean, however, is dependent on both historical con- tinuities and dramatic change. During the long colonial era (the 1600s to the late 1800s), travel to the Caribbean was also considered extremely danger- ous. Travelers wishfully dreamed of the region but, paradoxically, viewed it as a violent and diseased world, far from the comforts of a relaxing vaca- tion. Sickness and death stalked visitors. As the tourist historian Catherine Cocks has documented, at the end of the nineteenth century, "most Euro- pean and North American whites [still] regarded the tropics as the 'white's man grave.'" Yet by the early twentieth century, just a few decades later, this perception had begun to fade. By the mid-twentieth century, it was com- mon belief that the circum-Caribbean, from Florida to Panama, provided "ideal winter resorts for vacationers."[10] By the end of the century, leisure and luxury had solidified into seemingly timeless and natural parts of the tropical landscape. "The very sun itself," as one author noted on his vacation, "seemed preset for our comfort."[11]

Tourists now travel and imagine the circum-Caribbean as if it were always a place to vacation, detached from history. This mystification of the region has obscured the tourism industry's foundational history. There is, of course, precedent for this type of cultural amnesia. The Caribbean was not alone in its historic transformation from supposedly hostile (yet idealized) colonial territory to hospitable tourist destination. Similar developments occurred in the Middle East and on the African continent as Britain and France expanded and consolidated their colonial empires.[12] Likewise in Southeast Asia, as Eu- ropean powers and the United States expanded their geopolitical influence, so too did the possibilities for tourism. In the Americas, this imaginary and geographic shift also happened with the conquest of the western frontier. Yet most visitors and many scholars view the history of international rela- tions, which includes war, violence, and political intrigue, as separate from the cultural and economic development of tourism. This does not mean, however, that they were historically removed from one another. Analyzing the history of wilderness and its relationship to US continental expansion, the environmental historian William Cronon provocatively argued that "one of the most striking proofs of the cultural invention of wilderness is its thor- oughgoing erasure of the history from which it sprang."[13] Lack of societal reflection about the historical emergence of hegemonic culture can be proof of its ongoing power. Modern life, it seems, depends on forgetfulness. The anthropologist Clifford Geertz expressed a similar insight when he described the unique social ability to hide the human process of landscape creation: "As a chameleon tunes himself to his setting, growing into it as though he were part of it, just another dun rock or green leaf, a society tunes itself to its landscape . . . until it seems to an outside observer that it could not possibly be anywhere else than where it is, and that, located where it is, it could not be otherwise than what it is."[14] In short, only a culture and a people so intimately familiar with a set of social practices and beliefs could *naturalize* them out of history. "For him," as the author Jorge Luis Borges once put it, "they were part of reality, he had no reason to emphasize them."[15] Tourism appears to be no different. As postcolonial Caribbean scholars such as Angelique Nixon and Michel-Rolph Trouillot have argued, however, "we must uncover the silences of the past in order to understand our present."[16] Examining the Caribbean's particular history of tourism provides evidence for uncovering a global pattern of tourism development linked to the history of political and social power, landscape creation, and the economic inequalities of modern production and consumption.

Behind every historic event or process, though, we must remember the people. To make sense of tourism's emergence, we also have to learn about the stories of flesh-and-blood protagonists who created its institutions and its routes. Long before tourists ever arrived at their vacation destination, expectations formed and percolated in the mind, giving shape to what the sociologist John Urry called the "tourist gaze." This gaze is historically and socially organized. It depends on layers of history and "many professional experts" who "help to construct and develop one's gaze as a tourist."[17] This book deconstructs the gaze guiding tourists to the Caribbean by analyzing the mobile histories of "many professional experts"—exemplary travelers, state officials, explorers, naturalists, writers, developers, family members, and perpetual wanderers—who made and supported largely Western perceptions and practices of leisure. Scholarly efforts to categorically distinguish tourist from traveler, or explorer or colonial administrator, conceal more than they historically reveal. This is a history about the privilege of mobility, dependent on its opposite. Various forms of travel and work, from tour guide and colonial official to migrant laborer and service worker, conditioned the modern tourist experience. A whole host of transnational actors designed and participated in the Caribbean's tourism industry. *Unpacked* follows these diverse travelers and culture-shapers into the past, following a route linking the US East Coast with the Caribbean, from South Florida to Cuba to the Isthmus of Panama. By following intimate travel stories and analytically connecting them, we can see historical patterns essential to the emergence and experience of what has become a quintessential Caribbean vacation.[18] This history is neither a linear narrative nor a universal experience, yet it reflects "like to the sun in a small water-drop" key fragments of the present.

Defining Tourism

But before continuing, what do we mean by "tourism"? How should we define it? The first official appearance of the word in English, according to the Oxford English Dictionary, occurred in 1811. At its etymological roots, tourism derives from the Greek word *tornos*, which was a tool that made a circular motion. In this sense, its etymology differs dramatically and in a revealing way from the linguistic history of travel, which comes from the French word *travail* for hardship, with its roots in the Latin word *tripalium*, meaning "three stakes" used for torture. Travel as travail offered no guarantee of return and, as its genealogy suggests, no guarantee of pleasure or even survival. It was, at its essence, dangerous. Tourism, in contrast, implied a circular itinerary, leaving one place for another and then comfortably returning to one's original point of departure.[19] To be a tourist, by definition then, included significantly less risk than being a traveler in the traditional sense.

The tourism historian Eric Zuelow has argued that in its simplest and most contemporary form tourism refers to specialized "travel in pursuit of pleasure and an escape from everyday realities."[20] In short, a pleasure tour. Ascem Anand, author of the *Advance Dictionary of Tourism*, complements Zuelow's definition, describing tourism "as a composite phenomenon which embraces the incidence of [a] mobile population of travelers who are strangers to the places they visit. It is essentially a pleasure activity in which money earned in one's normal domicile is spent in the place visited."[21] The tourist, in this way, is a privileged traveler, someone who can safely leave home and become a stranger on the move spending money in search of escape and comfort. This mobile, comfortable search has become a trillion-dollar global industry. From Europe to Southeast Asia to the Caribbean, the tourism industry has become for many nations and communities their most important economic sector.

Although travel—for work, for food, for curiosity, for spirituality—is as old as human history, tourism on a mass international scale is a relatively new experience. John Urry and Dean MacCannell, leading scholars in the field of tourism studies, have characterized the industry as a modern phenomenon arising only in the past two hundred years. "Acting as a tourist," Urry famously argued, "is one of the defining characteristics of being modern. . . . It has become a marker of status in modern societies and is also thought to be necessary for good health and a cosmopolitan outlook."[22] The scholarly community continues to debate, though, when tourism as a social practice actually began. Some historians argue that tourism as an experience of comfort and pleasure dates back to the Roman Empire (and before then, the Greeks) when the wealthy sought "rest, meditation, and pleasure" in coastal and mountain villas such as Pompeii and Tivoli. Other scholars date tourism's modern origins to the era of the European Grand Tour. In the eighteenth and nineteenth centuries, as wealth accumulated in Europe's metropolitan cores, elites sent their sons and occasionally daughters to seek "enlighten-ment" and social status by studying and touring the European continent. "According to the law of custom, and perhaps of reason," a young Edward Gibbon claimed, "foreign travel completes the education of an English gentleman."[23] A small group of young elites from the new republics of the Americas also engaged in the European Grand Tour.[24] In general, however, in the early nineteenth century tourism remained an activity reserved for wealthy elites touring Europe.

After the American Civil War (1861–65), more tourists from the United States began to imagine and engage in overseas tourism, although still on a limited scale. In March 1867 a retired Civil War ship (the *Quaker City*) departed from New York City on a "great Pleasure Excursion to Europe and the Holy Land." Aboard was the author Mark Twain, who later re-counted his trip in the book *Innocents Abroad*. "It was," Twain wrote, "a novelty in the way of Excursions—its like had not been thought of before, and it compelled that interest which attractive novelties always command. It was to be a picnic on a gigantic scale."[25] By the end of the nineteenth century, urbanization and industrialization encouraged a growing mass of middle- and upper-class travelers to embrace this tourist mentality. Rather than travel in search of wealth or land or religious purity, more and more people began to travel as a means of temporary respite. Most of these tour-ists, though, remained within the confines of the traditional European tour or the national boundaries of their own home country.[26] To go abroad was still prohibitively expensive and required weeks, if not months, of free time. It was also viewed, especially outside temperate zones, as potentially deadly. Only in the twentieth century did tourism evolve from being an exclusive activity focused on Europe and a select number of resorts in the temperate zones of North America to become a societal rite of passage that stretched around the world, especially impacting communities in tropical and semi-tropical environments.[27]

I first began to wonder about the history of this global expansion of tour-ism while growing up in a small tourist town in Florida. How did my family, descended from the far corners of Europe and later the American Midwest and Northeast, end up here? And why did the tourists and retirees, in the millions, keep coming south? What is the history of this unfolding now? The story that follows is a microhistory dealing with these historical and

existential questions that hits close to home, which also embraces a genealogical approach for examining how the past accumulates into the present.

Grapevine of Tropical Paradise

In October 1961 city officials of Waukegan, Illinois, dined on 475 pounds of
"giant sea bass," along with Greek salad and French fries. The local newspaper, the *Waukegan News-Sun*, reported the massive meal and included a
front-page photograph of the collection of fish laid out on main street. The
story goes that Edward Havelka, a former Waukegan resident, had taken a
group of friends fishing near Key West, but they didn't have much luck. After his guests returned north to their families and responsibilities, however,
Havelka decided to go out and catch the fish himself. He then packed five
huge groupers, known as jewfish at the time (now goliath grouper), on dry
ice and drove fifteen hundred miles back to Illinois to share the fish with
friends and family. His trip home generated lots of interest in the community.
People crowded into the street to see the monstrous fish and listen to stories
of life in the "American Caribbean."[28]

Tuesday, October 10, 1961   THE KEY WEST CITIZEN   Page 5

FIGURE 1.   Pedestrians on a busy street in Waukegan, Illinois, stop to gaze at five goliath groupers
caught in the Florida Keys. *Waukegan News-Sun*, October 10, 1961. Scott Family Papers

Havelka was also my grandfather's favorite cousin. In the early 1950s Cousin Ed, as we knew him, had left Waukegan and moved to the island of Big Pine, thirty miles east of Key West. After having survived the horrors of World War II and a nearly fatal injury at the Battle of the Bulge, Cousin Ed balked at the idea of returning home to a steady and mundane job in the cold Midwest. After a brief time living in Mexico, he moved to the Keys. Cousin Ed, like the generation of veterans before him, wanted something more adventurous. He made a plan to buy undeveloped oceanfront land to build a small vacation and retirement development he named "Tropical Bay." "At that time," my grandmother recalled, "Big Pine had nothing on it. It was just the key deer. No restaurant, no tavern, no nothing. You had to go to Key West to go to the grocery store."[29] Cousin Ed planned to settle and develop the island. Back in Waukegan, he distributed promotional material to family, friends, and old neighbors. "At Tropical Bay," he explained, there will be "paved roads, city water, electricity and phones and school buses" and, most important, "no city taxes." Cousin Ed also promoted the health of the tropics. "Climate conditions are ideal. Sufferers from asthma, rheumatic fever, hay fever, arthritis, cardiac conditions experience relief in these healthful isles. . . . Frost has never been known on the Keys." Each homesite, he also assured, would have a canal and access to the ocean. "Your boat is docked at your doorstep and you may dive and swim at your property."[30] Tropical Bay would be their "paradise." Cousin Ed convinced my grandparents and dozens of other Waukegan residents to move to the southern isles of Florida. And like many developers and politicians, he saw tourism, retirement, and investment as part of the same process of development.[31] If he could get people to vacation and enjoy some giant seabass, perhaps they would invest in his plan and one day move there.

This particular story of tourism and migration, while influenced by their favorite cousin, depended on much more than a single man's plan. Cousin Ed's vision was part of a historically constructed cultural pattern, which depended on more than a half century of development. The tourism industry in Florida, and more specifically in the Keys, began to take root with the expansion of railroads and hotel construction. At the end of the nineteenth century, Florida, for the first time in history, was comfortably and efficiently accessible to northern white residents looking to escape cold winters and crowded cities.[32] The town where my siblings and I grew up, for example, was founded in 1885 by earlier midwestern developers, just as the railroad tracks arrived in Florida. Winter Park, as its name suggests, was a retreat from northern winters. In a travel brochure titled "Florida Cuba," published

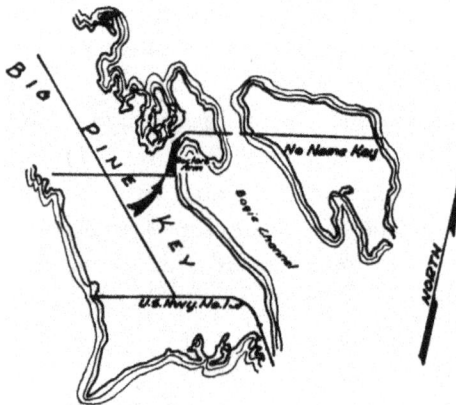

FIGURE 2.   The brochure Cousin Ed designed to promote his development project, Tropical Bay, on Big Pine Key, Florida. Scott Family Papers

in 1892, the railroad and hotel entrepreneur Henry Plant described the town and its Seminole Hotel: "This pleasant resort, situated on the line of the South Florida Railroad, among the Pines and the beautiful clear water lakes of Orange County surrounded by numerous orange groves and delightful winter homes of Northern visitors, is especially noted for its healthfulness, its balmy climate and dry atmosphere, affording relief from catarrhal and pulmonary affections."[33] Relief from an assortment of health ailments, which Cousin Ed also sold in the 1950s and 1960s, had begun to take rhetorical shape at the turn of the century. The lakes and swamps and balmy coasts of Florida, once the home of the Seminole people and seen by white travelers as dangerous and diseased, had been reinvented as health resorts for northern tourists. This historical process from disease to desire would, in geographic step by step, characterize tourism development across the circum-Caribbean from Florida to the Antilles to northern South America.

The route that millions of tourists followed was historically laid on the foundations of successive generations of political and environmental conquest. At the dawn of the twentieth century, another railroad developer, Henry Flagler, who was also cofounder of Standard Oil, sought to turn South Florida into a vacation destination and a Caribbean gateway. In 1904 Flagler announced that his Florida East Coast Railroad would extend across 150 miles of ocean, estuaries, and small islands to connect the island of Key West with the Florida mainland. His plan was well timed to link Caribbean trade routes from their northern to southern stretches. That same year, one thousand miles due south, the US government also began to dig the Panama Canal.[34]

Although Flagler's railroad infamously did not endure, being destroyed by a hurricane in 1935, the route remained and became the backbone of the region's emerging tourism industry. The countless tons of dirt moved, the drained swamps, and the bridges built for the rail line would be converted into a highway, an extension of US Route 1. Visitors who drove automobiles to the Keys in the following decades, including my family, traveled on the infrastructural remains of Flagler's dream.[35] Along the old rail line, hamlets also became bustling tourist towns and cities such as St. Augustine, Daytona Beach, and Miami. Before Flagler's railroad arrived in 1896, Miami was an agricultural and fishing village with an estimated population of three hundred. Yet by 1910 it was home to thousands of residents and visited annually by over 125,000 tourists.[36] Miami developed into a booming economy dependent on tourist and transportation services. Promotional literature described the city as the "Tropical Zone of Florida," the original "Magic City."[37]

The first generation of tourists to visit destinations in the circum-Caribbean were often of the wealthiest classes in US society. They were, in a way, the "vacation gentry." Leisure travel was still reserved for elite politicians, businessmen, and Victorian-like explorers and collectors. Early visitors to South Florida and nearby Caribbean islands included prominent individuals, such as

Harriet Beecher Stowe, Theodore Roosevelt, Thomas Edison, Henry Ford, and a young Franklin Delano Roosevelt. Vacationing in the tropical zones remained an elite activity until after World War II.[38] Yet before the "Great American acceleration" of the 1950s and 1960s, millions of middle-class people at home read, listened, and increasingly watched in theaters and on television the adventures and luxuries that privileged tourists and travelers enjoyed in the newly conquered tropics. As my grandparents' generation came of age in the early twentieth century, stories of tropical travel were everywhere: in the press and literature, in advertisements, on the radio, discussed at universities, and exhibited at public museums.[39] Tourist dreams and hopes were conditioned by the generation that came before them.

Following World War II, a new phase of tourism development began. In that moment, the other side of my family also arrived in South Florida to participate in the growing economy. During the war, my maternal grandfather had been stationed on a military base in Florida and fell in love with the state. He was not alone in his sentiments. "The establishment of wartime military bases in South Florida," as the social historian Chanelle Rose has explained, "ushered in the tourist boom in the tropic city as returning soldiers, tourists, celebrities, and war workers sought a permanent residence in the Magic City."[40] When the war ended, my grandfather looked to return to Florida and escape the orthodox expectations of his Russian-Jewish parents living in Atlantic City, New Jersey. They wanted him to work in their delicatessen. Instead, he bought a motorcycle and headed south. In Miami he found work in the emerging airline industry as a mechanic with Pan American World Airways. As a tourist destination and a transport hub to the Caribbean and Latin America, Miami promised employment opportunities.

The complementary elements of the tourism industry—the dream of tropical leisure, the transportation infrastructure, and the need for workers to support the service and transport economy—brought the two sides of our family together. I am, like so many, a product of tourism's history. By the time my parents met working at Holiday Hospital in Orlando, the region was experiencing a third wave of tourism growth: the Disney World boom. In the mid-1960s Walt Disney and his shell companies secretly bought up forty square miles in the middle of Florida. In 1971 the Disney Corporation opened the Magic Kingdom with six themed lands: Main Street U.S.A., Adventureland, Fantasyland, Frontierland, Liberty Square, and Tomorrowland. Here, echoing the expansionist history that made tourism possible, visitors would be entertained and, in a light-hearted way, educated about the world.[41] With the arrival of Disney, Orlando transformed from a southern town with no more than one hundred thousand people at mid-century

FIGURE 3. A brochure from the Florida East Coast Railroad owned by Henry Flagler. It includes a list of hotels and general information for tourists, 1904. Florida Ephemera, P. K. Yonge Library of Florida History, Special and Area Studies Collections, George A. Smathers Libraries, University of Florida, Gainesville, FL

into a twenty-first-century metropolitan area with over two million and an economy dependent on tourism. Disney's vision of the future, though, did not stop with theme parks or the Orlando area. They also formed a Disney film industry, a publishing firm, a television channel, outlet stores, and a cruise line taking tourists to Disney-owned islands in the Caribbean. What the Disney Corporation perfected in Florida—its "Mickey Mouse" version of history, development, and entertainment—became a model for the Caribbean region's economy. Like Disney, tourism providers worked to repackage centuries of violent history and cultural conflict into a pleasing vacation fantasy.

I tell this winding story of my family's migration and my community's history for a few reasons: to show the powerful and enduring pull tourism

FIGURE 4. A map included in a Florida East Railways and Hotel brochure highlights railway and steamship connections to the Caribbean, 1905–6. Florida Ephemera, P. K. Yonge Library of Florida History, Special and Area Studies Collections, George A. Smathers Libraries, University of Florida, Gainesville, FL

can have on families and community development, to acknowledge the autobiographical nature of my interests in this book, and also to introduce the historical methodology guiding my narrative approach. "One can never forget," in the words of the historian William Appleman Williams, "that it is people who act—not the policy or program."[42] History at its core is the story of people. Therefore, retracing their travel routes illuminates historical trends. Personal experiences reflect broader processes. Microcosms reveal macrocosms.[43] The chapters that follow embrace this microhistorical approach, telling travel stories that reflect broader patterns shaping the circum-Caribbean's history of tourism—from Florida to the islands to Central and South America. Narrative, though, is not mere storytelling. "All history becomes subjective," Ralph Waldo Emerson once wrote. "In other words, there is properly no history, only biography."[44] This book is a form of extended and comparative biography, describing what have I seen and felt from the past, from the archives and from my own travel observations.

Adapting the lessons of critical scholars such as Stuart Hall and Kimberlé Crenshaw, this book also argues that being a tourist or traveler is very much "an unstable identity, psychically, culturally, and politically. Something constructed, told, spoken, not simply found."[45] Tourism, like all social practices of privilege and inequality, is a composite phenomenon born out of history. Following Crenshaw's analysis of intersectionality, the history of tourism must be analyzed in the specific context of racial difference, gender, class, and nationality and seen in light of the ways identity politics have controlled one's access to transportation technology, capital, experiences of free time, leisure, and even healthful environments.[46] The hegemonic identity of a tourist—historically white, affluent, from the United States, Canada, or Europe—has depended on profound social shifts in the twentieth century, including understandings of tropical disease and health, transportation technology and infrastructure, US foreign policy, racialized immigration restrictions, visions of development and nature, and traveler imaginations of abroad and home. But the only way to see all of these elements coming together in one's life and a society's way of being is through the study of lived experience. People carried tourism's history within.

It is also worth remembering that no story, no destination, no place is really an island. This particular history is part of a bigger, global story. "Instead," in the words of geographer Doreen Massey, "of thinking of places as areas with boundaries around, they can be imagined as articulated moments in networks of social relations and understandings, but where a large proportion of those relations, experiences and understandings are constructed on a far larger scale than what we happen to define for that moment as the place itself, whether that be a street, or a region or even a continent."[47] Both biography and place belong to a larger field of time, space, and experience. One must look in multiple directions to understand the history of Caribbean tourism.

Producing and Consuming a Transnational Caribbean

The Caribbean region is an archipelago of cultural and historical diversity, but these diverse communities have been far from isolated. Looking closely, one sees that places and people—separated by geography, language, and ethnicity— share a common history. Communities assumed to be "insular," as the Caribbean historian Lara Putnam tells us, are actually "above-water fragments of submarine unities."[48] The transnational culture of tourism offers evidentiary "fragments" of "submarine" interconnection, although certainly not sameness or equality. Throughout the circum-Caribbean, from Florida to the islands to the coasts of Central and South America, tourism has become a leading economic activity.[49] This is not a coincidence of proximities. The tourism industry is both a local and transnational phenomenon defined by the politics and economics of mobility crossing borders.[50] Tourism in one locale is dependent on developments in another. To offer a recent example, in the 2010s between eight and ten million people annually embarked from ports in Florida to destinations in the Caribbean islands and Central America. As of 2015 three of the world's busiest cruise terminals were in the state: Port Everglades, Port Miami, and Port Canaveral. Their heading was almost always south, where the Caribbean led the world in cruise ship capacity, serving an estimated 37 percent of global cruise itineraries and 62 percent of US embarkations.[51]

Transnational connections between the mainland and the islands, though, precede the contemporary era. It is essential to contextualize and compare the current era of tourism with the types of movement that came before. There are countless precedent-setting episodes of transboundary travel from the Caribbean's past.[52] Colonial history also highlights "submarine" regional unity. When conquistadores arrived in the Americas at the end of the fifteenth century, Spanish ships began to navigate between the islands and the peninsula. The first governor of Puerto Rico, Juan Ponce de León, led an expedition to Florida. He was looking, like so many of his successors, for the mythical "Fountain of Youth." But on his last voyage to Florida in 1521, a group of Calusa warriors shot Ponce de León with a poison arrow. His expedition party escaped and sailed south to Havana, where he died of his wounds. The conquistador was a colonial-era microcosm of the region's border-crossing history. Ponce de León colonized Puerto Rico, fought in Florida, and died in Cuba. In violence and death, the region's history was also deeply connected.[53]

Pirates such as Francis Drake and Henry Morgan also sailed the Gulf Stream and attacked the Florida coast and then returned south to continue raids on colonies in Puerto Rico, Cuba, Jamaica, and Panama. European imperial powers and their privateers fought for centuries for control of Caribbean trade routes and its wealth of commodities. From Dutch Guyana to the Danish Virgin Islands to the French Antilles to English and Spanish colonies, the circum-Caribbean has experienced a dizzying history of colonial encounters. Although tourism to the region is relatively new, cross-cultural exchange via overseas movement is not.[54]

Today in Miami proud bankers and cosmopolitan businessmen claim their city as the new age capital of Latin America and the Caribbean. What most people do not seem to realize, however, is that for centuries Florida was already part of the Caribbean—not the capital but certainly an important link, a node, in a larger web of connections, which continued and evolved into the twentieth century. At the intersection of both US and Caribbean histories, Florida's history is a jumping off point. The peninsula, if it had feet, would have one on the mainland and the other in Caribbean waters. Retracing the historical movement of people and ships shows that Florida was as much a part of Caribbean history as that of the mainland United States. Likewise, Caribbean communities were intimately entangled with their colossal neighbor to the north, whether through the movement of tourists, migrants, or military personnel. This dual transit role, people coming and going shaping a place, is a defining characteristic of the region's transnational history. As a contemporary museum exhibition in New York described it, the Caribbean is a crossroads defined by "fluid motions . . . where human and natural forces collide."[55] On both sides of the Florida Straits, communities developed and defined themselves by mobile links—people, ideas, and goods shaping history on the move. The Caribbean's history therefore is defined by its *routes* as much by its historical *roots*.

In the late nineteenth and early twentieth centuries, as European imperialism slowly declined in the Americas, the US military and government, business, and tourists began to use the Florida Peninsula to expand into the rest of the Caribbean. So far, I have emphasized Florida's historical role in tourism, but as readers will see, this book will pay particular attention to the other geographic end of the circum-Caribbean. One thousand miles due south of the Florida Straits, the Isthmus of Panama also played an outsized role in the emergence of the Caribbean's transnational tourism industry.

Founded as a Spanish colony around the same time Florida was being explored (1510–13), Panama served for centuries as a crossroads for colonial trade in the Americas. Spaniards, Native American groups, English pirates, Scottish settlers, French entrepreneurs, and later US government officials and businessmen also claimed the isthmus between the Caribbean Sea and the Pacific Ocean.[56] With the building of the Panama Canal, US geopolitical influence reached new levels of hegemony and hubris in the Americas. As the canal project came to completion in 1914, the US government and the press claimed that the tropics had finally been conquered and made safe for the "white race." Journalists and expansionists argued that the canal had opened the region, from its far north to the far south, for tourists and commercial trade. US officials, along with private entrepreneurs and developers like Flagler, rushed to build railroads and modernize steamships and port facilities in Florida and the Caribbean islands because of the promise of this new maritime route. The US military also justified the development of naval bases from Charleston, South Carolina, to Key West, along with its century-long occupation of Guantánamo Bay, Cuba, and of Puerto Rico, with the need to protect the new Panama Canal. Passenger steamships in the early twentieth century sold some of the first packaged tours transiting the Caribbean, playing off the public's excitement for the construction project. One developer in the Florida Panhandle went as far as to change the name of the small coastal town of Harrison in 1909 to Panama City with the hope that popular interest in the canal project would spur tourism and investment. The town's population quadrupled in the decade that followed.[57] By the end of the century, Panama City was totally dependent on tourism and especially "spring-breakers." From Florida to Panama, tourism took on a regional character, and along the route from the peninsula to the isthmus, communities were pulled into a new orbit of economic and social activity focused on tourist consumption and production.

Transnational connections, however, go beyond the movement of people and their governments. In the realm of ideas and perceptions, diverse destinations in the circum-Caribbean have also forged a common story. Many communities depend on a tourist culture that is defined, in the words of the Caribbean author Derek Walcott, by its "high-pitched repetition of the same images of service."[58]

The Caribbean has played an outsized historical role in Western imaginations. The region was the realm of Shakespearean-like fantasies of romance and intrigue—of pirates and Indians, treasure and rum, of slavery, rebellion, and creative freedom.[59] These romanticized histories continue to influence the present: as a modern tourist, one can follow the path of (in)famous conquistadores, drink in the favorite bars of well-known travelers and writers, walk through the rain forest like a naturalist explorer, climb an old fort like a regular hero, and later enjoy the nightlife and casinos. As a tourist, one can escape the boredom or stress of home in search of a timeless and interesting past. Meanwhile, everyday life waits safely for one's return.

Central to this type of travel has been the feeling that one is following in the footsteps of history. The irony, though, is that the tourism industry also packages itself as an escape from reality. This is what Walt Disney sold at Magic Kingdom and what cruise ships do on their Caribbean voyages: the visitor gets to meet and play with a historical character—the pirate, the adventurer, the wealthy baron wining and dining, the "Peter Pan" free spirit who never has to grow up. In modern tourist culture, the pirates of the Caribbean have been reinvented as Disney characters and endearing eccentrics played by actors such as Johnny Depp. As one journalist reviewed the film *Pirates of the Caribbean*, "loopy but lovable Captain Jack Sparrow (Johnny Depp) relates the horrors of being marooned on a tiny deserted island. Later, he's dumped on the same spot, this time with the luscious Elizabeth Swann (Keira Knightley), who soon discovers that Sparrow's first visit involved nothing more horrible than sitting on a perfect beach and drinking rum— much like a modern Caribbean vacation."[60] In this highly limited vision of history's affect, pleasure and adventure overshadow the ugly and mundane, and the Caribbean remains a magical place.[61] It sounds appealing, yet is thoroughly problematic. History and culture transform into Mickey Mouse history packaged for mass consumption.[62] All the people's actual experiences, past and present, behind the fantasy get obscured in an epicurean haze.

The history of the Caribbean, its labor and race relations, its conquests and explorations, its economic activities, were more brutal than fantastic. For more than five hundred years the natural resources and people of Latin America and the Caribbean have served the desires of people consuming somewhere else, far away. As Uruguayan intellectual and journalist Eduardo Galeano famously argued, it "is the region of open veins. Everything from the discovery until our times, has always been transmuted into European— or later—United States—capital, and as such has accumulated on distant centers of power. Everything: the soil, its fruits and its mineral-rich depths, the people and their capacity to work and to consume, natural resources and human resources."[63] Galeano's observations capture the history of the capitalist world system in the Americas, where profit, greed, and pleasure coming from outside the region overly determined local history. In this sense, fantasies of paradise—whether colonial or touristic—have depended on material exploitation.

During the colonial era the insatiable foreign demand for sugar and other commodities such as tobacco and chocolate fueled centuries of wealth accumulation and plantation slavery. In *Sweetness and Power*, the anthropologist Sidney Mintz described in detail the violent labor system used for sugar production: the transatlantic slave trade, regimented plantation life, ecological devastation, and the millions of early deaths and miseries in the service of metropolitan desires for sweetness. The export of sugar dominated Caribbean life, with whole communities organized around its production.[64] For centuries, export industries and agricultural commodities were the economic base across the Caribbean and Latin America.[65]

By the late nineteenth century, bananas also became a sort of "green gold." International consumer demand for the fruit became a new organizing principle for many Caribbean communities. As the environmental historian John Soluri related, new towns formed around the needs of banana production, and new family and kinship ties were forged. Meanwhile, on the consumer end in the United States, an entertainment and food culture, featuring Miss Chiquita and "the Lady in the Tutti Frutti Hat," was born to sell tropical fecundity.[66] There is nothing natural, however, about patterns of mass production bringing the Caribbean into contact with Western consumer societies. We must study not only the history of production but also the influential relationship between changes in consumer patterns and processes of production. As Mintz explained, "one needs to understand just what makes demand work: how and why it increases under what conditions. One cannot simply assume that everyone has an infinite desire for sweetness, any more than one can assume the same about a desire for comfort or wealth or power."[67] How then does one learn to "desire"?

Consumer desires for agricultural commodities such as sugar, tobacco, chocolate, and bananas shaped the circum-Caribbean's relationship with the rest of the world. But not all industries geared toward foreign interest have been rooted in material goods. As Mimi Sheller eloquently argued in *Consuming the Caribbean*, "it is not only things or commodities that are consumed, but also entire natures, landscapes, cultures, visual representations, and even human bodies."[68] Services, experiences, even in love or friendship, in addition to landscapes and dreams could also be exploited by an industry or, as politicians and developers came to understand tourism, become an "invisible export." By the mid-twentieth century, the tourism industry had surpassed sugar, bananas, and other commodities as the most valuable economic sector in the Caribbean.

History is not made up of distinct phases, passing from one to the next. Rather, the past accumulates like layers of soil into the present. The same nations and people who historically profited and consumed Caribbean natural resources and also crafted colonial tropical fantasies not coincidentally became the region's tourist consumers. It was an historical process of succession.[69] Tourists and retirees did not one day wander out of the suburban and urban deserts of the United States to discover "tropical paradise." Their dreams were rooted in history. The travel decisions of countless individuals, including grandparents, emerged historically from ideas and practices forged over time, shared between kin and neighbor, from one generation to the next. Someone told them stories of adventure (who learned the stories from someone else), someone guided them to interesting sights, someone cut the trails, someone profited from their travels, and someone likely suffered. In this multifaceted historical process, a new way of travel and work took shape, connecting the people of the Caribbean once again with the desires of foreign consumers. As a result, an updated tradition of "tropical paradise," complete with white-sand beaches, wavy palm trees, smiling locals, care-free lifestyles, and fruity drinks, became the symbol of an industry transcending local difference.

Gilroy's Ship

Imagine now a cruise ship in motion: below the main deck oilers and wipers keep the big engines turning, while above guests are served elaborate meals on balcony cabins overlooking a beautiful blue expanse. Everyone on board is technically together, but their fates are profoundly different. The cruise ship, with its hierarchically organized crew and passenger groups, is a mobile microcosm of the asymmetrical yet interconnected experience of the Caribbean's history of tourism.

In his classic study *The Black Atlantic*, Paul Gilroy embraced a similar maritime metaphor to describe the history of the African diaspora. "The image of the ship," he wrote, is "a living, microcultural, micro-political system in motion."[70] The ship at sea represented the diverse routes of history's journey. With this in mind, what might a "pleasure cruise" reveal about history's turn into the present? Ships, the sea, and their ports of call have long stood as "paradigms of human existence."[71]

The history of the passenger line of the United Fruit Company (UFCO), the Great White Fleet, offers a telling example of tourism's transnational history.[72] Although traditionally known as an agricultural provider of bananas, UFCO, according to John Soluri, "also literally brought North Americans to the tropics via the same railroads and steamship lines that whisked bananas to consumers." Well before Hilton Hotels or all-inclusive resorts, "United Fruit's Great White Fleet carried tourists on Caribbean cruises."[73] From 1908 to 1913, as the Panama Canal was coming to completion, UFCO modernized its steamship service from small ships to luxury cruisers capable of carrying 160 passengers each. The company's new ships carried both passengers and, below in refrigerated hulls, bananas and other tropical commodities between the US mainland and the Caribbean. The Great White Fleet, which was the region's premiere tourist line in the early twentieth century, had a number of routes crisscrossing the region. One of the more popular routes—at one point called "route #1"—sailed from New York through the Florida Straits to Cuba, Jamaica, and Panama. Thousands of tourists traveled UFCO's Caribbean routes in the 1910s and 1920s.[74]

Each experiential aspect of the UFCO voyage, and each person aboard ship, was part of the social and economic relations of leisure travel. While tourists lounged on upper decks, the crew traveled with them in cramped quarters. On shore, more laborers catered to the ship's passengers. Taxi drivers, vendors of all sorts, guides, restaurant and store owners, and countless laborers depended on the arrival of tourists for their livelihood. In the mid-1920s, one travel writer with a heavy dose of prejudice described the scene incited by the arrival of a luxury ship to another Caribbean port of call:

> The news spread quickly that another horde of American tourists had come to the island, and every living inhabitant immediately picked a handful of fruit or found a handful of eggs and came out to offer his wares. The women, of whatever race, simply held up their wares in mute appeal. The men ran after us through the dust, leaping upon our running boards, insistent that we should purchase a bunch of bananas or a ripe breadfruit.[75]

Meanwhile, young boys swam out to the ship, begging tourists to toss coins into the harbor. As the Caribbean author Eric Walrond described such scenes, the dark-skinned boys would dive deep to retrieve the coins and implore the white tourists to throw more. "A penny, mistah . . . This way . . . as far as yo' like."[76]

The historical reality and the metaphor of a ship moving from port to port highlights the social boundaries of who could and could not travel as a tourist. Racial and economic injustices in the tourism industry were also entangled in some of the most contentious issues of the twentieth century. Racism in travel and tourism, for example, was the reason that the activist Marcus Garvey organized the Black Star Line Steamship Corporation. Garvey—who grew up in Jamaica and lived and worked in Panama before moving to the

United States—was highly aware of international racism. "The big companies that were engaged in the shipping business," Garvey explained, "were determined to keep the Negro off the high seas."[77] The Universal Negro Improvement Association (UNIA), founded by Garvey, worked to challenge racism at sea whether in travel for trade or leisure. UNIA's efforts, though, encountered intense white opposition. The technologies and infrastructures of international travel were viciously guarded. In 1924 UNIA purchased its largest vessel, SS *General Goethals*, from the US-controlled Panama Canal Company. Under UNIA ownership the *General Goethals*, originally named after the canal's chief engineer and governor, was renamed in honor of the African American activist Booker T. Washington. The day SS *Booker T. Washington* left the Port of New York headed for the Caribbean, however, the US Bureau of Investigation (later known as the FBI) charged Garvey with mail fraud. J. Edgar Hoover, who was the bureau's director from 1924 to 1972, led the campaign to prosecute Garvey on what looked like trumped-up charges. The Black Star Line had sent out a brochure with the picture of another ship it was in the process of purchasing. Hoover and the US government used this incomplete transaction as an excuse to attack Garvey and put him jail. With its leader in prison, the *Booker T. Washington* nevertheless proceeded on its one and only voyage under UNIA control, sailing to Virginia and from there to Cuba, Jamaica, and Panama.[78] The opposition faced during the ship's voyage epitomized white control of mobility. In Kingston and Havana, authorities detained the ship in the interest of creditors. Later, on its return to the United States, the Ku Klux Klan illegally occupied the ship in Jacksonville, Florida. To add insult, the ship was subject to fines for violations of US maritime regulations in Charleston. Eventually the *Booker T. Washington* made it back to New York, where it was forced to be sold at auction.[79] The history of a ship's failed journey was also a revealing metaphor.

Modern tourism depended on "power geometries" organized and controlled along racial, national, and class exclusions. It was the institutional sanctioning of resources and energy for the privileged few. This history, not yet past, requires critical reflection.

A Collage of Tourism

As hopefully made evident in this introduction, *Unpacked* is an historical collage. Each story and each chapter can be read by itself or in conversation. Each chapter explores a particular theme and a particular social group shaping modern-day travel culture to the Caribbean. The research and narrative method follow what anthropologist Claude Lévi-Strauss called "bricolage," bringing together an eclectic and heterogeneous collection of stories to illuminate historical signs pointing toward broader historical patterns.[80] This is a creative collage. Tourism, a multiexperiential activity, appears in this text as imperial history, as a dream of development, as scientific practice and knowledge-building, as urban discontent and escape, as a point of cross-cultural contact, as a source of rebellion, as ethnographic self-reflection, and as a constituted industry.

The narrative offers a genealogy of tourism, of historical events and people who guided the tourist's journey to the Caribbean. In the following chapters, readers will learn about colonial officials and frontier figures at the turn of the century becoming tour guides and entrepreneurs (chapter 1), elite politicians and revolutionaries turning to hotel and gambling development (chapter 2), sailors and aviators risking their lives to carve out new travel routes (chapter 3), scientists and explorers inspiring the tourist's gaze of tropical nature (chapter 4), traveling writers and "tropical tramps" envisioning and actualizing foreign escape from domestic responsibilities (chapter 5), and anticolonial activists intermingling with and rebelling against tourist privileges (chapter 6). This diverse cast of historical actors offers a collective biography of Caribbean tourism.

Many cultural and material aspects of vacationing, however, will not be discussed in the pages that follow. There will be no direct analysis of such classic vacation fetishes as daiquiris and margaritas or hammocks and tropical-colored shirts. A whole book could be written and has been on the history of the Panama hat, that headdress most people seem to wear only on vacation.[81] What this book does describe, however, is how "professional experts" constructed and popularized a hegemonic culture of leisure travel that allowed tourists to reimagine and reinvent themselves in dress, in forms of consumption, in their imaginations, and in their social behavior. The narrative, moreover, cannot take readers to every major port of call in the Caribbean, such as in the Bahamas, Barbados, the coast of Mexico, Aruba, and Trinidad. The chapters hold to one well-traveled route linking Florida, Cuba, Jamaica, and Panama. This historical narrative along a particular route, though, captures a *structure of feeling* that has been repeated again and again, standardized and packaged for mass consumption.

Traveling as a tourist has evolved from learned behavior, mimicked and embodied, marketed and disseminated from one generation of travelers to the next, from colonial times to the twentieth century into the present. It is story of cultural continuity despite tremendous historical change. The tourism industry in the Caribbean, I argue, is a mass copy, an imitation, of a colonial fantasy of travel. It depends on the "mimetic faculty"—that is, the cultural inclination to imitate previously observed human behavior.[82] Tourists have followed the social practices and beliefs of earlier travelers. The lessons have piled up, their origins often erased but still part of everyday social practice.

This book is also a form of travel: across time, from the early twentieth century to the beginning of the twenty-first; across space, from the Florida Peninsula to the Greater Antilles to the Isthmus of Panama; and across experience, from colonial officials to Caribbean elites to naturalists, writers, tourists, and service workers. Together these stories crossing time, space, and identity offer an historical mosaic of the present.

CHAPTER 1

Empire's Lake

Tourism in the Wake of US Expansion

The revisionist is one who sees basic facts in
a different way and as interconnected in new
relationships.

—William Appleman Williams, "Confessions of an
Intransigent Revisionist"

In anticipation of the Panama Canal's opening,
thousands of tourists began to travel south of the US border. Ports, streets,
and hotels in Cuba, Jamaica, and Panama swarmed with visitors. British author Winifred James chronicled this early wave of tourism to the tropics in
her travelogue *The Mulberry Tree* (1913). "The last year of the making of the
Panama Canal had begun," she explained, and because of this "all of patriotic America that had the time and the money was tumbling down through
New York as fast as it could to look upon the wonders of the nation's handi-
work."[1] "The Canal," as one tour operator summarized, had "created a new
interest in the Caribbean countries, their history, resources and future."[2]

The building of the Panama Canal from 1904 to 1914 was a watershed
moment in the Caribbean's transformation from disease to desire.[3] Tropical
vacationing as a cultural rite of passage, and as a regional industry, emerged
just as the United States secured its imperial control over the isthmus. Yet
today tourism and the canal are often viewed as separate issues and as separate histories. Scholars and the public remember the canal as an engineering
feat, one of the technological wonders or, depending on one's view, abuses
of the modern world.[4] On the isthmus, politicians, engineers, and migrant
workers had built a "path between the seas" for the movement of ships and
commodities. This is, as the anthropologist Ashley Carse called it, the story
of the "big ditch."[5]

The building of the Panama Canal, however, offers an historical beginning and geographic angle to make sense of regional change. The rhetoric
of tropical conquest associated with the canal was part of a shift in environmental thinking that would have long-term consequences for how tourists
experienced the tropics. "America," as one enthusiastic visitor noted in the
1920s, "made the Canal, but she overcame the forces of death first."[6] At the
dawn of the twentieth century, leisure travel to the Caribbean was still, in
most places, a nonexistent activity.[7] As late as 1896, the journalist and author
Richard Harding Davis reported a very different scene than what Winifred
James witnessed in 1913. When Davis and his two traveling companions arrived on the Caribbean coast of Panama, they described the experience as if
they had traveled to edge of the world or to the River Styx in Greco-Roman
mythology. "If Ulysses in his wanderings had attempted to cross the Isthmus
of Panama," Davis wrote, he would have "found this isthmus guarded by a
wicked dragon that exhaled poison with every breath, and that lay in wait,
buried in its swamps and jungles, for sailors and travelers, who withered
away and died as soon as they put foot upon the shore."[8]

Clearly this was not a vacation. In the 1890s there were a handful of efforts
to promote international travel to Caribbean destinations south of the Florida
Peninsula. But, as the historian Krista Thompson has explained, "tourism entrepreneurs faced a formidable challenge. Beyond the region the West Indies
were widely stigmatized as breeding grounds for potentially fatal tropical diseases." As an industry booster wrote in 1891, "to many old-fashioned people
at home to book a passage for Jamaica is almost synonymous with ordering a coffin."[9] It was, in the words of the historian Phillip Curtin, "death by
migration."[10] How then did tourist-environmental relations change from the
late nineteenth century to the early twentieth century, reinventing Caribbean
travel from a dangerous adventure into a potentially comfortable vacation?

The history of the Panama Canal highlights a cultural shift in tropical travel dependent on US empire-building and its associated advances in
tropical medicine. The canal construction project also supported the development of a fast and efficient transportation network. The railroads and
steamship lines that flowed south to meet the canal became the backbone
of the region's tourism industry.[11] Thousands of leisure travelers from the
United States arrived in the Caribbean by ship, often departing from New
York, New Orleans, or Key West. "Unless you deliberately choose it," James
wrote, "you cannot travel to Panama on the Atlantic side any other way
than comfortably."[12] Anticipating increased tourist and commercial traf-
fic following the canal, steamship lines such as the United Fruit Company,
the Hamburg-American Line, and the Panama Railroad Steamship Line

modernized their passenger services. Ships were redesigned specifically for tropical travel. As one passenger praised, some ships were even "cooled by a system of artificial ventilation which assures a comfortably night's rest even in the warmest weather."[13] Transportation providers, both private and government, expanded their services to meet the growing interest in tourism.

The expansion of the Caribbean's tourism industry on a regional scale was remarkably fast. Ten years after Richard Harding Davis visited Panama in 1896, whose coast he compared to the edge of hell, President Theodore Roosevelt embarked on a triumphant tour. In 1906 Roosevelt was the first US president to travel abroad during his tenure in office. During a seventeen-day trip through the Caribbean, the president visited Panama and then Puerto Rico. To a gathered crowd in Colón, Roosevelt gave a patriotic speech: "I go back a better American, a prouder American, because of what I have seen the pick of American manhood doing here on the Isthmus."[14] The thousands of tourists who visited soon after the president mostly agreed. James reported that among the crowds one could consistently hear the "parrot cry of the patriotic tourist whose good-morning and good-night is ever the same: 'Here, sir, you see one of the most marvelous engineering feats that the world has ever beheld.'"[15] Part of this feat was the supposed conquest of the tropical environment, making the region safe for leisure travel. This conquest of the tropics included both real material changes in public health and epidemiology and in the realm of ideas, about how tourists geographically and racially understood disease.

By the end of the canal project, the Caribbean had been repackaged as a health resort, a sign of victory over tropical nature. The journeys of Davis in 1896, Roosevelt in 1906, and in 1913 by James and tens of thousands of tourists also mark the evolving relationship between Caribbean tourism and US imperial expansion. In the most basic sense, US military and commercial efforts precipitated improved control of tropical diseases not only in Panama but also all along the route linking the isthmus to the US mainland. Those efforts, presented as successful, helped to dispel popular ideas that the tropics were dangerous to white people. Revisiting the history of the canal's construction therefore provides a revealing window into a larger story about how empire-building, medical science, and transportation technology came together in the early twentieth century to remake and reimagine the Caribbean environment into a desirable vacation destination.

From Disease to Desire

In June 1904 William Haskins, a native of Alabama, boarded a United Fruit steamer with eighteen other passengers bound for Panama. His fellow

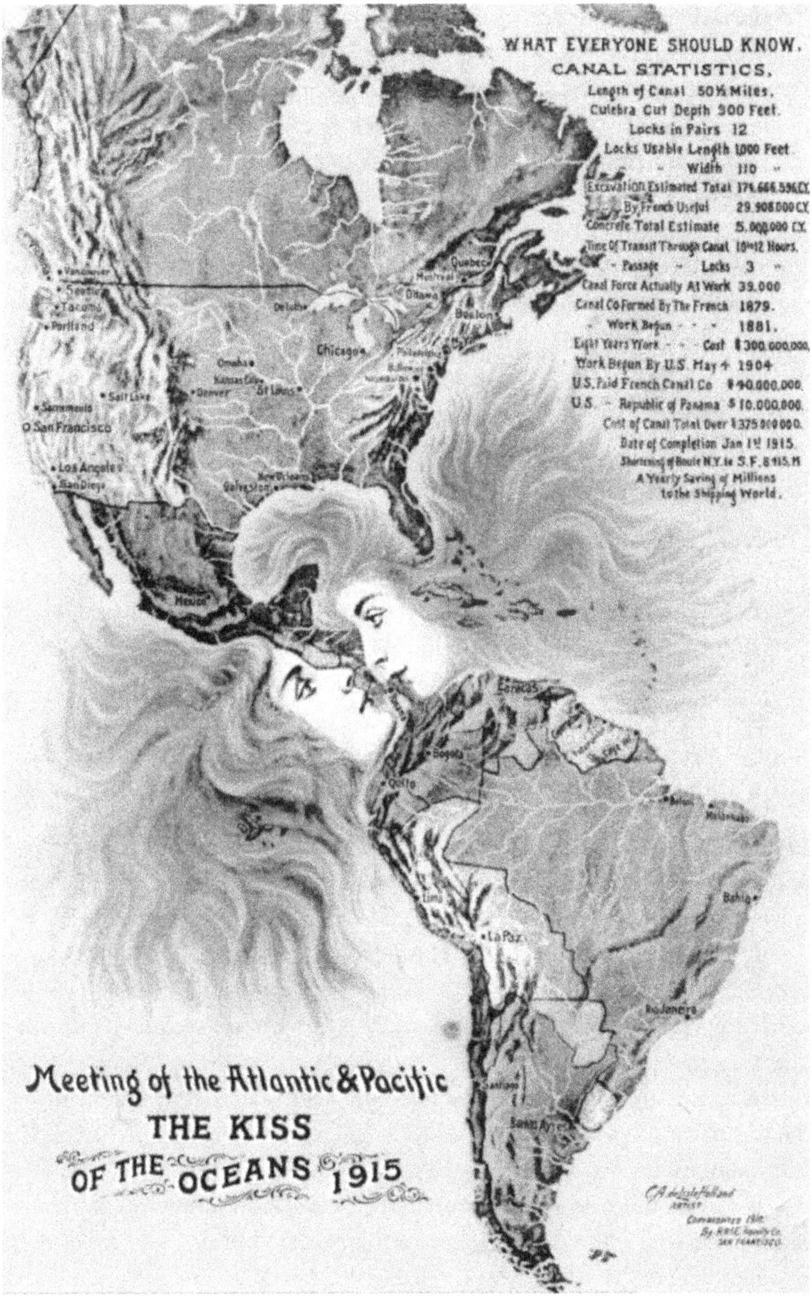

FIGURE 5. "The Kiss of the Oceans 1915," the meeting of Atlantic and Pacific Oceans at the Panama Canal, postcard, ca. 1915. Panama Canal Museum Collection, Special and Area Studies Collections, George A. Smathers Libraries, University of Florida, Gainesville, FL

travelers, he noted, "represented as odd a cross-section of humanity as one could expect to see. Most had never been to sea before, and were going to Panama hoping that the new land would produce rich returns." To participate in the canal project, they believed, was the chance to engage in adventure, to be part of history, and also make money. That summer Haskins traveled on behalf of the Alabama District headquarters of the Southern Bell Telephone & Telegraph Company. His manager in Montgomery, in coordination with an Alabama state senator, thought it would be a good idea "to get on the ground floor in Panama with a telephone system." As the promoters of overseas expansion had hoped, there was money to be made with the canal project. "One of these moves," Haskins remembered, "required someone to go to Panama to obtain an option on the telephone franchise held in the terminal cities." No one at the company, however, wanted to physically travel to the isthmus and negotiate the deal. The duty fell to Haskins:

> Finally, I said I would go. The rest applauded my nerve but warned that I was taking my life in my hands. But the die was cast, and in the interim prior to my departure, I tried to round up all the information I could about Panama. The Montgomery library afforded little of value and what there was wasn't encouraging. In consulting its section on Panama in the Encyclopedia Britannica I read the startling statement that "The climate is such that no white man can live there."[16]

At the time, the tropics (i.e., south of Florida) were still thought of as the "white man's graveyard."[17] When Haskins began his trip, his life insurance policy even expired because of a provision barring holders from tropical travel.

For centuries the Caribbean was home to vital trade routes and the source of vast wealth. But that history of exploits did not assuage fear. Travelers viewed a journey through the tropics as an experience that required one stare death in the face. In the mid-nineteenth century, for example, one traveler by the name of James Clark sailed from the US East Coast to California via the Caribbean-Panama route. Clark recorded intense hardships in his diary, a document that is now housed at the Library of Congress. Clark slept in the dirt and hiked miles on muddy trails in the tropical forest. He was not alone, though, on the arduous voyage. From the years 1848 to 1860, more than two hundred thousand people traveled from New York to San Francisco by way of the Caribbean Sea and Panama, more than those travelers who used the overland route across the North American continent.[18] The Caribbean offered the quickest route. But the trip was far from easy. In the nine days it took Clark to get from one ship on the Caribbean coast to find another on the Pacific Ocean, he attended multiple funerals for travelers who died on the trek. When Clark eventually arrived in San Francisco and found work, he himself fell ill. His journal entries end abruptly with reports of "vomiting and purging."[19]

During Panama's years under Spanish colonial rule (1513–1819), the isthmus had also played a key role in mobility and trade networks linking the Caribbean with Europe and its other colonies in the Americas. The Spanish Empire relied on Panama as a transoceanic land bridge for the movement of silver and gold from its mines in Peru to its treasury in Madrid. Royal ships transported silver up the Pacific coast to Panama City, where mules, men, and small river vessels carried the bullion across the isthmus to the Caribbean coast.[20] For that same reason pirates found the area an attractive stalking ground. Francis Drake in 1596 and Henry Morgan in 1671 built their infamous reputations attacking Panama's Caribbean coast. However, in all those centuries of movement and adventure, Spanish bureaucrats, English pirates, forty-niners, and an array of other travelers generally thought of Panama as a "corridor of infection," a quick and potentially deadly stopover along the journey. The isthmus was legendary as a treacherous, diseased shortcut between the Atlantic and Pacific Oceans.[21]

When thousands of workers began to dig the canal on the isthmus, these long-running predicaments had yet to be resolved. The French Canal Company, which initiated the construction project in 1881, lost an estimated twenty-two thousand workers, mostly to disease. Ferdinand de Lesseps, the company's president, had assumed that digging the Panama Canal would be an extension of his earlier success in Egypt with the sea-level Suez Canal (1859–69). It was simply an engineering problem that required know-how and capital. The French believed they had both, but their project ended in disaster. The combination of high mortality rates, engineering difficulties, and financial troubles bankrupted the French project in 1889.[22]

In the late nineteenth century, the United States also struggled to control disease outbreaks in the circum-Caribbean and the Pacific. During the Spanish-American War (1898–1902), the US military lost more soldiers as the result of disease than actual fighting.[23] Although fewer than four hundred US soldiers died in combat, approximately two thousand died from disease during the war. According to Gen. William Shafter, disease in Cuba was "a thousand times harder to stand up against than the missiles of the enemy."[24] Yellow fever in particular threatened the US ability to occupy the island of Cuba. "The health authorities were at their wit's end," Chief Sanitary Officer William C. Gorgas explained. "We evidently could not get rid of Havana as a focus of infection by any method we then knew."[25] When the United States began to dig the Panama Canal in 1904, it faced similar problems. Disease remained the main obstacle. It quickly became apparent to many workers that digging the canal was not worth an early and miserable death. When an outbreak of yellow fever occurred on the isthmus, workers fled by the boatload. As one official reported, "a feeling of alarm, almost amount to panic, spread among the Americans on the Isthmus."[26] During the first year of the project, the turnover rate for "skilled" laborers from the United States was 75 percent.

The spread of yellow fever caused the greatest fear. Symptoms emerged slowly. Victims developed a headache, back pain, and a flu-like fever. Then the virus would spread, attacking the liver and proteins necessary for blood to clot. Individuals bled from the eyes and nose and vomited blood. Growing frantic from the sight of their own decay, many of the sick had to be strapped down as medical professionals, unable to help, watched them die. Disease spread.

Because of the many dangers and poor working conditions, the canal would come to rely on a nonwhite and immigrant workforce for its construction. Of the fifty thousand workers on the project in 1907, 70 percent were "negroes" from the Caribbean islands. US officials on the isthmus claimed that black West Indian laborers were more resistant to tropical disease than white laborers. Black people, according to social Darwinist and climatological understandings of racial difference, were supposedly inherently adapted to hard labor in the tropics. Immunity was believed to be due to innate racial characteristics rather than personal disease history.[27] Although some Afro-Caribbean workers had built up acquired tolerance due to disease exposure in childhood, the reality was that the sufferings of black workers stirred considerably less controversy in the white-controlled and racist halls of government and the press. Workers of color died or grew sick, in fact, in much greater numbers than white workers on the isthmus.[28]

Recruiters for the Isthmian Canal Commission (ICC) paid for migrant workers to travel to the isthmus. The commission also used well-placed advertisements across the Caribbean to fuel "rags-to-riches" stories. "Colón-man-a-come," the story of a canal worker returning home with money in his pocket, was popularized in song and also in oral and written traditions.[29] The experience for most black workers when they arrived, however, was very different. Albert Peters, traveling from the Bahamas, was young and hopeful when he left for Panama in 1906. He explained:

> One day while reading the daily paper I saw where they were digging the Canal from ocean to ocean on the Isthmus of Panama and needed

thousands of men. I and two of my pals read it over and we suggested to take a trip over. We were all eager for some adventure and experience. My parents were against the idea. They told me about the Yellow Fever, Malaria and Small Pox that infested the place but I told them that I and my pals are just going to see for ourselves.

Peters was twenty-one years old when he and his friends arrived in Colón. But soon he was sick with malaria. In the hospital, he reported, "The first night in there the man next to me died and that's the time I remembered my parents' plea and wished I had taken their advice." Over the coming months Peters returned to the hospital several times with fever. Although he would survive and make a career in the Canal Zone, many of his friends did not. "Every evening around 4:30 one could see #5 engine with a box car and the rough brown coffins staked one upon the other bound for Mt. Hope which was called Monkey Hill in those days. The death rate was high. . . . If you had a friend that you always see and missed him for a week or two, don't wonder, he's either in the hospital or at Monkey Hill resting in peace."[30]

A generation of black Caribbean migrants looked for a better future at the Panama Canal. The urge to travel and earn a living encouraged thousands of West Indians to travel to the isthmus. The experience, though, was defined by hardship. Black laborers often earned no more than ten cents an hour and received the most dangerous jobs during the canal project. People of color dug and chopped away brush or served as waiters and cooks, but racism would not allow them to lead or fill skilled positions.[31] Farnham Bishop, a white southerner whose father served on the ICC, captured popular white sentiment in his 1916 book *Panama: Past and Present*. He wrote, "These big, strong, black men have to be looked after like so many children. They are very peaceable and law-abiding fellows, but exceedingly lazy, and unbelievably stupid. There is room in their heads for exactly one idea at a time, and no more."[32] This was the era of Jim Crow and intense racism in the United States. The canal project, in its need for cheap and expendable labor and also its desire to maintain social order, exported its uniquely US version of racism to the tropics. To many white southerners, in fact, the canal project and US imperial expansion into the Caribbean symbolized the reunification of the white-controlled South and North after the Civil War and the turmoil of Reconstruction.[33] Within this imperialist vision of reunification, people of African descent returned to the fields of hard labor.

The history of the canal is revealing of race relations at the turn of the century and its influence on the future of tourism in several important ways. The Panama Canal, which white Americans believed exemplified Uncle Sam's "conquest of the tropics," was carried out largely by the sweat and misery of black laborers from the Caribbean. The differentiated pay and accommodations for workers at the canal, listed on the Silver (nonwhite) and Gold (white) rolls, highlighted the significance of racial hierarchy for the development of US political, cultural, and economic power in the tropics. While white workers governed and set the rules as administrators and leisure consumers, black people were relegated to positions of dangerous and difficult work. The type of racism that governed the canal construction project would also come to characterize the identity and boundaries of the early tourist economy. US officials institutionally determined that welcomed visitors were white Americans and Europeans, while laborers and service workers were defined as brown and black.[34] However, before this racist social order could translate into tourist privileges, there was still the unresolved issue of disease for migrant workers and travelers of diverse racial backgrounds.

Scientific understandings of epidemiology were in transition when the United States invaded Cuba and a few years later when it initiated the canal project. In the early days, as William Haskins remembered, people were "still giving little credence to mosquitoes as being the cause [of malaria and yellow fever]."[35] In 1904, outside of the medical field, it was common belief that tropical diseases emerged from "miasmas"—that is, unhealthy air bubbling up from swampy and dirty soil. This theory dated back centuries and at the turn of the twentieth century still competed with the emerging germ theory of disease. The famous naturalist Alexander Von Humboldt, after visiting the isthmus in the early nineteenth century, concluded, for example, that decaying mollusks and marine plants on the beaches caused yellow fever, while malaria was due to "foul emanations" from overrank vegetation.[36]

Dr. William Gorgas, after serving in the military campaign in Cuba, was put in charge of the US sanitation effort on the isthmus. Gorgas, an officer in the Army Medical Corps who had grown up in Alabama in a military family, had also served as an army doctor in North Dakota, Texas, and Florida before the Spanish-American War. He and his wife had both caught and survived yellow fever in Texas in the 1880s and were thus immune to the disease.[37] Like his colleagues, though, Gorgas did not initially consider mosquitoes to be carriers of disease. His experiences in Cuba would teach him otherwise. In 1900, two years into the US occupation of Cuba, a special military commission on the island headed by Dr. Walter Reed concluded that female *Aedes aegypti* mosquitoes carried and spread yellow fever. Knowledge of the zoonotic transmission of yellow fever and malaria, from mosquitoes to humans, was beginning to increase at the turn of the century following important studies by British medical officials in India. A Cuban doctor, Carlos Finlay, had also theorized in the 1880s that mosquitos spread yellow fever. However, US authorities only began to accept these new theories in 1900 when it became a matter of geopolitical importance. When Gorgas was redeployed from Cuba to Panama, he traveled with these new lessons about mosquito species as vectors of disease.[38]

Yet in the early days of canal construction, members of the ICC overseeing the project held to the old miasma theory. They viewed Gorgas's unorthodox focus on insect control as an unnecessary and extravagant expense. His funding and authority were limited. In 1905, in the midst of a yellow fever epidemic during which one fourth of the white workforce fled the isthmus, both the ICC chairman and the governor of the Canal Zone asked for Gorgas's resignation. President Roosevelt, however, intervened to save Gorgas's position, against the wishes of ICC officials. "If you fall back on the old methods you will fail," Roosevelt's personal doctor, Alexander Lambert, told him, "just as the French failed. If you back Gorgas and his ideas and let him make his campaign against mosquitoes, then you will get that canal."[39] Roosevelt responded to the request for Gorgas's dismissal by granting him greater authority and financial resources. Roosevelt, who had witnessed the ravages of disease in the Cuba military campaign, feared the worst for the canal project if the problems of malaria and yellow fever were not resolved.[40]

With more authority and more resources, Gorgas intensified the campaign against mosquitoes. He called for an all-out war. More than four thousand men organized into "mosquito brigades" to destroy the insects' breeding grounds.[41] Female mosquitoes depended on standing fresh water to lay their eggs and allow larvae to develop. Teams drained surrounding marshes and cleared plants and brush where mosquitoes would gather. They equipped Canal Zone housing with screen windows and doors. The mosquito brigades also entered the private homes of Panamanians and, without authorization from individual residents, fumigated homes with chemical cleaning agents and insecticide powder.[42]

Oil, which would become the blood of twentieth-century progress, was the weapon of choice in the conquest of tropical disease. To prevent and kill mosquito larvae, the brigades sprayed thousands of gallons of oil onto fields and swamps around the canal and nearby communities. "Petroleum," Gorgas explained, "destroys the larvae by spreading over the surface of the water and smothering them, while phinotas oil acts as a direct poison. These are the chief methods for destroying larvae."[43] By 1914 the brigades had used over six hundred thousand gallons of oil, 120 tons of pyrethrum powder, and 300 tons of sulfur. As one enthusiastic visitor reported, "there was not a smell, or a mosquito, or a fly on Ancon Hill, but over it all was the odor of petroleum, with which the streams and marshes of the whole zone are spayed almost daily; and this has made the Canal and saved the workers."[44] Yellow fever outbreaks on the isthmus abruptly ended, and mortality rates among canal employees decreased from forty per thousand people in 1906 to eight per thousand in 1909. Mosquitoes, visitors claimed, had been eradicated from the populated parts of the Canal Zone. The landscape had been cleared (and smothered) for empire-building.[45]

The scale of the engineering project that paralleled the health campaign was unprecedented. By the time the transoceanic canal opened in 1914, the US government had built the biggest man-made lake and the biggest locks in the world, lifting ships from sea level and then lowering them back down as they crossed the isthmus. Workers and machine cut through swamps and mountains to connect the Atlantic and Pacific. The Chagres River, which flowed naturally into the Caribbean Sea, was diverted and dammed to create the main body of water for the canal. US authorities erased entire towns, displacing forty thousand Panamanian residents, as they flooded the lands to create Gatun Lake.[46] As British ambassador James Bryce saw it, the canal project was "the greatest liberty man has ever taken with nature."[47] It was, in a way, a war. When President Roosevelt visited, he cheerfully claimed, "I have felt just exactly as I should feel if I saw the picked men of my country engaged in some great war. I am weighing my words when I say that you here, who do your work well in bringing to completion this great enterprise, will stand exactly as the soldiers of a few, and only a few, of the most famous armies of all the nations stand in history."[48] The professed enemy was tropical nature, and by 1912 and 1913 it was clear that the United States was winning, although at great financial, social, and ecological cost.

It was at this historic juncture that the Caribbean's tourism industry began to expand. The success of the health campaign in Panama was headline news. Journalists and jingoists claimed that Uncle Sam had "conquered the tropics" and made the region safe for the "white race." Under the direction of Dr. Gorgas, the story went, the tropics had been transformed from a "pest-hole" into a "health resort." Canal chronicler Arthur Bullard claimed, "No American can visit either Colon or Panama without a large patriotic pride in the work of our sanitary engineers. These cities—not so many years ago—were called the worst pest-holes in the Americas."[49] The US government had defeated yellow fever and malaria, the plague of white travelers to the tropics. Modern technological know-how had flattened mountains and drained swamps, moving over 230 million cubic yards of dirt and rock, and white men now lived and governed in the tropics, the new gateway to global trade. As Bullard described it, "before very long the ships of the world will be passing through our Canal, and we will have to our credit a national achievement over which the old eagle may well spread and flap his wings." He added, "A visit to the Isthmus of Panama will make any American proud of his nation. The Canal is the greatest undertaking of the age."[50]

Dr. Gorgas, Col. George W. Goethals (chief engineer), and the canal workers became national heroes. After the campaign against yellow fever and malaria, the American Medical Association appointed Dr. Gorgas its president. At the association's annual meeting, Gorgas described the significance of their achievement. From his perspective, "the white man can [now] live in the tropics and enjoy as good health as he would have if living in the temperate zone. This has been demonstrated both by our two military occupations of Cuba and by our present occupancy of Panama."[51] Politicians and the public agreed with Gorgas's assessment. "The treatment of hygienic conditions on the Isthmus," as President Roosevelt put it, "has been such as to make it literally the model for all work of the kind in tropical countries. Five years ago the Isthmus of Panama was a byword of unhealthiness of the most deadly kind."[52] Now tourists flocked to the region.

The image of "the white man's graveyard" had become in the span of just a few years the image of a winter health resort. The public health practices and the narrative of tropical conquest attracted tourists not only to Panama but also to Caribbean destinations all along the route. Steamship and tour companies turned health and tropical conquest into a marketing tool to sell new Caribbean tours. "Today health and happiness are the treasures sought on the Spanish Main," the United Fruit Company advertised in 1915. "Great White Fleet ships, built especially for tropical travel, bear you luxuriously to scenes of romance."[53] The passenger steamship company Grace Line explained that "where fever and death once convinced the French that no canal would ever be built. . . [is] now one of the most healthful spots in the world."[54] Another steamship line advertised, "Here [in Panama] the humblest American will feel some of that imperial pride aroused in the citizen of ancient Rome or of modern Britain by the sight of his race carrying light to the dark places of the world."[55] Travel writers and tourists also reproduced and spread this ethnonationalist message of environmental conquest. "We landed," as one traveler noted, "and immediately started out to see the wonders performed by the genius of two great Americans, Dr. William Crawford Gorgas and General George W. Goethals. We found no mosquitoes anywhere, and very few flies—I think we saw only two or three in the two days we were in the Canal Zone."[56] After the conquest at the canal, old colonial fantasies of the tropics could be safely experienced for a rapidly growing number of visitors.

FIGURE 6. "The death song of the Mosquito, Canal Zone, Panama," a postcard capturing the work of the mosquito brigades, four thousand mostly West Indian laborers, who sprayed oil onto the fields and marshes surrounding the Panama Canal construction project. Doug Allen Postcard Collection

FIGURE 7. Tourists visiting the Panama Canal construction project. Doug Allen Postcard Collection

Yet strangely this conquest narrative fueling the early tourism industry has disappeared from popular memory. The story of malaria and yellow fever has submerged into a packaged timelessness of tropical paradise. It now appears as if the Caribbean had always been a fun and safe place to visit. A revisionist read of the Panama Canal's history, however, forces us to rethink the meaning of the gap in health perception between the past and present. Historians, particularly those working in the field of environmental history, have reevaluated the canal's triumphal narrative and its connection to US empire. The historian Paul Sutter explains that "the environmental management practices that had controlled tropical diseases there [in Panama] helped to alter American attitudes about the promise and perils of tropical nature."[57] Sutter proves, though, that scientific conquest was also the mitigation of unintended ecological consequences brought on by US imperial expansion. The waves of malaria and yellow fever during the war of 1898 and then in the early years of the building of the Panama Canal were not necessarily the result of an intrinsically hostile tropical nature. Instead, epidemics were the consequence of socially constructed landscapes and the ordering of work and living practices. In Cuba, army camps filled with thousands of men turned farms and forests into unsanitary mud pits. Human waste, sickness, and bodies were in close proximity. A similar transformation occurred at the Panama Canal. The project converted rain forests and hilly savannahs into war zones of man versus nature. The Culebra Cut, the most difficult and treacherous excavation site, looked more like Dante's inferno than the diverse tropical landscape it used to be. As one visitor observed, "now stretches a man-made canyon across the backbone of the continent. . . . Men call it Culebra Cut. . . . It is majestic. It is awful. It is the Canal."[58] To construct this artificial canyon, men trod and lived in a morass, the perfect breeding ground for disease-carrying mosquitoes. Human victims created and then worked in the middle of the mosquitoes' ideal habitat. These were not natural and hostile ecosystems eternally part of the tropics. Rather, they were part of a long-running history of human hubris and environmental folly.[59]

Tourism's twentieth-century rise, read in this reflexive way, is more complicated than the control of tropical pathogens. The mass organization of human labor and the use of industrial machines produced the need to tame nature. The conquest of disease was the US government engaging in one of its favorite foreign policy initiatives: fighting to solve a problem it helped to create, while denying any role in its creation. The desire to industrially engineer a new transportation route to feed economic growth at home instigated the ecological conditions (standing water for mosquito reproduction) and social relations (large migrant populations living in close proximity) necessary for epidemics.

Popular discourses that geographically and culturally pinpointed malaria and yellow fever as distinctly "tropical" diseases dangerous to white people misled as much as they explained about the history of the Caribbean and its relation to the mainland United States and the Atlantic World. People of European and African descent had been living in the Caribbean region for generations. Those residents, however, were not white citizens of the United States. The US government helped eradicate yellow fever and reduce the infectious rate of malaria in Panama and the greater Caribbean. But one must recognize that the natural habitat of mosquitoes and the pathogens they carry had never been isolated in areas south of the US mainland. In the summer, mosquitoes and their diseases were endemic from New England to the Carolinas to Florida. Malaria and yellow fever, in addition to other infectious diseases such as influenza, plagued urban and coastal communities. In the 1870s and 1880s, yellow fever epidemics regularly hit US coastal communities. As late as 1899, there were over fifteen hundred reported cases of yellow fever in Miami and Key West. Malaria, meanwhile, continued to plague communities in the South well into the 1930s. Circum-Caribbean nations before and after the canal project were statistically no more deadly or diseased than US mainland cities such as New Orleans and Charleston or even the industrial cities of Chicago and New York. The conquest of malaria and yellow fever in Panama and Cuba more accurately belongs to a broader shift in public health efforts across the Americas, from temperate to tropical zones, in the early twentieth century.[60] These epidemiological details, however, were lost on a public and a government eager to proclaim and justify victory in a foreign land. In Panama and Cuba, the United States had supposedly "regained" tropical paradise. Tourism and commerce flowed thereafter, and soon the traveling public would forget this triumphal origin story altogether.

Imperial Infrastructure

In addition to assurances of tropical health, advances in transportation speed and comfort encouraged tourists to travel farther south. It would be a long and arduous journey to newly sanitized tropical destinations without the parallel development of modern trade routes. New railroad and steamship lines, which supported US imperial and commercial expansion at the turn of the century, also made the region accessible to northern visitors.

Before the Spanish-American War and the building of the Panama Canal, the United States controlled no populated territories south of Key West, Florida. But by the time President Roosevelt embarked on his 1906 overseas tour, the United States had taken control of Cuba, Puerto Rico, Panama, and the distant Philippines and Guam. In 1898 the United States fought and won a war against Spain and in the process converted a series of national independence movements into an imperial transfer.[61] That same year, the US government also annexed the Republic of Hawaii. Five years later, in 1903, President Roosevelt sent a group of naval warships to the Caribbean coast of Panama, formally a province of Colombia. The Colombian government in Bogotá had refused to sign a treaty allowing the United States to dig a transoceanic canal across the isthmus. In response, the US Navy supported a bloodless revolution to create the new Republic of Panama. The resulting Hay-Bunau-Varilla Treaty, signed without a single Panamanian in the room, granted the US government the right to build the Panama Canal and total control over the Panama Canal Zone, a ten-mile-wide strip of land that ran from the Caribbean to the Pacific Ocean, which the US claimed to lease "in perpetuity."[62]

In the halls of government, and in close dialogue with the nation's most powerful capitalists, it was reasoned that if the United States was to continue on its path to industrial progress, it had to be a player in the imperial race for colonies and new markets. The historian and political theorist Brooks Adams summarized this expansionist ideology in 1898, arguing that the United States "stands face to face with the gravest conjuncture that can confront a people. She must protect the outlets of her trade, or run the risk of suffocation."[63] The naval strategist Alfred Thayer Mahan also advocated overseas expansion, explaining, "Americans must now begin to look outward. The growing production of the country demands it."[64] The United States, officials argued, needed to develop new markets in Latin America and the Pacific that would also serve as strategic stepping stones on the path to the wider "open door" of the coveted "Asiatic markets."[65]

With imperial territorial grabs from 1898 to 1903, the United States gained control of the most important shipping routes in the Americas, acquiring strategically located bases in Cuba, Puerto Rico, and the future Panama Canal. These military actions modeled the established naval strategy of the British Empire in the Mediterranean and the Indian Ocean. As Mahan argued, the British navy was the source of the island nation's development into the world's most powerful empire in the nineteenth century. Controlling the sea and strategic shipping locations such as narrow straits, canals, and well-placed coaling stations was essential to the future success and security of a growing nation. US expansionist designs in the Caribbean, from the Florida Straits to the Isthmus of Panama, paralleled the British naval strategy, which controlled shipping lanes at the Straits of Gibraltar and the Suez Canal.[66] As one early canal observer noted, "the Caribbean is to be the American Mediterranean, and the visible and effective power of the United States in those waters must be equal, probably vastly superior, to that of England in Europe's great inland sea."[67]

Military and commercial expansion proceeded in successive fashion from one conquered territory to the next. The ports, railroads, and even the hotel accommodations of Florida, as discussed in the previous chapter, became points of departure for the US invasion of Cuba. In the mid-nineteenth century, the US government considered much of Florida to be Indian frontier, the site of brutal wars with the Seminole people. But by the 1890s, the state had become the settled staging ground for another wave of expansion. "For some time before the opening of actual hostilities between the United States and Spain," one journalist observed, "Key West bore the appearance of a war port."[68] The battleship *Maine* steamed out of Tampa and anchored in Key West before arriving in Havana Harbor where its fiery destruction sparked war. Soon afterward, Roosevelt and his Rough Riders trained for combat in the field adjacent to the Tampa Bay Hotel, owned and operated by the Plant System of Railways and Hotels. The Florida East Coast Railway owned by Henry Flagler also grew alongside US political and military expansion. When the US government began the canal project in Panama a few years later, the railroad expanded all the way to Key West. In a brochure for passengers, the railway's management explained:

> When the road is finished it will be a strong factor in handling the rapidly-increasing passenger business to Cuba. It also will be the nearest rail point in the United States to the eastern end of the Panama Canal. It is believed the possibilities of the road in connection with the rapidly-growing commerce of the United States with West Indian and Central American points will warrant the great outlay for construction. . . . A line drawn from Miami to the [sic] southward would pass midway through Cuba and strike Colon, one of the terminals of the Panama Canal.[69]

The voyage by rail and sea, according to the line's brochure, promised to be "a veritable trip through wonderland." The brochure, titled "Paradise Regained," included a map of the Caribbean and an image of heaven-like pillared gates, flanked by two smiling black men in servant uniforms carrying golf clubs and a suitcase (see figure 3 in the introduction), followed inside by a list of hotels and general information. Imperial infrastructure, public health initiatives, and racist social orders were merging into a new industry.

The development of roads, pedestrian walkways, and modern hotel accommodations followed a similar pattern of imperial piggybacking. In Cuba, Col. Leonard Wood, former commander of the Rough Riders, was appointed US military governor of the island. The infrastructure he commissioned became the scaffolding of Cuba's early tourist economy. Wood ordered the construction of Havana's famous ocean promenade, the Malecón, still admired by both tourists and Havana residents. The goal of the military government, he believed, was to bring US business and development to the island. "When capital is willing to invest," Wood declared, "a condition of stability will have been reached."[70] Sanitary conditions, infrastructure, and US-style government would bring investors and visitors. In Panama, the canal and its supporting infrastructure also served the movement of leisure travel. The Canal Zone had all the creature comforts of a newly formed suburb, with restaurants, recreation facilities, movie theaters, and welcoming neighbors to interact with and entertain visitors. "The Canal Zone," as one traveling writer saw it in 1913, "is an outpost of high civilization in the tropics. It affords object lessons to the neighboring republics . . . in architecture, sanitation, road building, education, civil government and indeed all the practical arts that go to make a State comfortable and prosperous."[71] The US government, under the orders of the president of the United States, even built several luxury hotels for tourists visiting the isthmus. The Hotel Tivoli, overlooking Panama City from Ancon Hill, was constructed in anticipation of Roosevelt's 1906 visit. In the years immediately following the presidential visit, additions were made to the hotel to accommodate "those persons connected with, or interested, in the construction of the Canal who were constantly arriving from the United States."[72] The Hotel Tivoli emerged as one of the more popular hotels on the tropical tourist scene in the first half of the twentieth century. "Here," as one writer noted, "practically all of the tourists come and stay while on the Isthmus."[73] The US government also commissioned the construction of the Hotel Washington in Colón. Colonel Goethals, governor of the Canal Zone, reported that

> the lack of suitable hotel accomodations [sic] in the vicinity of the Atlantic terminus of the Canal was brought to the attention of the President during his visit to the Isthmus in November last, and he authorized the construction of a suitable fire-proof hotel by the Panama Railroad Company in Colon on the site of the present old "Washington Hotel," both to supply this want, and as a revenue producer for the Panama Railroad Company.[74]

In sum, the development of hotels and transportation infrastructure for the early tourist scene in the Caribbean followed the route of US empire. In the 1890s there was no serious tourism industry south of Florida, nor were there any US colonial possessions. But by 1912–13, multiple steamship and railroad lines raced south. Tourists "in the midst of the wildest orgies of imperialism" had begun to embrace tropical vacationing.[75] The connection between the growth of tropical tourism and US imperialism, however, ran deeper than overlapping chronology or shared science, technology, and infrastructure. The beliefs and ideologies guiding US foreign policy and tropical travel culture also emerged from the same history.

Empire as a Way of Life

As one canal worker cheerfully rephrased the exhortation, "A generation ago, Horace Greeley said, 'Go West, young man, go West!' Tomorrow the word may be, 'Go South!' "[76] Following US history from the early nineteenth century to the early twentieth century, one can trace the real and imaginary lines of expansion shifting from the American West to the tropics of the Caribbean and Pacific. In the nineteenth century, as settlers and soldiers moved farther west, they often traveled through the Caribbean and across the Central American isthmus on their journeys. They normally, though, did not stay very long. Filibusters such as William Walker tried to carve out their own republics, like they did in Texas, but farther south the local populations of Central America and the Caribbean effectively pushed back against foreign intruders from the United States. Walker died by firing squad in Honduras in 1860, while his attaché, Col. Henry Titus, escaped and later founded a small town in Florida, which he named after himself (Titusville). The US military also put troops on the ground in Panama no fewer than thirteen times before the beginning of the canal project. The main thrust of US settler expansion in the nineteenth century, however, remained continental. By 1904, however, the Isthmus of Panama had become the southern edge of a new tropical "frontier" for the United States. The movement west, then south, was part of the same mentality of expansion.[77] Canal workers saw themselves as the next generation of pioneers. As Arthur Bullard described them in 1914, they were the "modern frontiersmen of our day, undismayed by the odds against them."[78]

The soldiers who had earlier engaged in the conquest of the American West also led the conquest of the tropics. Dr. Gorgas, for example, was stationed in North Dakota, Texas, and Florida before being sent to Cuba and Panama.[79] The ICC called on white workers and military officials, who had conquered US continental frontiers with violence, dynamite, steel, and concrete, to build the canal. Colonel Goethals, who also served in the Cuba campaign and oversaw the completion of the canal as chief engineer, began his career conducting surveys for the Army Corps of Engineers in the Pacific Northwest. John Frank Stevens, Goethals's predecessor in Panama, helped build the Great Northern Railway in the 1880s, which ran from Saint Paul,

Minnesota, to Seattle, Washington.[80] Colonel Wood, who would become the US military governor of Cuba and later the Philippines, had earlier in his career participated in the last official army campaign against Geronimo and the Apache in Arizona and New Mexico. White men all down the hierarchical line of the Spanish-American War and the Panama Canal project had similar migration histories, moving from the West to the tropics—from the president of the United States to engineers to military men to low-level colonial officials.[81]

Soldiers, engineers, and government officials moved water and earth and people to reshape tropical landscapes to serve the demands of US production and metropolitan consumers. The Caribbean's transition from conquered land to vacation destination, in this sense, echoed environmental, technological, and political changes that occurred earlier with the continental frontier. Expansion, however, involved not just economic interests and military strength. The frontier fed the industrial machine, but it also offered an outlet of escape and rebirth for the curious travelers and discontents of society. "That restless, nervous energy," in the words of Frederick Jackson Turner, "that dominant individualism, working for good and evil, and withal that buoyancy and exuberance which comes with freedom, these are the traits of the frontier." In 1893 Turner captured this popular belief in his famous essay "The Significance of the Frontier in American History."[82] He argued that the frontier was "a magic fountain of youth in which America continuously bathed and rejuvenated. . . . This perennial rebirth, this fluidity of American life, this expansion westward with its new opportunities, its continuous touch with the simplicity of primitive society, furnish the forces dominating American character." Politicians, businessmen, and soldiers agreed with Turner that if the frontier ended, so would the nation's greatness. "His personal influence," according to the historian William Appleman Williams, "touched Woodrow Wilson and perhaps Theodore Roosevelt, while his generalization guided subsequent generations of intellectuals and business men who became educational leaders, wielders of corporate power, government bureaucrats, and crusaders for the Free World."[83] The culture of manifest destiny, the necessarily always expanding frontier, was an accepted and celebrated part of US culture.

The far edges of "civilization" provided a space to experience and confront nature and, as Turner theorized, feel free from the constraints and rules of home. The frontier was a region, a nature, a culture that did not fit into preconceived US notions of what it meant to be modern.[84] The American West, and even Florida, had been a frontier because Native Americans and Hispanic settlers did not live and use the land the same way white settlers and soldiers from the United States viewed the proper relationship between man and community, man and nature. It therefore had to be conquered, settled, and civilized. The tropics were part of this paradigm of thinking.[85] US officials and military personnel in Cuba and Panama, and also in the Pacific in Hawaii and the Philippines, saw their mission and way of being as part of an expanding frontier of civilization. The Spanish Empire and mixed-race and dark-skinned "natives" followed a different way of being, one that was supposedly hostile to white American values. It, too, had to be conquered for the sake of progress. Yet at the same time, there was something appealing about uncivilized life. It was both abominable and liberating. The rules of civilization did not entirely apply to the frontier during its conquest. It was a liminal zone between civilization and barbarism, and those frontiersmen living or visiting that zone felt they had the privilege of being able to have one moral foot in each.[86]

White workers at the canal often viewed themselves as "roughnecks" living in the untamed tropics. Clubs and societies that embraced rugged manhood became famous in the days of construction. The Society of Chagres, an exclusive white-male club of canal workers, encouraged unchecked freedom. Founding member John K. Baxter celebrated:

> Three cheers, my brothers, three rousing cheers for Pagan Panama.
> What other city on all the seven seas is so plenteously provided with bars, breweries, brothels, bodegas, barrel houses, cantinas, clubs, groggeries and gin mills? Where is Scotch Whiskey more plentiful or more vile? Where so complete a collection of topers, tipplers, tanks, panhandlers and pimps? Where is the Sunday night souse in such esteem, or the Monday morning headache so habitual?[87]

Tropical frontier life was hard-drinking, individualistic, and supposedly free from the constraints of civilized conformity. Nightlife in Panama City and Colón lived up to this reputation. The US Canal Zone, inhabited overwhelmingly by men, banned bars and "unmarried" cohabitation with women. But in nearby Panamanian cities there were no such restrictions. Canal administrators outsourced worker desires for fun and vice. Stories of cross-cultural debauchery became infamous and encouraged many repressed travelers and tourists to see it for themselves.[88] As Baxter advertised,

> if you are persecuted in arid Kansas, in Russia or in Maine, if you are parched and thirsty and the Pharisees will give you no vital drop to ease the burden of your woes, there is a refuge for you in Panama. . . . We will welcome you with wassail and good cheer, and speed you merrily

on the road to Hell! Many of us have traveled the way, and some of us have reached the goal!—and our end is in Panama![89]

Tourists from the United States could visit occupied territories in the circum-Caribbean and be proud of their nation's conquest of the tropics, while still getting a taste of the liberating revelry of frontier life. This ethnonationalist view of the "pagan" frontier paved the way for the comfortable escapist culture of the tropical vacation. The frontier mentality, in all its effort to escape and be free from restrictive responsibilities, was the forerunner of a hegemonic culture of leisure travel. Tourism's emergence embodied the geographic expansion and cultural standardization of empire as a way of life.[90]

Not only did tourists and tropical frontiersmen share a freewheeling culture, but soldiers and colonial officials also worked as cultural mediators between domestic norms and travel experiences abroad. The agents of empire, who led the "conquest of the tropics," subdued the region to make visitors feel safe in terms of health, but they also established the attractions and facilities to accommodate the tourist's visit. Individuals with entrepreneurial ambitions developed bars, restaurants, tour companies, newspapers, and attractions, big and small, to serve the rapidly growing class of leisure travelers. Canal workers and soldiers, living in the tropics, became guides in the emerging tourism industry. They invited and entertained the next round of travelers, playing a similar role to the frontiersmen-turned-showmen of the American West, like Buffalo Bill and his peers, who went from cowboys and soldiers to tourist entrepreneurs.[91] Charles Wesley Powell, for example, a former canal worker, organized a botanical garden, which developed into one of the more popular attractions on the isthmus, later forming a partnership with the Missouri Botanical Garden. According to one visiting botanist from the Smithsonian Institution, Powell's collection was "unsurpassed."[92] The *Panama News*, an English-language newspaper geared to visitors, also published a number of articles about Powell's garden:

Undoubtedly, the Panama Canal has a rival for honors. "Have you seen the 'Big Ditch?'" will not be the only question put to tourist's [sic] who pass through these parts. One does not need an extraordinary amount of foresight to predict that without doubt both local people and visitors will soon be exclaiming with pride and admiration, "Have you seen POWELL'S ORCHID GARDEN, the TROPICAL STATION of the MISSOURI BOTANICAL GARDENS?" If you haven't, you should, for it is one of the prettiest places in the world.[93]

The newspaper that covered Powell's story was run by former canal workers and also veterans of the Spanish-American War. The *Panama Times*, according to its editorial board, "reflects the scenic charm, historic interest, tourist attractions, business opportunities and commercial advance of Panama and neighboring republics." John K. Baxter, who was also a secretary in the ICC, was the chief editor of the *Panama Times*. Baxter, a native of Tennessee and a Harvard graduate, was a canal employee turned writer and entrepreneur.[94] In addition to writing for the *Panama News*, Baxter was the first editor of the English-based newspaper the *Panama American,* whose motto was "Panama, A Play-Ground for 365 Days in Every Year."[95] Colleagues remembered Baxter as an "outstanding writer" who often attributed his daily inspiration to his favorite drink, Azuero rum.

Other Society of the Chagres club members, in addition to Baxter, were deeply involved in the promotion of tourism. John O. Collins, who compiled the society's annual yearbook, was one of the main authorities for tourism information on the isthmus, publishing *The Panama Guide* (1913) and *Recreation in Panama* (1914).[96] Like many of his peers, Collins joined the canal project after serving in the military campaign in Cuba. Another member of the club, W. M. Baxter, was the Canal Zone government's official tour guide. Baxter accompanied tourists on their railroad sightseeing tour of the canal, which had become a highly efficient and profitable business. In 1912, according to the Canal Zone newspaper,

> the sightseeing business has therefore been systematized and its conduct is now a regular part of the work. There is no better way to see the Canal than the trips of the sightseeing train, and none that requires so little time. . . . The train moves slowly through Culebra Cut, and about the locks and Gatun Dam, while the guide explains in clear and authoritative manner all phases of the work and answers all questions.[97]

Among the Society of Chagres members, however, Baxter regularly complained that the tourists were "generally comfortable men and women of 50 or more, a few spinsters, an occasional girl of near 20 years. Men between 25 and 45 are few. I suppose they are too busy to take three weeks for Panama." To rough canal men like Baxter, the visitors were sometimes irritating. "The male fool is annoying only when he becomes excited," Baxter noted. "He has read a book, or perhaps two books, about the Canal on his way to the Isthmus."[98] Nevertheless, he admitted, tourists did help pay the bills.

A tight-knit community of educated white men, as seen in the Society of Chagres, moved between various social positions—in war, colonial governance, and tourism. Empire as military might or engineering infrastructure was on the everyday scale bound up with touristic services. The story of individuals like Baxter and Collins, so closely connected, show how US imperial expansion became entangled with the tourism industry. Both men fought in Cuba, lived in the same Canal Zone community, worked in the same offices, and were members of the same exclusive clubs, and both of them promoted and profited from the growth in tropical tourism.

It was not, however, just white officials and ex-soldiers from the United States who entered the new tourist economy. The industry also involved local elites, small business owners, and a whole legion of service-sector entertainers and workers of color from across the circum-Caribbean. Black West Indian migrants who participated in the construction project also became service and maintenance workers in the emerging industry. Their experience with the US canal project and their knowledge of English, coming from British Caribbean colonies, facilitated the transition to tourism work.

In the highly racist colonial system, however, people of color were severely limited in terms of socioeconomic mobility. Black laborers went from digging ditches for white foremen to serving drinks at the Hotel Tivoli and Hotel Washington for white tourists. This hierarchy of labor, combined with the culture of the imperial frontier, translated into social practices and privileges for a burgeoning yet racially exclusive tourism industry.

In sum, the Caribbean's transformation from a diseased to a desirable region emerged out of the crucible of US imperial expansion in a number of important ways: as a nature to conquer and make safe, as a frontier to enjoy and exploit, as an extension of US commercial and political interests, and as a revenue source for maintaining the infrastructure and influence of empire. When the United States expanded into the Caribbean, the region was reimagined for touristic consumption. In the twenty-first century, however, this crucial relationship between imperialism and tourism seems to be forgotten. Harry Franck, a travel writer who journeyed all over the Americas and worked in Panama during the final years of the canal's construction, predicted this eventual erasure:

The swift growth of the tropics will quickly heal the scars of the steamshovels, and palm-trees will wave the steamer on its way through what will seem almost a natural channel. Then blasé travelers lolling in their deck chairs will gaze about them and snort: "Huh! Is that all we got for nine years' work and half a billion dollars?" They will have forgotten the vast hospitals with great surgeons and graduate nurses, the building of hundreds of houses and the furnishing of them down to the

FIGURE 8. The Culebra Cut, the most intensive site of the Panama Canal construction project, which was formerly called the Galliard Cut, after US Army engineer David du Bose Galliard who oversaw its excavation. Doug Allen Postcard Collection

FIGURE 9. After the canal's completion, the Galliard Cut was depicted as an idyllic passage for passenger steamships. Doug Allen Postcard Collection

last center table, they will not recall the rebuilding of the entire P.R.R. [Panama Railroad], nor scores of little items like $43,000 a year merely for oil and negroes to pump it on the pestilent mosquito, the thousand and one little things so essential to the success of the enterprise yet that leave not a trace behind. Greater perhaps than the building of the canal is the accomplishment of the United States in showing the natives how life can be lived safely and healthily in tropical jungles.[99]

Although the historical scars and injustices have submerged into the tropical landscape, excavating this history raises serious questions about the meaning and practice of modern leisure travel. What type of regional development did the intersection of imperialism and tourism promote for the long term? What type of travel culture did this historical connection encourage? Our answers begin here in the crucible of US empire-building.

CHAPTER 2

Service Sector Republics

Transnational Development in Panama and Cuba

> If you have a lot of what people want and can't get,
> then you can supply the demand and shovel in the
> dough.
>
> —Meyer Lansky

On October 28, 1928, Guillermo Andreve—a Panamanian intellectual and national hero—sailed from Colón, Panama, to Havana, Cuba. Andreve traveled as a first-class passenger on SS *Ulua*, a six-thousand-ton reefer ship in the United Fruit Company's Great White Fleet. Aboard ship he was surrounded by luxury. The Great White Fleet, "built especially for tropical service and for the most exacting of passengers," was the most famous cruise line in the Caribbean's early tourism industry. The *Ulua* and its sister ships were known as "the largest and finest ships that sailed the tropics."[1]

Andreve, however, was no tourist. He traveled for another, yet related, purpose. In early November he arrived in Havana as a diplomat for the Panamanian government. His official task was to "study the organization and development of the tourism industry in the Republic of Cuba." It was, in the words of Panama's president, a "mission of the highest importance."[2] The Caribbean's tourist economy was growing exponentially in the 1920s. An estimated hundred thousand tourists visited Cuba in 1928, and Panama was experiencing a similar influx of visitors. That year more than seventy-five thousand tourists came to the isthmus, not counting the thousands of sailors and soldiers who also took shore leave or were temporarily stationed there. According to a report by the National City Bank of New York, "the tourist business is the most important factor [for Panama's economy], and is certain to grow from year to year."[3] During his trip, Andreve met with Cuban officials to discuss tourism-development strategies that could also be implemented in his own country. Tourism was becoming a model of international development for local and national governments in the circum-Caribbean.

In a short book, *Cómo atraer el turismo a Panamá* (How to attract tourists to Panama), published in 1929, Andreve outlined Cuba's approach to the tourism industry. He explained that the Cuban government, in its efforts to maximize profits, organized an international publicity campaign and promoted the development of first-class hotels and attractions, such as casinos, cabarets, and horseracing. Andreve's report focused in particular on Cuba's tourism law of 1919, which created the island's first National Tourism Commission, and outlined a series of tax incentives to attract foreign investors. Most important, and with long-term effects, the law legalized gambling and casinos on the island; it became known as the "Monte Carlo Bill." It was the first step in the Cuban government's effort to turn tourism into a tool for national development.[4] It was also the beginning of Cuba's state-sanctioning of touristic desires (or vices), which would come to characterize a region-wide industry.

Following this legislation, a cast of unsavory figures—Meyer Lansky, Lucky Luciano, Frank Costello, and lesser-known gangsters and opportunists—also began to invest in the tourist economy. Organized crime from the United States would come to finance the hotel-casinos, tourist resorts, and clubs that would make Havana famous in the years before the Cuban Revolution.[5] Andreve, seemingly unaware of this impending social storm, recommended that Panama and other circum-Caribbean nations follow similar legislative steps to promote foreign investment. He explained that the tourism industry offered "naturally beautiful and exotic" countries, with underdeveloped agricultural and industrial resources, a path to economic growth. The state, he argued, should support tourism development. His colleagues in government agreed. Upon his return to the isthmus, Panama's National Assembly passed a tourism law modeled on Cuba's, legalizing gambling and casinos.[6]

On the surface, Andreve's policy recommendations looked like a radical departure from his earlier public career. A revolutionary hero, national literary figure, and politician was now a tourist planner. During Panama's struggle for political autonomy, Andreve had served as a colonel in the Thousand Days' War (1899–1902). He was an outspoken critic of Colombian centralized rule. "Among the group of men, who took it upon themselves to create and organize the republic," according to the historian Rodrigo Miró, "Andreve exhibited characteristics that gave him a special profile." After the nation's founding in 1903, Andreve served as president of the National Assembly and during the presidency of Belisario Porras (1912–24) as secretary of education and later as secretary of government and justice. Andreve developed a reputation as a "militant liberal" in the fight for national sovereignty. In addition to his political career, he was also a respected author. According to Miró, Andreve was "the creator of our national literature."[7] He was a sojourning intellectual, revolutionary, and liberal in the classic nineteenth-century Latin American sense. But by the 1920s he was also a man of tourism.

The story of Andreve's visit to Cuba highlights a historic contradiction within Caribbean and Latin American development strategies emerging in the first half of the twentieth century. Politicians who fought for national sovereignty and often espoused the rhetoric of anti-imperialism quickly embraced policies that worked to attract investors and visitors from the empire.[8] How was it possible to be a revolutionary and nationalist and also a promoter of an economy dependent on foreign consumers? As the United States established geopolitical control over the Caribbean, local elites sought to turn US interest in the region to their own favor. If they could not stop the United States militarily and politically, they could culturally and economically embrace, in the words of the historian Michael Gobat, the old idea of "empire by invitation."[9]

Elite strategies focused on both short-term monetary gains from visitors and long-term economic development through foreign investment. These national policies were transnational political efforts. As the journey of Andreve shows, tourism development in one locale was connected to developments in other parts of the Caribbean. Panama modeled policies in Cuba, but tourist developers traveled in both directions. Politicians and businessmen in South Florida were also part of this elite network, in dialogue with their neighbors and forging close ties of economic and cultural exchange.

By the 1920s the growth of tropical travel and elite dreams of progress converged. State efforts to promote tourism in the Caribbean began much earlier than scholars and the public have typically recognized. Liberal legislation, put in place in the first decades of the twentieth century, allowed for highly unregulated economic growth for the rest of the century. The classic post–World War II era of development, traditionally studied by tourism scholars, depended on the foundational policies of the preceding half century. Although tourism may seem to belong to a more contemporary current of thinking and mobility, distinct from turn-of-the-century liberal visions of the nation-state, the industry was actually part of a long thread of development ideology running from the nineteenth century into the twentieth century. Elites updated old liberal ideals of free trade and mobility to justify and promote tourism. In the context of neoliberalism, they are still used today.[10]

Politicians and developers reasoned that foreign tourists would become important consumers for emerging economies. And with the right incentives, visitors might decide to stay and invest their cultural and economic capital for the long term. As one economic report from Panama explained in the late 1920s, "there is more to the development of the tourist business than the mere expenditures of visitors. . . . The chief value of this travel is the publicity value. . . . Men of all lines of business and varieties of interests will be visitors here in increasing numbers, and business men of experience, even on vacation trips, have their eyes open to opportunities."[11] Tourism could also translate into foreign direct investment.

In the quest for national development, political leaders viewed tourists as capital investors, desirable immigrants, and as sources of interconnected and competitive development linking regional economies with the rest of the "civilized" world. Despite the threats of imperialism, Caribbean and Latin American leaders continued to valorize European and US ways of life. Political philosophies of positivism remained common belief. There were debates about details, but in essence it was a shared belief that Western Europe and the United States offered universal models of progress for Latin American and Caribbean nations.[12] Inheriting a liberal tradition rooted in nineteenth-century thinking, elites in the twentieth century acted to promote a transnational and economically dependent model of tourism. "The dreams of this elite," as the historian Peter Szok documented in the case of Panama, "was a bustling center of business that would attract Europeans and civilize the isthmus."[13] What follows in this chapter is an intellectual history of how tourism became part of this particular vision of the future, another spoke on the wheel spinning toward progress.

Liberal Development in the Era of Imperialism

In the wake of US political and economic expansion, Caribbean tourism became a highly profitable industry—for those in the right position to take advantage of it. Business owners and politicians found quick profits in the new tourist economy. The industry also supplied work to chauffeurs, wait staff, maids, cooks, bartenders, musicians, prostitutes, and a variety of other service sector workers catering to the desires of visitors. By the mid-1920s, coastal cities such as Miami, Key West, Havana, and Colón had become bustling destinations for tourists and US military personnel.

Advances in tropical medicine and transportation technology, as described in the previous chapter, opened Caribbean communities to a new form of economic development. Most of these changes were beyond the control of

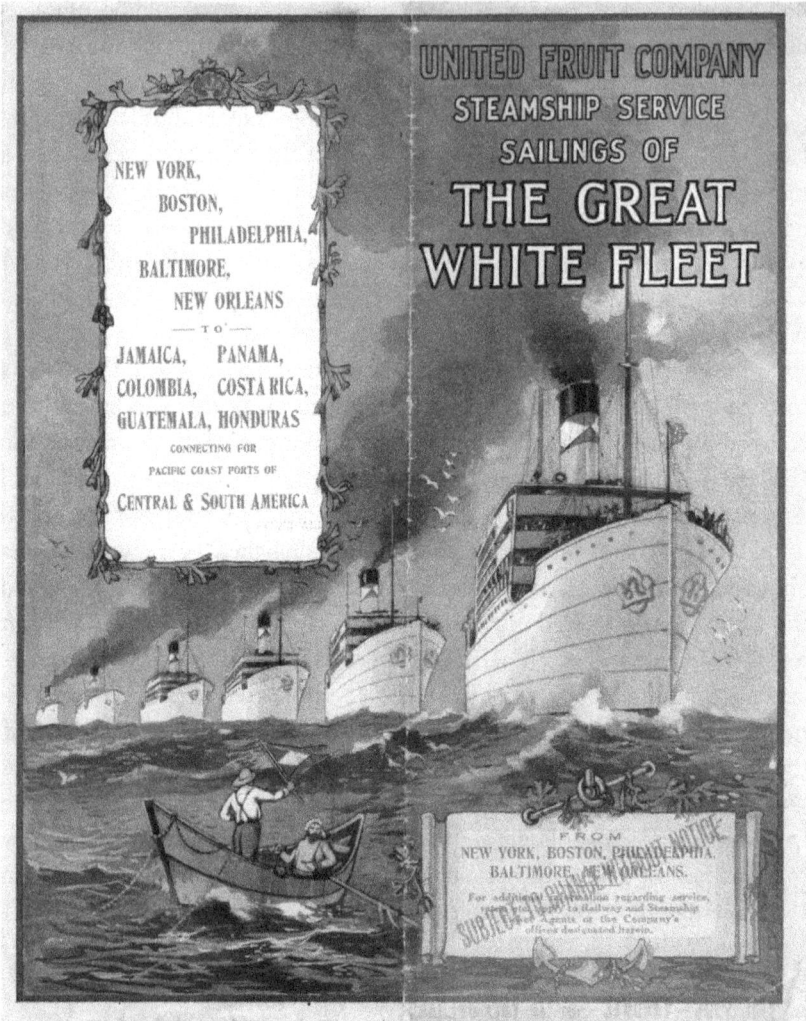

FIGURE 10. "Sailing List No. 16, January–July 1912," lists the United Fruit Company's steamship departure points in the United States and ports of call in the Caribbean and Central and South America. Collection of Björn Larsson.

local people. Part of the reason for Andreve's 1928 trip to Cuba, for example, was the decision by Pan American Airways to begin air passenger service connecting Miami and Havana with Colón. More and more tourists were expected to come to the isthmus by air in addition to steamship.[14] These international forces influenced what economically mattered and what did not, but as the anthropologist Sidney Mintz asked, "at what point does the prerogative to bestow meaning move from the consumers to the sellers?"[15]

Scholars critical of tourism, however, have hesitated to recognize the role of local leaders in the rise of the Caribbean's tourism industry. As the anthropologist Amanda Stronza summarized it, "often our assumptions have been that locals were duped into accepting tourism rather than having consciously chosen such an option for themselves."[16] The historical record, though, challenges preconceived notions that national and local community leaders passively accepted international tourism.

Politicians and business owners did not simply wait for the tourists to arrive. In the case of both Cuba and Panama, leaders embraced their new position as tropical vacation destinations and international models of sanitation and hygiene. Looking for opportunity in the era of US expansion, they decided to welcome the possibilities of tourism. "People on contested territories," according to the historians Frederick Cooper and Jane Burbank, "could resist, deflect, or twist in their own favor the encroachment of a more powerful polity."[17] State officials and private citizens sought to "twist" the influx of foreigners. They worked to expand the Caribbean's appeal, building new hotels and consumer attractions and promoting an identity that held up the region as a desirable destination, which would economically and politically benefit their nation-building projects.

To historically ground this strategy of national development, this chapter examines policies during the administration of President Belisario Porras (1912–24), remembered today as the "architect of Panama's modernization."[18] Events on the isthmus during that particular time have much to tell about broader patterns shaping tourism development across the region. The life history of Porras also exemplifies the tensions and possibilities of national development emerging from within the crucible of US empire.

In 1903, as the United States took control of the canal project, Porras spoke out against US military intervention. He was a committed anti-imperialist in the tradition of figures such as Cuba's revolutionary hero José Martí.[19] In the 1880s and 1890s, Porras traveled throughout the Caribbean, Central America, and Europe, speaking and writing about the fundamental importance of progress directed by and for Latin Americans. He believed in the sanctity of both liberalism and national sovereignty. Porras grew up in a small town in western Panama, the son of a politician committed to the Colombian government. As a young man, he studied law in Bogotá, a city he fondly remembered as the "Athens of the Americas." After graduating with his doctorate in law from the National University in 1881, he traveled to Europe as a diplomat with "a thousand projects in mind." Inspired by his formal studies and his foreign travels, he hoped to bring progress and civilization to the Colombian nation. According to his autobiography, he considered the renowned Colombian liberals Gil Colunje and Buenaventura Correoso as the sources of his political aspirations. "It was in the hands of these two illustrious sons of the isthmus," Porras recalled, "that I crossed the threshold of adolescence and I joined the ranks of the party, and which later motivated me to stand on the battlefield, to enter government, and defend the party in the press and in the courts, when it was still a crime to think."[20] In the Thousand Days' War between conservatives and liberals, Porras joined the liberal cause. He became a general, leading Panama's fight against the centralizing government of Bogotá. He had no intention, however, of Panama becoming a separate nation. He viewed the war as an internal dispute between political parties. In the face of US imperialism, Porras argued that "Colombian sovereignty should be maintained at all cost."[21]

Following the US intervention, though, Porras found himself isolated in his nationalist commitments. The majority of Panamanian liberal and conservative politicians "gave unconditional support to the idea of independence" after the Colombian Senate refused to ratify the canal treaty with the United States.[22] Pressured by US government officials, his opponents in the new Panamanian government revoked his citizenship, and Porras was forced into exile, to El Salvador. When he was allowed to return to the isthmus three years later, he came back with a more conciliatory perspective toward the United States and its hegemonic role in the region. He explained his shift in opinion by way of a parable, describing how US officials invaded the home of family friends forcing them onto the street in order to fumigate for mosquitoes. The family was upset. US officials, his friends argued, were "the enemies of the country." But a few years later, the family came to see things differently, according to Porras. "Have you seen the streets, Doctor?" they cheerfully asked him. "Now we can walk them without getting dirty." Nationalists like Porras remained opposed to US imperial control, but they also began to recognize new opportunities. The gringos had brought modern sanitation and transportation technology. Perhaps, despite the humiliation, they had laid a foundation for future development. Porras concluded that "progress and innovation are resisted by those who do not understand their potential benefits. Today we proclaim a great good what we believed before to be a terrible ill."[23]

Elected president of Panama in 1912 and again in 1918 and 1920, Porras would continue to criticize US control in the region but more tactfully and selectively. The US government and its control of the canal were there to stay. Porras and subsequent presidents would instead focus on negotiating with the US government to leave room for more locally controlled development.[24] Accepting the reality of the US military presence but still fighting for national sovereignty meant finding the means to prosper while under imperial control. It was within this compromised context that tourism appeared to be a potential middle ground between foreign domination and nationalist desires to guide the economy. Under the Porras administration, Panamanians began to reimagine US citizens as "tourists," invited guests of the republic. To assuage nationalist and commercial interests, tourism boosters also regularly relabeled US military personnel and sailors stationed on or visiting the isthmus as tourists. Panama's Association of Commerce even argued that the arrival of US naval vessels represented the "economic redemption" of the country.[25] Bars and cabarets earned huge profits when sailors took shore leave. In just two months in 1929, more than 180,000 US sailors visited the isthmus. This was a routine occurrence in port cities in the Caribbean. "Panamanian cities," according to the historian Jeffrey Parker, "belonged to a broader Caribbean world that shared a history of entertaining North American tourists and U.S. military personnel."[26]

Marketing Canal Triumphalism

As president, Porras looked to convert US tropical triumphalism into an instrument of the economy. The opening of the Panama Canal, he believed, had drawn the world's attention to the isthmus as "one of the great centers of universal commerce."[27] The Panamanian government joined the celebrations. In anticipation of the Panama-Pacific International Exposition in San Francisco to be held in 1915, an event that would receive an estimated nineteen million visitors, the Porras administration began to organize its own National Exposition of Panama. Expositions, international conferences, and fairs on the grand scale were seen as a way to promote development and investment.[28] Officials reasoned that tourists departing from the East Coast of the United States would coordinate their trip to pass through the actual canal on their way to the San Francisco exposition.

The national exposition had two goals: one, to attract foreign visitors to spur short-term monetary gains and, two, to stimulate long-term economic growth in national industries by inviting European and Euro-American immigrants and capital investment. In 1913 the Porras administration set events in motion, hiring journalists and a publicity company to advertise in the United States. The government hired W. W. Rasor, the editor-manager of *Pan American Magazine*, to publish full-length illustrated articles. The magazine would report on the republic's progress and its role as "the travelers' Hub of the Universe." Later that year, Gerald Hamilton, a journalist working at the *New York Herald*, also signed a contract to develop a promotional campaign. Hamilton would write a weekly chronicle about the exposition to circulate to major US newspapers.[29] The government also coordinated with steamship companies to advertise the exposition in Panama as part of the San Francisco exposition. The United Fruit Company promoted a special trip from New York to San Francisco by way of the canal. In a promotional flyer, UFCO officials explained that traveling "through the Panama Canal acts as a fitting prelude to the expositions; perhaps in no other way can the purpose and meaning of these commemorative expositions be so well understood."[30] In Panama's capital, meanwhile, an elaborate building project began to develop the rural outskirts of the old colonial city into a neighborhood with broad, paved streets and sidewalks to host the upcoming event. The neighborhood, still known today as La Exposición, would become the home of new government buildings of Commerce, Education, Agriculture, and Entertainment, in addition to a new stadium and horseracing track. La Exposición, moreover, became the location of foreign embassies. The new neighborhood, state officials argued, confirmed the nation's position as a modern republic and a center of commerce. "From a purely business point of view," the exposition's director explained, the construction project was "bound to give quick and many returns."[31] The new neighborhood also provided Panama's wealthiest residents the opportunity to move into more spacious and luxurious homes. "It will," according to one journalist, "become the residential district for the higher classes."[32]

There was also a clearly nationalist twist to Panama's celebration of the canal. The national exposition honored the US engineering feat but, unlike the San Francisco event, focused on the republic's *hispanidad*. In its framing of the exposition, the Panamanian government emphasized its historic relationship with "Madre Patria Española" (the Spanish motherland) and connections to other Spanish Caribbean and Latin American nations. State promotional material reminded visitors that King Charles V of Spain had originally proposed to build the canal in 1534, long before the French or US efforts. Exposition officials also notably shrouded the celebrations in the four-hundred-year anniversary of the Spanish "discovery" of the Pacific Ocean. Vasco Núñez de Balboa, after plundering throughout the Caribbean, became the first European to cross the isthmus to the "south sea."[33] This effort to memorialize Spanish colonial history was significant in light of the newly established US government and military presence in the region.

Yet at the same time, the exposition sought to attract US interest. James Zetek, a former Canal Zone employee and US Department of Agriculture scientist from Chicago, was appointed the national exposition's director. Zetek, who later became the director of the Smithsonian Institution's tropical research station in Panama, was a close friend of Porras. He advised the president that the exposition should cater to wealthy tourists from the northern parts of the United States, who annually escaped the winter cold and vacationed to warmer climates. "We should not forget," Zetek wrote, "that in all Expositions attractions and entertainment are the principal factors that bring the success we desire. If we have a good horseracing track, an athletic field for baseball, etc. . . . we will have nothing to fear in respect to a good turnout. [The isthmus] will be the place tourists choose to go." He added that "it is the foreigner with money that we want to interest. . . . which will bring to Panama the much needed capital and genius to develop the resources that lie latent in her bosom." Officials in the Ministry of Development and Public Works agreed: "If our character closes us off from finding the necessary elements to fertilize our fields and develop our national wealth, then why not attract foreign capitalists, agents of economic activity, and tourists . . . who we may win over by objectively demonstrating our commercial, agricultural, and industrial opportunities?"[34] This was becoming an established political-economic view among liberal elites in the early twentieth century. It presented an externalized model of tourism development. Officials in both Panama and Cuba, eyeing events in other tourist destinations, particularly on the Florida Peninsula, noted that tourists who escaped the cold climate of the North for one season often returned the next year to purchase lots and build winter homes. A good tourism industry could entice desirable visitors to become investors and perhaps permanent residents.[35]

A key component of this particular vision of development, however, was the racialized notion that progress depended on the "white race." President Porras was direct about his own vision for the nation: "I consider the actual population of our Republic to be insufficient to carry out her development." He reasoned, therefore, that the country needed to promote the "healthy" immigration of people of European descent, who possessed ready-to-use capital. The indigenous and black populations of the country were viewed as inferior to those of European background.[36] Social Darwinism and the ideas of sociologists such as Benjamin Kidd held wide appeal among liberal progressives in Latin America and the Caribbean. Kidd argued that the tropics remained underdeveloped because the dark-skinned majority was of "low social efficiency."[37] Elite minorities in the circum-Caribbean, like those represented by Porras, believed they needed more "white" people to become modern communities. As the historian Aviva Chomsky documented, "many Latin American nationalists embraced so-called 'scientific' racism and urged European immigration and racial whitening as building blocks to national dignity and independence."[38] Even the Cuban intellectual Fernando Ortiz, famous for his studies of Afro-Caribbean culture, argued as early as 1906 that "white immigration is what we should favor" because it would "inject in the blood of our people the red blood cells which tropical anemia robs from us, and sow among us the seeds of energy, of progress, of life . . . which today seem to be the patrimony of colder climates."[39] Like previous generations of Caribbean and Latin American liberals who had tried to attract European immigrants, the next generation of elites did something similar with tourism. In the early twentieth century, state and commercial developers began to interpret the promotion of migration, foreign investment, and tourism as mutually inclusive projects. European and white US tourists fit the mold of desirable immigrants. This close relationship between older development strategies and the promotion of tourism can still be seen in contemporary economic policies, an approach to development that transcends political difference. Governments across the Caribbean today still view tourism as a prelude to long-term investment.[40]

As a set of ideas about economic trade and modernity, however, the intellectual framework for the development of tourism actually preceded the arrival of tourists by several centuries. The economy of the circum-Caribbean as early as the sixteenth century revolved around the international movement of people and goods. Newly arrived Europeans believed the Caribbean's geographic position linked to a larger web of Atlantic world trade was the region's greatest resource. Colonialists, rather than focus on the production of goods for domestic consumption, specialized in export industries and the maritime service economy to support commercial trade with Europe. The historian Alfredo Castillero Calvo, in a seminal essay about Panamanian history, argued that three key historical periods defined this development model, which he called *transitismo*—that is, dependence on a transit-based economy: (1) the period of Spanish flotillas in the sixteenth and seventeenth centuries, when an incredible amount of New World gold and silver crossed the isthmus to the Caribbean on its way to Spain; (2) a brief surge period in international trade right before the Spanish colonial independence movements of the 1810s and 1820s; and (3) the California Gold Rush of 1848–55, when more "49ers" traveled through the Caribbean and across the isthmus on their way to the West Coast than those who crossed the vast interior of the North American continent.[41] The rise of US imperialism in the early twentieth century, and the resurgence of a service economy, appeared to be the next chapter in this evolving history of transitismo.

Generations of elites in Panama believed in, and tried to implement, transitismo as national development. Belisario Porras as president did and so did his son, Hernán Porras, a well-known historian and political figure in the mid-twentieth century. The younger Porras, who would also serve in government as minister of trade and industries, offered perhaps the clearest articulation of his father's vision. "White capitalists," he argued, were best equipped to politically control the country and turn the nation's privileged geographic position into a path of economic progress.[42] Transnational development, rooted in ideals of foreign trade and scientific racism, justified the concentration of the republic's economic and political power in the hands of a small group of elite families. The canal project and the international attention that followed reenergized this long-held belief.[43] It provided a means to develop a modern transit economy, one in which new types of travelers, especially tourists, would play an essential role.

Panamanians were not alone in the belief that their location on the world map was their greatest asset. Elites across the circum-Caribbean shared this geographically determined view. In Cuba, political and commercial leaders also claimed that more tourism incentives needed to be pushed forward in order for the country to receive "the benefits it deserved due to its climate, natural beauties, and its geographic position."[44] Residents of Havana, who had long argued that the colonial city was the key to the New World and the Caribbean, believed that the city was also essential to the region's new tourist trade. In South Florida, the rhetoric of tourism development was similar. Flagler extended his East Coast rail line to Miami and then Key West, claiming that Florida's "geographic position" warranted the massive construction investment. In the 1920s Pan American Airways also initiated regular international air service, from Miami to Cuba and then to Panama, justifying its choice in location because Miami's "geographic position" made it the gateway to the Americas.[45] The Caribbean had always been a crossroads—a place of transit—for travelers. But with that many destinations claiming the same geographic importance, the question became how to stand out on the route.

The "Second Harvest"

Following plantation industries such as sugar, citrus, and bananas, tourism became the next industry of development in the Caribbean region. Planners and developers in Cuba, Panama, and in neighboring islands such as Jamaica first began to call tourism their "second harvest" in the early twentieth century. The industry, as they hoped and planned, would become the source of a "vast quantity of new capital."[46] The machines and labor regimes of agricultural work were slowly giving way to an economy of luxurious hotels, entertainment, and refined service.

This new economy depended on a new system of production. Tourist consumers obviously crossed borders but so did industry promoters looking for development models. When Andreve traveled to Cuba in 1928, he went to study the new tools being developed for this second harvest. He traveled abroad in search of tourism and economic connections. Andreve, though, was just one of many travelers studying the new possibilities of tourism. Luis Machado, a respected Cuban diplomat, traveled in the other direction to the isthmus. Machado was the president of Cuba's first tourism commission in the 1920s and 1930s, Cuban ambassador to the United States in 1950–52, and later a director at the World Bank.[47] During multiple visits to Panama, his task was to help national leaders form a plan to boost tourism revenue. Machado argued that the state had an important role to play in the development of tourism. "Only the government," he claimed, "is able to make and execute a coordinated tourism plan, such as the construction of roads, the facilitation of communication technology, and the regulation of prices and tourist services." He concluded that "to develop tourism is to develop the nation's wealth."[48] The governments of both Cuba and Panama followed the approach that Machado outlined, investing in hotels, transportation infrastructure, and attractions.

While tourism in Cuba was a continual source of inspiration for Panama, at the same time Florida served as a model for both nations. Meetings and exchanges occurred between tourism boosters on both sides of the Florida Straits as early as the 1910s and continued into the 1950s. In August 1929, for example, a group of Cuban businessmen affiliated with the Rotary Club "were entertained in Miami."[49] Visitors learned about tourism and commercial developments in the "Magic City." There was also considerable discussion among Florida businessmen about developments in Cuba and the greater Caribbean. Representing the Greater Florida Association, A. T. Moreaux contacted the president of Cuba, praising the Cuban state's efforts to promote tourism. "I am convinced," he wrote, "that the hour has arrived for Cuba. The whole situation, this great continental trend to travel and invest, is unprecedented."[50] In November 1929 Florida's Rotary Club also sent a delegation to Havana, where it met with a young Luis Machado, Havana's Rotary Club's president, and Gen. Gerardo Machado, president of the republic. "I also am a Rotarian," the president told the invited guests. "As we help your financial institutions [in the United States], which are practically in many cases Cuban institutions, so you must help in the development and progress of our country, and in the expansion of our economic activities. Our purposes and our ideals are the same."[51] Well before the famous tourist boom of the 1950s, pro-Cuba-Miami partnerships formed to facilitate the movement of tourists and capital. Local authorities in Miami agreed to advertise the island in their tourist publications, and Cuba's tourism commission agreed to reciprocate.

Authorities from Panama also cultivated close relations with tourist officials in South Florida. Because the tourism industry had been established earlier in Florida, since at least the 1890s, the state's tourist economy offered a sort of blueprint for development. South Florida depended on outside tourist dollars for real estate and infrastructure development. In less than two decades, Miami had transformed from a small town to a cosmopolitan winter resort with tens of thousands of inhabitants. After the completion of the canal, Panama was cultivating a similar model of growth. The Panamanian government set up a consulate in Miami with the hope of funneling tourists and capital farther south. The consulate's main task involved attending festivities and events with information in hand about the isthmus's own tourist attractions and commercial possibilities. Panama's first consul in Miami was Howard Brown, a former United Fruit Company employee and a US citizen who had lived and worked in Panama. Brown claimed to have strong ties with Miami's mayor and chamber of commerce. To the Panamanian press, he reported that he took the consulate job "to serve Panama however possible. I am proposing to open a permanent exhibition of Panamanian articles in Miami, a city that is visited by thousands of tourists each month and has played an important role in her progress." To Panama's president, he wrote, "I have devoted much of my time to preparing exhibits of Panama and talks before various clubs and other organizations." In the early 1930s, Brown organized exhibits for the Miami Chamber of Commerce and at popular stores such as Sears and Burdines and at social organizations such as the Rotary Club, the Kiwanis Club, and the Woman's Club of Miami. In his public speeches, Brown claimed "that Panama and Miami have much in common as tourist centers."[52]

Tourism development in the circum-Caribbean—from Miami to Havana to Panama—involved generous concessions to private developers. Tax breaks and the distribution of cheap or free land, political leaders believed, was essential to reaping the second harvest. Governments at the national and local levels passed law after law, and handed out contract after contract, in an effort to support privately financed tourism projects.[53] In 1922, for example, the Panamanian state conceded a tract of land to an investor, Raul Espinosa, to construct a stadium for "all classes of spectacle," though primarily for horseracing, "to stimulate the arrival of tourists to the isthmus." The state exempted Espinosa from having to pay taxes on supplies for the construction and maintenance of the stadium in exchange for "indirect benefits" to the republic. The contract required Espinosa to pay only a small annual fee for the use of the land.[54] The government offered similar concessions for the development of hotels and casinos. After the legalization of gambling in 1928, the Panamanian state received a flurry of investment propositions. "A modern tourist hotel and casino for Panama," the Panamanian press reported, "seems almost certain." A New York investor, Ben Gray, obtained one of these state concessions to build several hotels and casinos. The contract stipulated that Gray had free use of government lands to construct hotels and casinos and access to any neighboring lands for "beautification" projects. The state moreover exempted Gray from national taxes. That same year, the government also received a major development proposal from the Union Hotel Corporation of New York to "build a modern $1,000,000 hotel and casino" in La Exposición. The National City Bank of New York would finance the new hotel, and Minor C. Keith, one of the founders of the United Fruit Company, would "furnish the land for the proposed structure."[55] Members of Panama's Association of Commerce praised the state's role in this promotion of privately financed tourism development. Thanks to this newly organized plan, the association was now "confident" that "none of the world's touring centers offers greater attractions to the traveler."[56]

Similar and parallel investment schemes occurred in Cuba. In 1924 the Biltmore Company, which also built luxury hotels in New York and Coral Gables, Florida, completed a ten-story luxury hotel in downtown Havana. The hotel, designed by the US-based architecture firm Schultze & Weaver, would become a gathering place not only for wealthy tourists but also organized crime networks operating in Havana. In 1930 the same architectural firm completed construction of the famous National Hotel and its casino, built atop an old Spanish fort guarding the port of Havana. The hotel project, like in Panama, was financed by the National City Bank of New York. The National Hotel, overlooking the ocean and with five hundred rooms, was modeled after the well-known Breakers Hotel in Palm Beach, Florida. Mobster Meyer Lansky, already involved in the casino-nightclub business in South Florida, received a concession from the Cuban government to operate the casino at the National Hotel in the early 1930s. Soon afterward, Lansky and his fellow Mafia bosses founded a company called Cuba National, which took over partial ownership of the National Hotel and merged with the development firm National Cuba Hotel Corporation. As the journalist T. J. English described the events, "the mob funneled dirty money into Cuba to build casinos and hotels, which in turn generated the funds used to facilitate the corrupt political system."[57] It was the accumulation of injustices and corruption associated with these private-Mafia-state partnerships in Cuba that eventually helped ignite the Cuban Revolution. This is a well-known history in Cuba and abroad, but few people recognize that the process of tourist corruption had begun decades before Fidel Castro and his bearded revolutionaries fought in the mountains of the Sierra Maestra.[58]

Tourism development worked as an incentive for the expansion of state projects that on the surface did not seem to be related to the industry. Road-building and construction projects, for example, took off with the promise of tourism. Luis Machado and other promoters advocated the expansion of roads as a form of development that would extend tourism into the interior of the country (not just in the main cities). Highway construction, Machado explained, "will provide the tourist an easy, comfortable, cheap and safe means to travel in his own vehicle and with his own resources."[59] The government, he proposed, should also set up regional tourist boards to manage and regulate attractions and businesses along the new routes.

The most lucrative tourist activities, however, continued to take place in the port cities, in their restaurants, bars, and nightclubs. Alcohol sales, gambling, and tobacco became the largest tax revenue sources in Panama. Depending on the year, according to the historian Matthew Scalena, alcohol taxes accounted anywhere from 20 percent to 50 percent of Panamanian state revenue.[60] Meanwhile, state fiscal agents explained that "the government should give every incentive to grow and develop these attractive activities."[61] The state, with a traditionally weak domestic tax base and no direct commercial control over the Panama Canal, found an alternative source of revenue and investment from foreign demands for alcohol and gambling. During the era of Prohibition in the United States, bar owners, smugglers, and officials in Cuba also grew rich from the trade in alcohol, attracting thirsty US residents to the island. Cuba also became a key source of illegal northbound shipments.[62]

The desires of foreign visitors encouraged the development of bars and cabarets in Cuba's and Panama's urban environments. Both local and foreign commentators, though, complained of the brutality and "immorality" of this increasingly cosmopolitan nightlife. Narciso Garay, a longtime public servant in Panama, lamented that "the spectacle of the streets of Colón was something almost painful for me."[63] Visitors found the port and tourist cities of Panama, Cuba, South Florida, and more broadly the Caribbean to be ideal destinations for the fulfillment of vice: drunkenness, gambling, and paid sex. By the early 1930s, it was estimated that more than seven thousand prostitutes worked in Havana. "For many men," according to the journalist Mark Kurlansky, "a visit to a prostitute was one of the celebrated features of a trip to Havana, along with music, rum, and cigars."[64] In Panama, the writer

Demetrio Korsi expressed his own critical sentiments about these touristic desires. In a poem, "Vision of Panama," published in 1953, Korsi wrote (originally all in Spanish):

> Gringos, gringos, gringos . . . negros, negros, negros . . .
> Shops and stores, a hundred races in the sun.
> Square-faced *cholitas* and clumsy *mulatas*
> Fill the lobbies of brothels
> A decrepit taxi passes with tourists.
> Soldiers, sailors, come and go
> And women in short skirts, the cabaret workers
> Panama, where the gringos have discovered the land of Adam.
> Panama the easy, Panama the open,
> Panama of Central Avenue,
> The crossroads, bridge, port, and door
> Where one enters through the Canal.
>
> Movement. Traffic. All the bars,
> All the drunks, all the foxtrots
> And all the rumbas and all the crooks
> And all the gringos that God sends us.
> Thousands of foreigners and thousands of wallets. . .
> Spirits, music . . . how awful!
> The millions dance their macabre dance
> Gringos, negros, negros, gringos . . . Panama![65]

The cross-cultural and exploitative experiences referenced in this poem were often guided by foreign perceptions of tropical exoticism and sexuality. Nonetheless, the state sanctioned and profited from these desires.[66] As the historian Jeffrey Parker has documented in Panama, "the majority of proprietors in both the Cocoa Grove and Navajo districts [the red light and tourist districts] consisted of elite Panamanian families." Even the mayor of Panama owned property in Cocoa Grove, which he leased out and authorized as a bar and brothel.[67]

Political and commercial leaders, it seemed, were willing to do almost anything for "progress," regardless of the moral implications. The question is, why would Andreve, Porras, Machado, and other elites be willing to allow and in fact promote development, and particularly tourism development, in this way? What type of state-building project was this? What did hotels and casinos and tourist desires have to do with national progress? The answer seems straightforward: there were quick profits to be made in the sanctioning of vice, and there had been a long tradition of a service-port economy dependent on supplying travelers' desires. To paraphrase Meyer Lansky, if you have something people want, find a way to supply it and then collect the profits.[68] This idea, which would become known as "Lanksy's law" in the world of organized crime, was the same principle guiding international capitalism and international tourism. As rational businessmen, they simply provided what visitors wanted. The complicated part, however, was that these economic activities emerged within a highly controlled context. In the Panama Canal Zone, where everything was run by the US government, commissaries sold nonessential and luxury items, despite local protests. Panama's government received $250,000 in annual rent from the US government on land for the canal but had no say in the canal's logistical or commercial operations. Panamanians, though, had one clear economic advantage: the Canal Zone prohibited bars and gambling. The selling of vice was a lucrative alternative for the nation's service economy to develop, away from US government-subsidized competition. This relationship represented in microcosm the type of socioeconomic exchanges that linked the United States with the Caribbean more generally. The legalization of gambling, the ready supply of alcohol, and the extraordinary expansion of the Caribbean's tourist economy of vice took off during the righteous era of US imperialism and puritan progressivism.

The Caribbean's early tourism industry became an outlet for travelers in search of drink and activities made illegal in the United States. Cuba's tourism law passed the same year that the Eighteenth Amendment, establishing Prohibition, was ratified. Entire bars and businesses, such as Harry's New York Bar, the Texas Bar, the Chicago Restaurant, and the Manhattan Café, picked up and moved from the United States to Cuba, Panama, and other Caribbean locales.[69] Max Bilgray, known as "the cabaret king of Colón," claimed to have converted Panama's cabaret scene in the 1920s from a "frontier style" to a "rallying place for genial comrades." Bilgray previously owned saloons in Chicago until Prohibition. Relocated to Panama, he opened The Tropic, which would become one of the Caribbean tourist scene's most famous bars. Another bar and cabaret entrepreneur from the United States, Mary Lee Kelley, found financial success running "one of the most famous whorehouses in the world."[70] In a 1926 profile in the *Panama Times*, Kelley described herself as a "rags to riches" woman of Irish descent. "Why I'm as Irish as Patty's pig. I came from Boston where everybody's Irish including all the politicians and policemen."[71] The United States, with its restrictive laws, had exported a culture of hard drinking and outlaw living farther south. Rumrunners, expatriate liquor distributors, and bar and cabaret owners like Bilgray and Kelley became romantic and heroic figures in the era of Prohibition.[72]

When Panama voted on its own tourism law in 1928, the US federal ban on alcohol sales and its crackdown on the domestic vice economy was still in effect. "Gambling," Andreve noted, "would become a primary revenue source and our main tourist attraction."[73] At the same time, though, he acknowledged the potential risks involved in this type of tourism development. He argued that locals should be prohibited from visiting the new casinos and hotels in order to protect them from moral corruption and financial ruin. "In order to benefit the nation rather than damaging it," he wrote, "it should be absolutely prohibited for national citizens, who are not employees, from visiting the gambling rooms. . . . If we let our countrymen gamble, I foresee many misfortunes and unfortunate events."[74] The misfortunes nonetheless arrived. The tourism law that Andreve recommended for Panama was essentially the same law that Lansky and a whole slew of gangsters and crooks would exploit to build their gambling and hotel empires. National tourism policies opened the floodgates to the most creative, ruthless, and transnational developers of vice. According to T. J. English, "Lansky was a big shot on the island [of Cuba], a friend of government officials going all the way to the top."[75] Lansky's partner Lucky Luciano also came to have influence in Panama. After being deported from the United States and later kicked out of Cuba, Luciano decided to base his narcotics-running operations in Panama.

Elite politicians were not immune to the social consequences of this organized crime. In January 1955, Panama's President José Remón was shot and killed at the Juan Franco Racetrack (built in 1922 during the first wave of tourism development). Although the assassins were never found, many believed that Luciano and his international narcotics ring were responsible for the president's death. Remón, his wife, and his brother had all been implicated in drug- and arms-trafficking scandals linked to mob activities stretching from the isthmus to South Florida. President Remón, according to US government accounts, had previously provided protection to drug-running and Mafia activities in Panama when he was a police officer in Colón in the 1930s and 1940s. His wife supposedly participated in these illegal activities as well. During a visit to Puerto Rico, Mrs. Remón was found with a bag of narcotics and forced to pay a $50,000 fine by US customs officials. Emblematic of their transnational lifestyle, Mrs. Remón was in Florida when her husband was assassinated.[76] At the same time in Cuba, the government of Fulgencio Batista was deeply entangled with the Mafia operating on the island. The ties between drug traffickers, the owners of hotels and casinos, and government and military authorities ran historically and transnationally deep in the Caribbean.[77]

But for national leaders, tourism was more than a corrupt industry of foreign sin and US dollars. The arrival of visitors promised to stimulate their economies, but it also buttressed more culturally infused state projects. The tourism industry served as both an economic and cultural resource. Under the pretext of tourism development, elites became the authorized gatekeepers of national culture. The promotion of folklore as a tourist attraction was very much connected to a nationalizing and whitening project. While US tourists often thought of the region as impoverished nations of dark-skinned and primitive "natives," the state used cultural events and the protection of Spanish colonial ruins to emphasize the "lighter" side of their national heritage. Early tourism brochures and pamphlets reflected this position, overwhelmingly ignoring the Afro-Caribbean elements of national life.[78] In this way, the industry operated as an ideological platform, as much for domestic as foreign audiences. With tourism as an economic resource and a means to distribute information abroad and at home, elites could articulate what it meant to be a citizen of the republic. Modern visions of culture and history solidified, in part, within the tourism industry. Particular commodities, histories, and identities took on new values and forms. Historical sites and traditions ignored for centuries received state funds, private investment, and renewed cultural lore. The possibility of tourism encouraged the Porras government, for example, to pass the republic's first law of historic preservation in 1912 at the height of the isthmus's first tourism boom.[79] Efforts to turn colonial buildings and ruins into historic districts and tourist attractions also occurred in Cuba and Florida. Tourists willingly paid to see and experience the Caribbean's colonial history of pirates and conquistadores. Yet parallel to historic conservation and national identity was always economic interest.[80]

Tourism and Racial Exclusion

While Caribbean and Latin American elites created extremely liberal and generous incentives for white people of European descent to visit and invest, they intensely discriminated against nonwhite travelers and migrants. As the historian Lara Putnam explained, "the story of the making of outsiders is thus also the story of the making of insiders and of the naturalization of the barriers—ideological, institutional, physical—between them."[81] Putnam was referring to racialized restrictions that limited black mobility in the Caribbean in the 1920s and 1930s. Her observation, though, also pertains to the history of tourism. The making of "insiders," the making of privileged tourists, was also the making of "outsiders," undesirable immigrants. Tourism development was part of the history of defining desirable and undesirable people, potential insiders, and inherent outsiders.

State authorities encouraged the development of hotels and casinos and created new ways to attract tourists and investors. At the same time, they patrolled the borders and coasts to keep "undesirables" out because of their racial and ethnic backgrounds. In 1926 Panama passed an immigration law, mirroring US immigration restrictions, that excluded the entry of people of African descent in addition to "Chinese, Gypsies, Armenians, Arabs, Turks, Hindus, Syrians, Lebanese and Palestinians." This type of racial discrimination was as old as the republic. As the historian Marixa Lasso has shown, the state "constantly questioned the right of the Chinese and West Indian community to become Panamanian."[82] Laws as early as 1904 declared people of African and Asian descent as races of "prohibited immigration." Article 20 of the 1926 law reaffirmed these exclusionary practices, declaring that "those individuals to whom the present law refers, who find it necessary to come to the territory of the Republic, in transit to other countries, must solicit special permission from the Department of Foreign Relations through the Panama Consul at the port of departure."[83] Meanwhile, white tourists from the United States did not even need a passport to enter the country.

The Republic of Cuba maintained similar racialized immigration laws in the 1920s and 1930s, while allowing white US citizens to travel to the island without a passport. Restricting mobility along racial lines was widespread. "According to a survey of Latin American countries" conducted by black West Indian activists, "it was revealed that besides Panama, seven countries exclude Negroes entirely . . . and others set up extremely difficult entrance qualifications."[84] These racialized structures of mobility and immobility did not distinguish between rich and poor or between well-known and unknown people of color. In 1930, when the author Langston Hughes planned a trip to Cuba, officials in New York initially denied him passage. "The [steamship] companies claimed," according to the historian Frank Guridy, "that they could not sell him a ticket because the Cuban government banned 'Chinese, Negroes, and Russians,' from entering the country." Other prominent black travelers, such as the African American educator Mary McLeod Bethune and the activist William Pickens of the National Association for the Advancement of Colored People (NAACP), experienced similar discrimination when visiting Cuba. "There is a policy," Pickens wrote to the US secretary of state, "inspired and supported from some sources to harass, hinder and discourage Negro citizens of the United States, when they seek to exercise their privilege of coming to the republic of Cuba, even as tourists for a week or a month seeking education and knowledge, or on business or pleasure."[85]

The problem was similar in Panama. George Westerman, a Panamanian journalist and activist of black West Indian descent, consistently and passionately denounced racial injustice in the tourism industry. Westerman asked, "Why has the law still been permitted to operate to the detriment of thousands of non-white peoples who wish to spend a brief vacation with Isthmian relatives or friends, or visit this Republic en route to other Central American countries?"[86] Westerman documented case after case of discrimination. An African American nurse from Harlem on her way home from a conference in Brazil, for example, tried to stop in Panama for a brief vacation. Authorities told her, however, "that she could not come to Panama as American Negroes are not permitted to land in Panama." Into the mid-twentieth century, the Panamanian state continued to require African American tourists to have a passport to enter Panama and put down a $500 deposit, while white Americans could enter with $1 tourist card and no passport. Westerman explained in 1953, "Our present policy toward tourists causes resentment which is affecting our democratic standing abroad, at the same time that it is debilitating our friendship with all non-white peoples whose opinion in present world affairs cannot be ignored. Panama must give proof to the outside world that it does not subscribe to a double standard in applying the principles of democracy."[87]

Outsiders, in this way, did not exclusively define the privileged identity of tourists to the Caribbean. Elites in the region also defined who could and could not be a desirable guest. White travelers and investors easily crossed international borders, while so-called undesirable races were shut out or even thrown out. "Every age has its Inquisition," the traveling writer B. Traven wrote in 1926, and "our age has the passport to make up for the tortures of medieval times."[88] The tourism industry, however, also had its share of hypocrisy and rationalized exceptions for the immoral and privileged. Local and national governments opened their communities to a tourist economy rooted in gambling, drinking, and prostitution and simultaneously tightened the reins on nonwhite travelers, who often had direct familial connections in the region. Mob and drug dealers such as Meyer Lansky, Lucky Luciano, and Santo Trafficante were welcomed, while black travelers, educators, and intellectuals such as Langston Hughes, George Westerman, and Mary McLeod Bethune were harassed and put under suspicion.

These types of racial exclusions in the early tourism industry had historic consequences. For one, state policies that privileged white foreigners and tourists would fuel popular resistance against colonial and minority rule.

It was no coincidence, for example, that Fidel Castro and his band of revolutionaries turned the Havana Hilton hotel into the revolution's headquarters and renamed it "Free Havana." It was no surprise that the 1964 revolt against US rule in Panama would turn its rage on the tourist economy. The area around the famous Hotel Tivoli became embroiled in an intense street battle. The seeds of national development policies rooted in a monocultural vision of tourism in the early twentieth century sowed their own undoing in the mid-twentieth-century era of decolonization and antiracist rebellion.

Yet despite these lessons from the past, another generation of Caribbean elites, after the social upheavals of 1960s, has returned to (neo)liberal policies of tourism development. The development strategies of the early twentieth century and the early twenty-first century, in this sense, are remarkably similar. Continuity remains in planning and action. Although there is now in theory more national and local control over the tourist economy, in practice the end goals are similar: attract foreign direct investment, despite the social costs, to encourage "progress" and development. As one recent government sign in the streets of Panama claimed, "More tourism, better country!"

For the privileged tourist, these historical consequences still present in the industry should cause one to pause and reconsider: why is whiteness so often associated with being a tourist in the circum-Caribbean, while to be black, regardless of one's nationality, still seems to represent someone, something else? Racialized definitions of who could and could not be a desirable visitor from the past play an outsized contemporary role in classifying acceptable and unwanted visitors.[89]

In sum, the expansion of US imperialism into the region, in combination with local efforts to twist and profit from the influx of foreigners, opened the Caribbean to a new era of exclusive and racialized travel culture in the twentieth century. Tourism development was not simply imposed by the outside. It was also invited. But once the political and economic stage was set, how would the masses of tourists get there? For centuries, shipping had been the main mode of transnational mobility, but by the late 1920s that, too, was shifting.

CHAPTER 3

Changing Routes from Sea to Air

The Rise of Pan American World Airways

> How many times have you stood on the deck of
> a steamer, tossing in a rough sea and enviously
> watched the gulls wheeling and dipping 'round the
> vessel. What swiftness and lightness, what ease, while
> you suffered the agonies of the endless rolling and
> pitching of a spiteful sea. How you longed for the
> smooth, quick flight of the gull. But now man has
> mastered the principles of flight and may enjoy the
> comfort, speed and safety of aerial transportation.
>
> —*The Air-Way to Havana*, Pan American Airways
> brochure
>
> That is the terrible thing—the curious illusion of
> superiority bred by height.
>
> —Anne Morrow Lindbergh, "Airliner to Europe"

Early in the morning of October 28, 1927, a
crowd of seven hundred spectators gathered to witness the first flight of Pan
American Airways. One hour and twenty-five minutes after taking off from
the sandy dirt runway on Key West, the three-engine Fokker F-7 airplane
landed in Havana with three crew members and their cargo of mail. It was a
watershed moment for the development of international air travel.[1]

Within three months, Pan American Airways (Pan Am) was not only flying mail to Cuba but also paying passengers. In early 1928 the airline inaugurated passenger service, carrying eight people for $50 a seat from Key
West to Havana. It was, without hyperbole, the dawn of a new era of leisure
mobility. From its inaugural route, Pan Am grew into the world's largest international airline carrier, expanding rapidly from Florida to Cuba and across
the Caribbean. By 1931 Pan Am had extended its services to twenty-three
countries in the Americas. A decade later, its reach was global: flying to sixty
countries and covering an impressive ninety-eight thousand route miles. As
the airline's executives recalled later, "Our first flight [to Havana] was a short

FIGURE 11. Pan American World Airways' first scheduled passenger flight from Key West to Havana on January 16, 1928. University of Miami Special Collections

one . . . but it was long on history, as it opened America to worldwide air travel."[2]

The rise of aviation is a well-documented history, yet most authors tend to tell narratives of "technological triumph" and focus less on the complex cultural impacts when considering the development of air transportation.[3] In fact, for most modern travelers, flight has become a taken-for-granted aspect of mobility. This chapter, however, reinserts cultural context into the historic wonder of flight. Building on the insights of the historian Jennifer Van Vleck, it documents how the "logic of the air" rejected the significance of the ocean's territoriality, not only for US political, economic, and military interests but also for tourism.[4] The transition from sea to air mobility restructured how and where tourists would travel on vacation. Although air travel remained an economically elite form of leisure mobility until well into the "jet age," the development of air routes in the first half of the twentieth century foreshadowed the future experiences and destinations of mass tourism. No longer would a vacation require weeks and multiple ports of call before one arrived at a desired locale. Aviation, combined with growing economic prosperity at home, would make it possible for the United States to send more tourists to the Caribbean and other international vacation destinations than any other nation in the twentieth century. The revolution in transportation as expressed in the air embodied technological change but also a much wider transformation in how travelers experienced time, space, and cross-cultural connection. Aviation, in short, created a powerful force for "the annihilation of space by time" and, as a result, dramatically altered tourism to the Caribbean and, more broadly, around the world.[5]

The history of aviation is a remarkable story of expansion, all the more interesting when brought into dialogue with the long history of transportation technology. By examining and comparing the forms of overseas mobility that came before, we gain a deeper understanding of the importance of what came next. Before Pan Am's first flight to Havana, the only way to visit Caribbean nations from the mainland United States or the Florida Keys was by steamship and not long before that by sailing vessel.[6] It was a journey dependent on the sea, ships, and the knowledge of seasoned sailors. This maritime history, though, has faded into nostalgia or, worse, has been forgotten in today's jet age of travel. As tourists gather in crowded airports hoping for a routine and monotonous flight, they should remember when, and with what consequences, the act of overseas travel changed from sailing at sea to flying thousands of feet above the surface of the earth.[7]

Travels across the Gulf Stream

The transition from maritime to air travel was a huge leap in hemispheric relations and in the history of globalization. Flight altered the way people crossed borders, but it did so in ways not well remembered today.[8] The phenomenology of transnational travel has radically changed: the speed, distance, time, relation to natural elements, smells, sights, and sounds are significantly different now when compared to travel experiences at the beginning of the twentieth century. According to foundational scholars such as Edmund Husserl, phenomenology is the phenomena making up everyday life—the structures of experience.[9] In the context of tourism and travel, the structures of experience include and are often overdetermined by the means of getting there—that is, the tourist's form of transport. Comparing the history of air and maritime travel, it becomes clear that the phenomenological sensations of nature and machine, in addition to fear and adrenaline, dramatically differed depending on the mode of mobility.

Modern aviation quickened the journey, but at the same time it disconnected people from the places and communities they traversed. The early years of aviation were a romantic and adventurous time. But as technology advanced and became more accessible to civilian travelers, flight also began to foster the sense that the waters separating the mainland United States from the islands and nations to the south were merely a short hop. The perils and geography of the sea—literally and figuratively—became vertically distant from modern sensibilities. The sea mattered much less to the travel experience when one was thousands of feet above its surface. This twentieth-century aerial view, though, was a new way of imagining what was long considered a potentially perilous maritime journey.

By analyzing the history and culture of maritime travel, we get a better sense of the radical revolution that would be aviation. Consider, for example, one well-known and dramatic voyage from Florida to Cuba just thirty years before Pan Am began flying to the island. On New Year's Eve 1896 the writer Stephen Crane boarded *SS Commodore* in Jacksonville, Florida, headed for Cuba. Crane was on his way to cover the outbreak of war on the island. But in rough seas off the central Florida coast, the *Commodore* began to take on water. With the ship slowly sinking, the surviving crew made it into a small lifeboat, which they struggled to keep afloat. Crane would later write of his ordeal in a short story he called "The Open Boat":

> None of them [including himself] knew the color of the sky. Their eyes glanced level, and were fastened upon the waves that swept toward them. These waves were of the hue of slate, save for the tops, which were of foaming white, and all of the men knew the colors of the sea. The horizon narrowed and widened, and dipped and rose, and at all times its edge was jagged with waves that seemed thrust up in points like rocks. . . . These waves were most wrongfully and barbarously abrupt and tall, and each froth-top was a problem in small boat navigation.[10]

Although most sea journeys in the late nineteenth century did not end in disaster like Crane's, his story nevertheless highlights the vulnerability, excitement, and sensory perspectives of "going to sea."[11] The possibility of being lost in a storm, blown off course, swamped by a wave, or shipwrecked were concerns deeply embedded in the cultural experience of maritime travel. Indeed, the waters between Florida and Cuba were historically a treacherous sea route for sailors and fishing crews. "The Gulf Stream," as the author Ernest Hemingway liked to remind readers, was "the last wild country there is left."[12]

Travelers took to the ocean dreaming of distant lands, but the journey itself was an important "site of imagination."[13] Revisit, for example, the experiences of another maritime adventurer and writer who went to sea fifty years before Crane. In the 1840s a curious twenty-two-year-old sailed as a crewman from New Bedford, Massachusetts, through the Caribbean and around Cape Horn to the South Pacific. It would be more than three years before he returned home. Young Herman Melville's journey at sea would also become his writing material. His literary characters, like him, longed for maritime travel. The author's most famous novel, *Moby-Dick* (1851), opens with how despair and boredom on land sent him to sea:

> Some years ago—never mind how long precisely—having little or no money in my purse, and nothing particular to interest me on shore, I thought I would sail about a little and see the watery part of the world. There is nothing surprising in this. If they but knew it, almost all men in their degree, some time or other, cherish very nearly the same feelings toward the ocean with me.[14]

The watery world that Melville sought and wrote about embodied an adventurous "world between worlds." It was, as the historian Eric Zuelow described it, "a third place that existed between one's point of origin and one's terminus."[15] The ocean passage and the ship was a destination and an experience in itself. When sailing from the north into the tropics, one observed the first signs of environmental difference from the changing conditions of the ocean rather than from the land. As ships headed south from the United States in the winter sailing season, the north wind would blow bitterly cold, and the seas were rough and intimidating. Once off the coast of Florida and the Bahamas, however, the color of the water would shift to deep blue, almost purple, and the weather would warm, a sign for passengers to don white clothing and for sailors to go barefoot. If the weather was fair, it was a moment of celebration. Seasoned sailors who safely entered the tropics would often practice rituals of "tropical baptism," such as bathing new crew members with warm seawater and plying them with strong drink. Such rituals when entering the torrid zone, according to the historian Paul Sutter, demonstrated how "the qualities of its waters, its weather, its place in relation to the sun and stars, even its sea life—was critical to broader perceptions of the region as discrete and exotic. It was on the high seas that expanding Europeans [and Euro-Americans] most precisely honored the tropics as a geographical abstraction."[16] Long-distance mobility—from the earliest colonial encounters to the whaling adventures of Melville to Crane and his contemporaries in the age of steamships—depended on the nature of the ocean's power. The sea and its environment were a wonderous and intimately felt part of international travel.

The technology of sail dates back thousands of years, crossing geographic and cultural differences. But among all sailors, black or white, European or Polynesian, going to sea was a risky and therefore revered affair. According to the United Nations Educational, Scientific and Cultural Organization (UNESCO), some three million shipwrecks lie on the ocean floor. The Florida Straits, one of the most heavily traveled shipping lanes in the world, is riddled with sunken vessels.[17] The ocean was synonymous with travail. For most of maritime history it was difficult to predict approaching weather, precisely identify one's location, or even know the depth of water beneath one's vessel. In fact, the arrival of Christopher Columbus and his crew in the Americas in 1492 is less remarkable as a "discovery" but as a story of survival. Departing the Spanish port of Palos in August 1492 and arriving in the Bahamas some two months later on October 12, the *Niña, Pinta, and Santa María* had sailed across the Atlantic Ocean averaging less than four knots per hour in the heart of hurricane season, yet they experienced no serious storms. Luck as much as skill made Columbus the "admiral of the seas."[18]

Improvements in oceangoing travel were the most important technological developments of the early modern world. The sea's power was both mode and potential obstacle.[19] During the era of European colonial expansion, it was a race to distant seas, and whoever had the safest ships and the fastest ships would be the most powerful. An impediment to international travel or forming an overseas empire, however, was the ability to get to one's destination. State-sponsored mariners and scientists as a result invented an astounding and creative multitude of navigational technologies. In the mid-eighteenth century, for example, the British government sponsored the development of the sextant and the standardization of the geographic coordinate system, with precise latitude and longitude, which allowed sailors and travelers to measure their location on the surface of the earth in relation to Greenwich, England, the prime meridian, or longitude 0.[20] The sextant and the geographic coordinate system together helped build the British Empire. But the British were not alone in their research efforts. Competing European empires funded maritime expeditions, research, and design to support political, military, and commercial expansion. For centuries—from the colonial conquest of the Americas in the early sixteenth century to the industrialization of naval fleets in the nineteenth century—science and technology at sea were intimately entangled with imperial expansion. The geopolitical interests of empire relied on maritime travel.[21]

At the end of the nineteenth century, the US government also began to expand its overseas reach, not so much for colonial settlement but for access to strategic ports to resupply its merchant and naval fleets.[22] The control of shipping lanes was an established and guiding rationale for overseas imperial expansion, from the Caribbean to the Pacific. But whereas in the past maritime powers required coastal way stations to repair wooden vessels (with lumber) and gain fresh provisions (of water and food), the nineteenth-century development of steamships industrialized the notion of a port of call. Although it took decades of technological advances before steamships could surpass oceangoing sail technology, the logic of coal demanded a new form of industrial maritime expansion and work: the coaling station.[23] In the Spanish-American War of 1898 and the subsequent Platt Amendment of 1902, for example, the United States asserted its control over Guantánamo Bay, Cuba, because it was an important stopover in its network of coaling stations between the US East Coast and the soon-to-be-built Panama Canal. The invention of steam engines, associated with the industrial revolution and factory work on land, also revolutionized the sailor's experience at sea. As the author and sailor Joseph Conrad explained, "the machinery, the steel, the fire, the steam . . . stepped in between man and the sea. A modern fleet of ships does not so much make use of the sea as exploit a highway."[24] Steam engines, powered by external combustion engines, required an immense amount of coal to keep the boilers pressurized, pushing against wind and wave.

The age of coal-powered shipping, however, was short-lived compared to the centuries of sail. In the 1910s and 1920s, naval and merchant vessels transitioned from coal to oil. Oil-powered ships could carry more fuel, weighed less, burned fuel slower, and generated greater hull speed. During each phase of technological development, though, the old means of mobility paralleled and competed with the new for decades. Sailing vessels plowed alongside steamships or became hybrid vessels with both sail and steam power in the nineteenth century, and for a short time coal-burning ships stayed in use even though oil-burning ships were faster and more efficient. Nothing was inevitable, except for the certainty of movement and change. With the twentieth-century arrival of aviation, it was a similar pattern of the new replacing the old, essentially for the same goal. The rise of air travel was part of the same historical trajectory of new transportation technologies being developed to annihilate space and time for geopolitical and economic expansion.

Pan Am and the Age of Aviation

Airplanes contributed to a wide array of phenomenological changes in travel, not all of them universally appreciated. Writing about his experience on a Pan Am flight for the *Havana Evening Telegram* in 1928, the journalist A. Edward Stuntz remarked, "A trip from Havana to Key West and return by one of the big Fokker planes of the Pan-American Airways is novel enough but not exciting." Rather he claimed boredom, observing, "Now I've heard

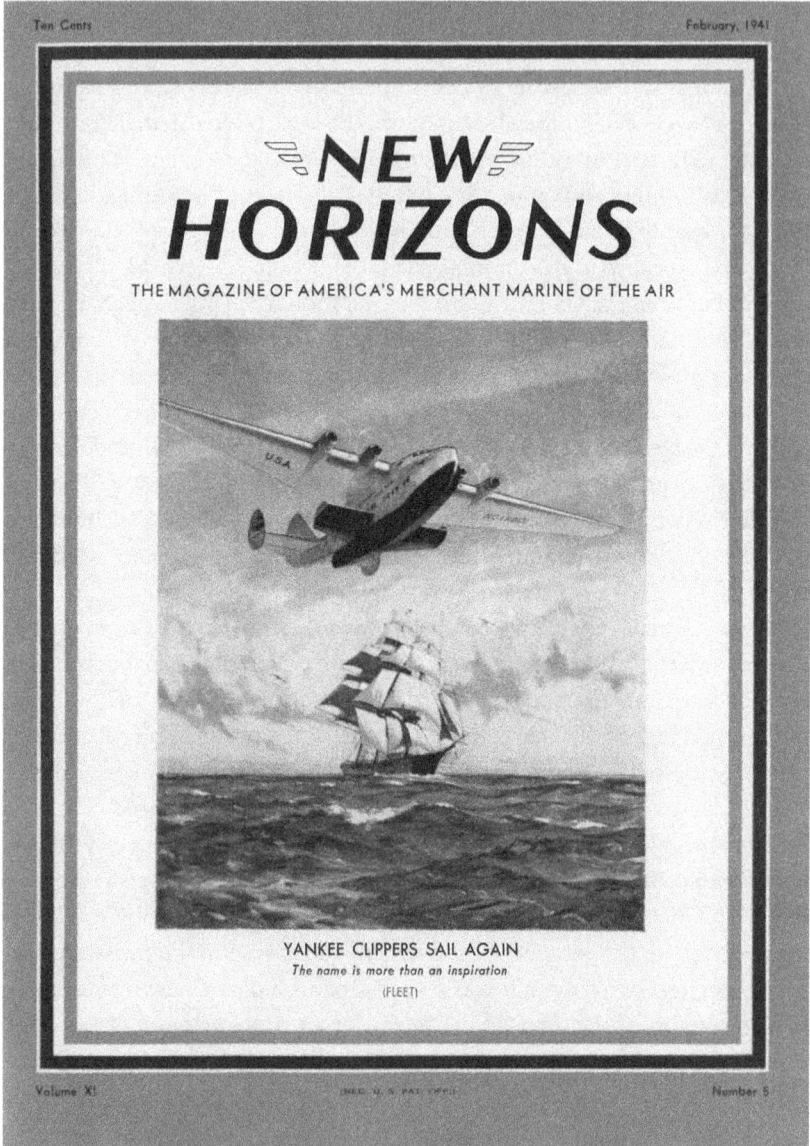

FIGURE 12. A cover of *New Horizons* magazine from February 1941 featuring the iconic painting *Yankee Clippers Sail Again* by Gordon Grant. University of Miami Special Collections

about squalls in the air and I'm disappointed. . . . Here in the cabin, there is no dramatic business. It is all about as fearful as a trolley ride and not half as bumpy." Stuntz apologized to readers hoping for more adventure: "I am sorry I couldn't adequately write this trip from the air. But how can anyone conjure the proper phraseology for a sparklingly interesting experience in an hour and a half. Let's call it short and sweet and let it go at that."[25] Stuntz's perspective, though, was in stark contrast to triumphant and futuristic views in the 1920s that depicted the development of aviation as an escape from the drudgery of earthly existence. The aviator Charles Lindbergh reflected on his early flying experiences, claiming that in an airplane "it seemed I had partially escaped mortality, to look down on the earth like a god."[26] Airplanes would supposedly be the source of a magical new world of adventure and power. But Stuntz—certainly not as influential and famous as Lindbergh— saw a present and predicted a future of something more mundane.

Whether it was the observations of a bored journalist or an aviator imagining quasi-divinity, it was clear that traveling thousands of feet up in the air would be a dramatically different experience than overseas mobility dependent on the ocean. In addition to changing travel experiences of space, flying of course shortened the transit time. Depending on the ship and the weather, sailing from Key West to Havana could take anywhere from fifteen to twenty-four hours. Meanwhile, by steamship the trip could take from sunrise to sunset. But by 1928 air travel reduced the trip to just ninety minutes. It was a new form of time-space compression. "The air," *Fortune* magazine argued as early as 1943, "is a [new] blue-water ocean to which every nation potentially has access for trade and high strategy in all directions. Under its intoxicating implications the ancient ideas of a world divided by land and sea seem to be as outmoded as the Chinese wall."[27] With this new "logic of the air," travelers were no longer bound by nor necessarily aware of the geography and environment between their point of origin and their destination.[28]

Modern flight evolved into a form of sensory dislocation or, in the words of the anthropologist Arjun Appadurai, "deterritorialization."[29] The natural elements, while physically still in place, had little to do with the air traveler's perception, or lack thereof, of the journey. Over the course of the twentieth century, air travel increasingly isolated passengers from the outdoors. Ask travelers today about what they do on an overseas flight, and the list of activities is rather standard: sleep, watch a movie, listen to music, drink, eat, read, maybe talk, and rarely getting out of one's seat except to use the lavatory.[30] In contrast, at the level of the sea, countless generations of sailors and passengers witnessed the tiniest of ecological events—a flying fish, a visiting bird, a ship in the distance, a change in the wind or waves.

The twentieth-century shift from to sea to air mobility, however, did not fully erase the social practices of sea-travel culture. Maritime history and technology, along with geopolitics, set the stage for the era of air travel. The emergence of the air route from Key West to Havana demonstrates how new transportation networks and infrastructure depended on the maritime routes of empire. Havana was only a short flight from Key West, but the island of Cuba was also a protectorate or, as critics understood it, a neocolonial possession of the United States. Getting people and information quickly from the mainland to the island was essential for US imperial governance. Federal contracts paid for Pan Am's early operations, and thus it was no coincidence that the location of US military and naval bases abroad guided the development of Pan Am's aerial routes.[31] This relationship was part of an established pattern linking state power with transportation advancements.

At the start of World War I in 1914, however, the US military owned a mere forty-nine aircraft. But soon the necessities of war pushed officials to embrace technological innovation, resulting in an aviation boom. In March 1915 Congress used the Naval Appropriations Act to create the National Advisory Committee on Aeronautics—later to become the National Air and Space Administration (NASA).[32] By November 1918 US firms had manufactured 13,894 airplanes. The number of production firms had expanded from sixteen, employing 168 workers, to more than three hundred companies, with approximately 175,000 employees. Airplane design evolved rapidly as well, transforming slow, wood-and-wire-frame, fabric-covered biplanes into sleek, aerodynamic aluminum monoplanes capable of landing on water or land. The speed of these new aircraft, moreover, doubled from a maximum velocity of 75 miles per hour to nearly 150 miles per hour by the end of the war.[33] Aviation innovations, in this way, mirrored in rapid fashion the earlier improvements in maritime technology, which also relied on collaboration between private interests and the state during times of global military conflict and competition.[34]

Following the war, the Americas and Europe had entered what aviation scholars now call the "golden age of aviation." In 1919, less than three months after the Treaty of Versailles, Germany (despite its defeat) began the world's first passenger airline service, with routes linking Berlin, Leipzig, and Weimar. The British and French similarly converted former military bombers for commercial service between London and Paris. There was also a period of European investment in regional air travel in the Americas. Peter Paul von Bauer, a German ace pilot in World War I, opened the first South American commercial airline, the Colombian-German Air Transport Association. In the early 1920s the US aviation industry, domestically and abroad, still lagged behind German, French, and British efforts. However, increasing business investment and military involvement in Latin America and the Caribbean encouraged the US government to develop its own international air transport system. Between World War I and the mid-1920s, according to the historian Rosalie Schwartz, US foreign investment in the Caribbean and Latin America grew by nearly 300 percent.[35]

In support of US military and economic expansion, Pan American Airways received the first US federal contract to deliver air mail to the Caribbean, beginning with Cuba. The airline was founded by four military aviators, veterans of the Great War. But after a series of selling and buying, the company was taken over by Juan Trippe, who was also a former US Navy pilot and aviation entrepreneur. Trippe would run Pan Am for the next four decades, cultivating close government ties. He negotiated to assure the airline's position as the US government's "exclusive international" carrier and claimed proudly that his airline was the "chosen instrument" of the state.[36]

Pan Am carried passengers, mail, and express shipments vital to the US government. It also worked as a symbol of US power abroad. The inauguration of the airline's international passenger service was timed to coincide with President Calvin Coolidge's visit to Havana for the Sixth Pan-American Conference in 1928. Coolidge and Cuban president Gerardo Machado greeted the plane when it landed, claiming it a sign of hemispheric unity.[37] On January 17, the day after Pan Am's passenger flight, President Coolidge gave a speech to conference participants in Havana, declaring that "no citizen of any of the Americas could come to the queen of the West Indies without experiencing an emotion of gratitude and reverence. These are the outposts of the new civilization of the Western Hemisphere."[38] Listening to that message were thousands of US officials, Latin American dignitaries, and tourists who were also in Havana that winter season.

The next major Pan Am stop, after the Florida-Cuba connection, was the Isthmus of Panama. The US government had completed and now governed the Panama Canal. Hundreds of thousands of sailors and soldiers annually passed through or were temporarily stationed on the isthmus in the 1920s.[39] Pan Am's role was to support the US colonial outpost, assuring fast and efficient communication between Canal Zone officials in Panama and leaders across the Caribbean and back in Washington.

In February 1929 Charles Lindbergh—Pan Am's newly appointed technical adviser—began his survey of the route. Departing Miami at six in the morning on the eve of his twenty-seventh birthday, Lindbergh flew first to Havana and then across the western tip of Cuba to the coastline of Belize (then British Honduras). After an overnight stop, he continued on to Costa Rica and Nicaragua before arriving in Panama (having covered two thousand miles in nineteen hours of flying time). Lindbergh's survey flight provided expert advice to Pan Am but also generated publicity for it along the way.

Having completed the first solo nonstop transatlantic flight two years earlier, Lindbergh was an aviation celebrity. "Whenever Colonel Lindbergh moved," according to reporters covering his circum-Caribbean journey, "there was an eager crowd following him: persons were eager to shake his hand or even be close enough to have him brush past them."[40] Pan Am and its pilots were carving out a new "frontier" of aviation.

The airline's regularly scheduled passenger service, though, still depended on the sea. In 1934 Pan Am opened Dinner Key Terminal on Biscayne Bay, Miami, the largest marine air facility in the world.[41] The new terminal would serve fifty thousand passengers annually in the 1930s and early 1940s and attract even more curious visitors. The new terminal's fleet of aircraft were called "clippers," a nod to the heyday of fast sailing ships that dominated transoceanic trade in the previous century.[42] Pan Am clippers of the time were also called "flying boats" because they took off from and landed on water. They were designed in this way because many of Pan Am's destinations in Latin America and the Caribbean had yet to develop the runways and infrastructure necessary for terrestrial landing.

The culture of air travel mimicked not only the technology and geographic routes of maritime travel but also its cultural traditions and training protocols. Flight crews rigorously prepared as if they were part of a ship's crew, with a captain in command and learning seaplane anchorage, marine tides and currents, celestial navigation, and overwater navigation. The discipline of sea travel provided the foundation for aeronautics.

The ports of the past linking distant places were giving way to the "air" ports of the future. By 1935, less than a decade after its inaugural flight, Pan Am also began to expand beyond the Americas—to Hawaii, the Philippines, and China. In 1939 it also inaugurated regular transatlantic service to England and continental Europe. The international and US press closely followed and reported on the development of these new routes via radio, newspapers, and film. As Pan Am expanded, so did public interest.[43] Yet for most travelers in the 1920s and 1930s, travel by ship remained the more affordable and reliable means of venturing abroad. Air travel was expensive, and although the trip was fast and sometimes mundane, it was also seen as uncertain. Stories of aviation catastrophes captured headlines. In 1927, the year before Pan Am began passenger service, nearly half of all pilots attempting long-distance overseas flights "either lost their lives or had their flights end in near disaster."[44] As one airline executive admitted in the early 1920s, "he never flew in his company's planes when he could avoid it—and his wife flatly refused to fly at all."[45] The public had gone "plane crazy" in interest, but many were still unsure about flying in one for their vacation.

After the devastating unleashing of airpower during World War II, how-ever, there began a new era of safer, faster, and more affordable civilian air travel. Following the war, the United States became the world's leader in aviation technology. The Boeing Company, which had developed Pan Am's most famous and advanced flying clippers and much of the US bomber fleet, came out of the war committed to bringing jet travel to the masses.[46] The US government had also begun to invest heavily in new jet technology and research, including employing the ingenuity of Europe's early aviation lead-ers, particularly from Germany. In Operation Paperclip, which ran from 1945 to 1959, the US government relocated more than sixteen hundred German scientists, engineers, and technicians to support US military and technologi-cal programs. During the Cold War air and space race, notable German sci-entists, such as Adolf Busemann, helped the US aviation industry develop new aeronautical designs, such swept wings, which would become essential in the postwar jet age. As Col. Donald L. Putt explained to his boss, Maj. Gen. Hugh Knerr, deputy commander of US Strategic Air Force in Europe, Ger-man scientists "would be of immense value in our jet engine and airplane development program."[47] Like previous eras of transportation advancement, the interests of war and national security pushed human engineering to new heights (and moral ambiguities) that would later serve civilian purposes.

In 1954, after years of planning, Boeing opened a massive factory in Renton, Washington, for the development of its 707 passenger jet. At the factory's opening, more than eight thousand employees and community leaders gathered, waving US flags while a brass band played the US Air Force anthem. Pan Am, still the government's exclusive international airline, was the first to use Boeing's new jets for passenger service. The 707 could carry 150 passengers at speeds up to 600 miles per hour.[48] In a television adver-tisement released in 1958, Pan Am promoted its new jet service, claiming "there is no feeling of movement at all, no vibration, hardly any sound. . . . The travail has been taken out of travel. . . . This is the atmosphere on a jet clipper flight." Footage included happy passengers, all racially white and finely dressed, sitting comfortably, reading a newspaper, and having a quiet experience with family.[49] The 707 transformed the dream of comfortable and privileged travel to the skies. In its first year of operation, Pan Am's fleet of twenty 707s carried more than a million passengers. Passengers and pilots alike commented on the smooth, relatively noiseless journey. The "travail" had indeed finally been removed from travel.[50]

In thirty years, from 1928 to 1958, Pan Am grew exponentially from one thousand annual passengers flying on small propellor planes to over a million annual passengers with its 707 jet service. Pan Am celebrated and advertised this historic growth, claiming "modern civilization in the broad sense came to Latin America on caravels during the Golden Age of Explorers—Columbus, Cortez, Pizarro and their ilk—but it really took the air age to unlock the rich storehouse that daring had discovered."[51] International travel had entered the jet age, but this change was not the result of technological "destiny." Instead, it was the result of precedent-setting imperial travel routes, overseas military interests, technological investments, and postwar consumer affluence.

The expansion of jet travel in the 1960s also led directly to the demise of the era of great ocean liners. Maritime passenger service could not compete with the public fascination and speed of the jet age. It would be decades before the shipping industry was able to repackage itself with luxury cruise ships—becoming a "throwback" novelty in comparison to increasingly routine air travel in the late twentieth century.[52] Flight, like so much of consumer culture, evolved from an elite, expensive, and novel activity to being a mainstay of middle-class tourist culture. This great acceleration and phenomenological shift in mobility happened in just a few decades, from the early to mid-twentieth century. With the mass of travelers moving from the sea to the air, though, we have to remember: how did this technological transformation change cultural experiences of space and time?

The New Era of Globalization

Shipping was the lifeblood of transnational cultural and economic connections in the Americas—from the colonial era to the age of revolutions to the early twentieth century. Ships and sailors linked producers and consumers, farmers and grocers, colonial subjects and citizens, tourists and hosts, and travelers of all sorts. But by the mid-twentieth century, the cultural logic of the sea had given way to a new logic of mobility. Scholars of globalization have argued that this shift in technology intensified social interactions, bringing once isolated communities into more direct and intimate contact. Both admirers and critics have heralded the airplane as one of the most important manifestations of the modern era.[53] The airline industry seems to agree. A US Airways advertisement told its customers before its 2013 merger with American Airlines, "It is a big world. We've got it covered." When reevaluated in historical context, though, this idea of global interconnection via air travel becomes less certain. Is the world really all so "covered" in the era of globalization? Compare for a moment the age of sea travel with the age of aviation, as described by the journalist Dea Birkett in 1991:

> The borders of the world's greatest ocean have been joined as never before. And Boeing has brought these people together. But what

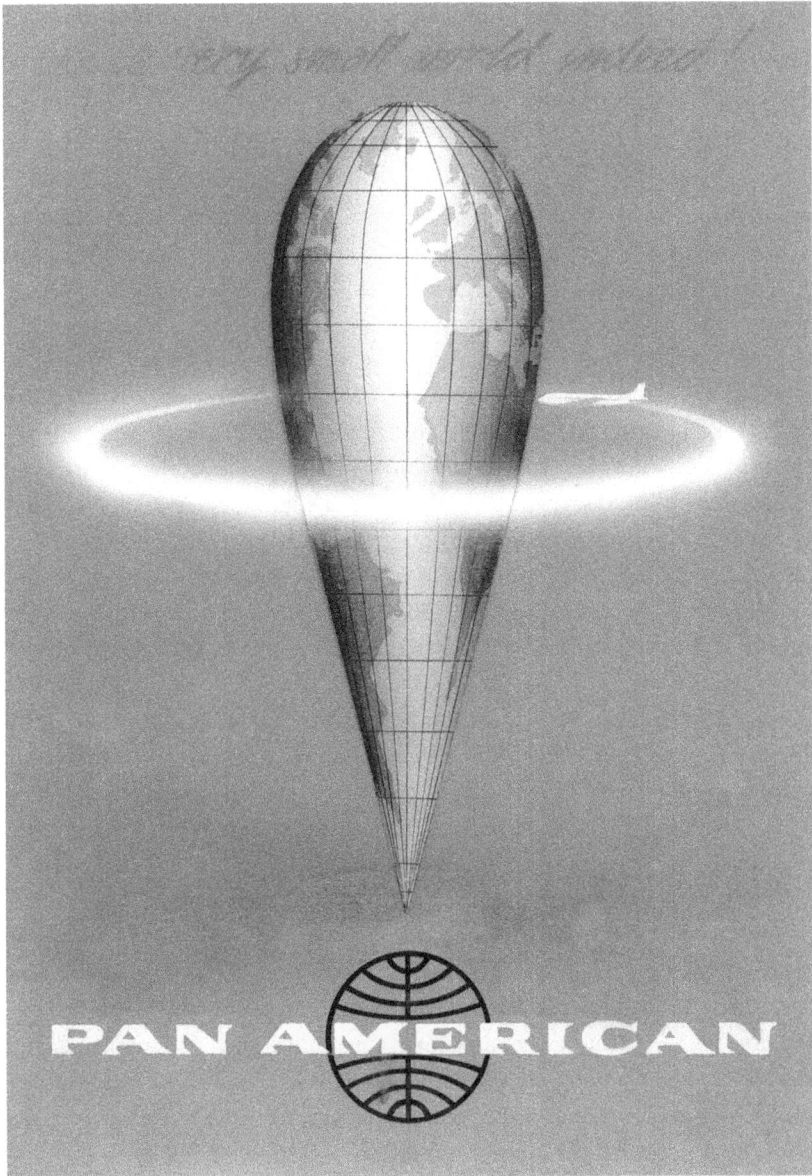

FIGURE 13. Pan American World Airways, "A Very Small World Indeed," ad sketch, original by Paolo Garretto, University of Miami Libraries Digital Exhibits

about those they fly over, on their islands five miles below? How has the mighty 747 brought them greater communion with those whose shores are washed by the same water? It hasn't, of course. Air travel might enable businessmen to buzz across the ocean, but the concurrent decline in shipping has only increased the isolation of many island communities.[54]

The geographic dislocation of the majority of international passengers from the sea accentuated rather than decreased social inequities of mobility. As more travelers flew and as the shipping industry increasingly mechanized and centralized its services, international transportation networks began to bypass smaller ports of call.[55]

This leads to three concluding observations about the effects of "flyover" culture and its impact on international tourism. First, the ability to fly directly from New York City or Miami to Havana may be convenient to the traveler, but it disconnects communities along the route. Two cities gain a direct link allowing for both tourism and emigration, while the entire US eastern seaboard, along with communities in the Florida Keys, the Bahamas, and farther south, disappear from the traveler's itinerary. People, ideas, and goods departing and arriving, from one port to the next, become moored to the past. Technology and wealth as a result have concentrated in fewer and fewer locales. Meanwhile once bustling port and tourist towns such as Port Antonio (Jamaica), Santiago (Cuba), and Colón (Panama) have economically declined and lost employment. The rise of air travel for many communities has actually been a process of geographic isolation. Rather than the story of increasing unity, globalizing technology can also create vast swaths of flyover territory.[56]

Second, for the curious traveler—is it possible to be more conscious of the world thirty thousand feet above its surface? The energy exerted by traveling across space varies depending on whether one walks, sails, rides, drives, or flies over it. The reflections of the German philosopher and critic Walter Benjamin are insightful when considering this issue. Writing in the late 1920s, Benjamin mused that "the person in the aeroplane sees only how the lane moves through the landscape, unwinding in conformity with the laws of the surrounding terrain. Only someone walking along the lane will experience its dominion."[57] To walk the terrain or, in the case of overseas travel, to sail the sea is instead, in the words of Benjamin, "to know the new prospects of his inner being that the text, that lane through the ever-denser internal jungle, opens up." The higher the technology mediating one's experience, the more difficult it would be to understand the magnitude or the magnificence of the immanent world. For many travelers this is what made the hardship of the sea worthwhile and made the Gulf Stream the scene of both adventure and literary imaginings. In the case of land-based travel, a similar phenomenological shift had also occurred in the nineteenth century, as railroads took over from equestrian mobility, and in the twentieth century, when the automobile outpaced them both.[58]

In the modern era, with less awareness of the environment and the communities between destinations, the Caribbean's waters have been reimagined as a sort of sanitized marine park. As the Caribbean poet and Nobel laureate Derek Walcott put it, it is "a blue pool [seen from a distance] into which the [American] republic dangles the extended foot of Florida as inflated rubber islands bob, and drinks with umbrellas float towards her on a raft."[59] The Caribbean, once seen as an adventurous and dangerous sea, has been reinvented as a crystal-clear lake of paradisiacal islands welcoming tourists.

The speeding up of travel may also mean the loss of "real time." If one can get to a Caribbean destination in just a few hours from the mainland United States, there becomes less need to stay. A thirty-six-hour stay, the *New York Times* tells readers, is more than enough.[60] As we fly and rush, from work to leisure and back, there has been a deep and profound shrinking of time to interact with local communities and ecologies. Technology has been an excellent vehicle of mobility and efficiency but can also have unanticipated social and ecological consequences. The old adage "it's not the destination that matters; it's the journey" has been turned upside down.

Despite all the modern comforts of health and safety and the accelerating technological speed in which tourists accessed them, the social practices and beliefs feeding the habits and behaviors of the tourism industry still retained deep roots in the Caribbean's colonial past. To be a tourist was to be "modern," while at the same time wishing for and mimicking seemingly timeless experiences. The next two chapters offer collective biographies of social groups that embodied and helped spread a hegemonic tourist culture to the Caribbean in the twentieth century. Once the historical structure was in place—empire, visions of development, transportation—privileged actors stepped into the scene and taught countless spectators how to play on vacation.

CHAPTER 4

The Nature of Tourism

Naturalist Explorers as Scientific Guides

> If you have health, a great craving for adventure, at
> least a moderate fortune, and can set your heart on
> a definite object which old travelers do not think
> impracticable, then travel by all means. If, in addition
> to these qualifications, you have scientific taste and
> knowledge, I believe that no career, in time of peace,
> can offer to you more advantages than that of a
> traveller.
>
> —Francis Galton, *The Art of Travel*

His bedroom resembled a small nature mu-
seum, a "cabinet of curiosities." In the room there were skulls, shells, feathers,
stuffed birds, pressed plants, and minerals: an assortment of animal remains
and natural objects. As a child, he loved to study and collect nature. It was
a passion, perhaps an obsession. Young Theodore Roosevelt accumulated
hundreds of specimens, which he proudly called the "Roosevelt Natural History Museum."[1] Traversing and possessing nature, he believed, would make
him strong in body and mind. "There is a delight," Roosevelt explained, "in
the hardy life of the open. There are no words that can tell the hidden spirit
of the wilderness, that can reveal its mystery, its melancholy and its charm."[2]

Roosevelt spent his childhood exploring the forests and waterways of
North America in search of "ornithological enjoyment and reptilian rap-
ture."[3] But as an adult this fascination with discovery expanded to new geographies and environments. As the United States expanded overseas in the late
nineteenth and early twentieth centuries, Roosevelt's curiosities also crossed
national borders. The trajectory of his life mirrored US territorial expansion.
Roosevelt's adventures took him from the Adirondacks of New York to the
American West to the American tropics and eventually sub-Saharan Africa.
Naturalist exploration and international travel for Roosevelt and many others were intimately entangled with war and politics.[4]

The desire for adventure embodied by Roosevelt's experiences also came to shape the nature of tourism. Many of the environmental values of modern tourism have their roots in the culture of the naturalist explorer. The president's childhood interests in nature collecting, along with his exploits in war, foreign travel, and big-game hunting, highlight an often-ignored aspect of modern travel culture: deep-seated colonial desires for discovery and adventure influenced the way tourists would dream of and experience tropical nature. Countless children in the twentieth century dreamed like Roosevelt of travel to far-off places in search of "wild" nature. Like him, they searched for a nature seemingly more authentic and pristine, the opposite of increasingly urban industrial life.[5]

The twenty-sixth president of the United States claimed to follow an established and noble tradition. He saw himself as a man of action, travel, and science. In the process, he also helped form the route of US empire and also the route of tropical tourism. In 1898 Colonel Roosevelt and his unit of Rough Riders sailed from Tampa, Florida, to the southern shores of Cuba where they fought against Spanish forces near the city of Santiago. They returned home as national heroes. Their victory in the war in Cuba transferred into political capital.[6] After returning home, Roosevelt was elected governor of New York. A few years later, as president (1901–9), Roosevelt continued to engage in and publicize the value of foreign travel. In 1906, for example, he was the first sitting US president to travel abroad, marking a new era of leisure travel.[7] After running for president for a third term and losing in 1912, Roosevelt returned to the tropics, this time to the Amazon on an expedition sponsored by the American Museum of Natural History.[8] These activities are a snapshot of a long career and cultural phenomenon.

The president's overseas experiences reflected a common culture embraced by tourists and travelers who grew up on stories of colonial exploration. Wild nature, and uniquely its tropical version, promised an escape from the mundaneness of modernity."[9] As technology and science increasingly made life more comfortable and mitigated risks to human health and as families increasingly migrated from the countryside to the city, nature-based tourism and travel offered temporary adventure. Roosevelt's journeys also offered a high-profile model. His social position ensured that his ideas and practices of mobility were well known by the public. His stories inspired a generation of hopeful travelers. A young Ernest Hemingway, for example, dreamed of going on a naturalist expedition after seeing the president. "When Roosevelt came to Oak Park on a whistle-stop tour after his African safari," according to Patrick Hemingway, "Ernest, in his own little khaki safari outfit, was standing alongside his grandfather Anson, cheering on the great African hunter and rough rider of San Juan Hill."[10] Roosevelt brought home a vision of an intriguing tropical world and, in the process, laid out a path for future travelers to follow.

Roosevelt was one of many who, through the power of example, taught tourists how to wonder and wander through the tropical environment in the modern era. In the twentieth century, institutions such as the Smithsonian, the National Geographic Society, and the American Museum of Natural History also shaped how tourists would understand and appreciate the tropics.[11] From the microlevel to the institutional, this chapter retraces the journeys of naturalist explorers affiliated with institutions of scientific research to give *feeling* to the environmental values and practices of tropical travel. It offers a phenomenological read of the naturalist journey to describe how explorers influenced future tourists not exclusively through their use of language but also by their behavior, their actions, by the totality of their deeds.[12] Tourists in search of tropical nature would come to mimic the naturalist's experience. The explorers of the past became touristic examples.

The history of exploration in the tropics has not so much passed, or faded away, but instead accumulated into modern travel culture. As the historian of science Robert Kohler argued, naturalist expeditions "gave countless consumers instructions in understanding nature in a naturalistic or scientific way. They were the cultural software of the middle-class outdoor vacation, giving a simulated experience of nature-going and endowing it with intellectual purpose."[13] Explorer-scientists taught the public that visiting nature could be more than just "leisure." It could be "recreational," spiritually and intellectually uplifting. Tourism was also active. The journeys of explorers, once reported home, helped assemble the ecological fabric of modern tourist culture. Behind every naturalist, behind every expedition, and behind every museum exhibit, as historian and scholar Donna Haraway reminds us, there "lies a profusion of objects and social interactions which can be recomposed to tell a biography embracing major themes for the twentieth century."[14] Naturalist exploration and its engagement with tropical nature are essential elements of tourism's twentieth-century biography.

Diffusing Knowledge at the Smithsonian

"The foundation of our success as a country," Roosevelt argued, depended on "scientific imagination."[15] US foreign policy, foreign travel, and research were profoundly linked. Roosevelt himself traveled and explored, but he also believed that it was the responsibility of government and society to foster interest in both travel and scientific study. As early as 1882, at the age of twenty-four, Roosevelt donated his childhood natural history collection to the Smithsonian Institution's National Museum of Natural History; the same year, he was elected to the New York State Assembly (his first political office).[16] The ambitious politician, over the following decades, would become one of the Smithsonian's most powerful supporters.

As president, Roosevelt advocated for an unprecedented increase in federal funding for scientific exploration and nature education. In 1904 he allocated funding for the construction of a new National Museum of Natural History, the same building that stands today. The museum's exhibition halls, completed in 1910, expanded to 220,000 square feet dedicated entirely to natural history.[17] The Smithsonian, which critics such as Mark Twain had earlier mocked as a "poor, useless, innocent, mildewed old fossil" of the nineteenth century, emerged in the new century as the nation's premier research and educational center.[18] Over the course of the twentieth century, the Smithsonian would serve as the leading US institution to study, explore, collect, and make sense of the tropics. The Smithsonian is now the biggest museum complex in the world, housing natural history specimens and cultural artifacts from around the globe. Pamela Henson, the director of the Smithsonian Institution Archives, told the press in 2007, "We [at the Smithsonian] are what I call a temple of national identity. What we put on center stage says a lot about what the U.S. is—our culture, history, what we believe in terms of science."[19] The Smithsonian's history also reveals what it has meant to be a US tourist and traveler abroad.

Museums, naturalist exploration, childhood dreams, and tourism have fed off each other. They were and they remain interdependent. To study the Smithsonian, then, is to study a history linking exploration, scientific research, and education with the nature of tourism. Its institutional history helps explain how the tropical environment became a fundamental part of touristic imaginations.[20]

Established in 1846, the Smithsonian received its original funding and its name from an Englishman. James Smithson, an amateur scientist and a student of the European Enlightenment, died in 1829. Despite never having set foot in the United States, Smithson decided to leave his entire estate to the US government with the specific request that the money be used to found in Washington, under the name "Smithsonian Institution," an "establishment for the increase and diffusion of knowledge among men." Twenty-seven years after his death, in August 1846, Congress finally passed legislation bringing the Smithsonian Institution into existence. The question remained, though: what type of "knowledge" would the Smithsonian "increase and diffuse," for whom, and for what purpose?[21]

As the United States expanded its territorial reach in the mid-nineteenth century, the Smithsonian became the collecting house for the possessions of conquered lands. The museum's first natural history collections focused on western North America. Research and exhibit strengths paralleled the growth of US geopolitical and commercial expansion along the frontier. As the secretary of the Smithsonian (1945–52), Alexander Wetmore, believed, this pattern of museum growth and interest was "natural because of the military and other expeditions that were going off into the far reaches of our territories."[22] Military and railroad surveyors, working with professional scientists, assembled natural history specimens and also Native American artifacts for the museum to share with the public back home.

The focus of Smithsonian research and its collections began to shift, though, in the early twentieth century. After the Spanish-American War and President Theodore Roosevelt's self-proclaimed taking of Panama in 1903, the tropics also became of national interest. There emerged an immense desire for knowledge about the nature and culture of newly acquired or occupied overseas territories in the Caribbean, such as in Puerto Rico, Cuba, Panama, and Haiti, and in the Pacific, such as in the Philippines and Hawaii. The Smithsonian, which essentially had no collections or researchers focused on the tropics in the mid-to-late nineteenth century, refocused its efforts to become a center for tropical research. Charles Walcott, secretary of the Smithsonian from 1907 to 1927, noted for instance that "the construction of the Panama Canal aroused so greatly public interest in the aboriginal remains of the West Indies that the bureau has arranged for more extended studies in West Indian archeology."[23] Research and collection efforts would also include extensive biological studies of the region's flora and fauna. As a result, by the mid-twentieth century the overwhelming majority of staff scientists at the United States National Herbarium, a branch of the National Museum of Natural History, were interested in tropical plants in the Americas. One Smithsonian scientist remembered, "Looking at that group, I don't think there was anyone who was interested in [anything] other than the American tropics."[24]

How could the nation govern, exploit, or enjoy the fruits of expansion in the circum-Caribbean without intimately knowing the region's nature? Museum growth and US imperial expansion occurred side by side, mimicking earlier European colonial encounters with the tropics. Territorial conquest, as the historian Richard Grove has documented, encouraged Europeans "to understand unfamiliar floras, faunas and geographies, both for commercial purposes and to counter environmental and health risks."[25] What Europe had done before—merging science, commerce, and knowledge production to govern overseas colonies—the United States embraced and built upon in the twentieth century. The institutionalization and popularization of international scientific research depended on expansionist concerns.

Institutions such as the Smithsonian in Washington, DC, and the American Museum of Natural History in New York took on educational roles in this new era of US overseas expansion. They viewed themselves, as the historian Philip Pauly explained, as "a medium of expression between authoritative science in America and the people."[26] The Smithsonian and its staff of scientists offered practical knowledge about the tropical environment, but scientific research could also have a profound influence on popular travel culture. The so-called objective instruments of science provided a rationale for more subjective constructs as well. "Ideas about the natural world," the historian David Arnold has argued, "have developed and informed our very understanding of history and culture."[27] The tropics, not unlike the American West before it, became the symbolic location for US twentieth century imaginations of "wild" and "pristine" nature.

Storytelling and popular entertainment were woven deeply into the fabric of scientific research. Scientists gained a new field of study, and the public found a new natural object of desire. "From the most scientific point of view," as the ecologists Warder C. Allee and Marjorie Hill Allee told young readers in 1925, "there is still the glamour of romance in the tropics. The beauty of the golden-flowering tecoma tree, the absurdity of the great bill of the toucan, the drama of the long struggle between white men and yellow fever—these are as keenly fascinating when seen with wide-open critical eyes as ever they were in any legendary tale."[28] Reports of scientific expeditions and research in the tropics became new-age parables of adventure.

The twentieth century began with an intense push to expand the role of museums in educating the public about natural history. Children visiting the halls of museums, as Henry Osborn of the American Museum of Natural History claimed, "become reverent, more truthful, and more interested in the simple and natural laws of their being and better citizens of the future through each visit."[29] In the context of rapid urbanization and the loss of everyday contact with nature, museums could also bring nature and history to urban residents and teach young people about the natural order of life.

Scientific influence, however, did not just manifest itself in museum exhibits, published articles, or headline stories of adventure. In the back-and-forth process between individual and society, scientists also shared their stories of collecting and traveling with the public through more intimate mediums—radio and film, public and university lectures, and everyday conversations with people in their community. Their network of influence was extensive.

Famous explorers, well-endowed research institutions, humble professors and teachers, and relatively forgotten travelers all played a role in circulating scientific and environmental ways of engaging and consuming the tropics.[30]

Wetmore's Explorations in the Age of Imperial Expansion

The travels of one explorer-scientist at the Smithsonian, Alexander Wetmore, form a biography linking tourism, science, and the US military in the circum-Caribbean. His journeys, rather than being a unique adventure, exemplified a growing and influential web of US exploration increasing and diffusing knowledge about the tropics. Wetmore's travel and research experiences are documented at the Smithsonian's archives, from his first recorded observation in Florida in 1894 to his final collecting trip to Panama in 1966. The arc of his professional career paralleled US international and tourism histories in the twentieth century. As a highly productive taxonomist and collector of birds, Wetmore traveled throughout the Americas, though predominantly in the Caribbean region. For the Smithsonian's National Museum of Natural History, he collected over twenty-six thousand bird and mammal skins in addition to 4,363 skeletal and anatomical specimens and 201 clutches of bird eggs.[31] Because of his collecting work, his publications, and his role as an administrator and public advocate for nature education, Wetmore's colleagues nicknamed him the "Dean of American ornithologists."[32] Over his long career he published hundreds of articles, books, and essays. As a scientist, Wetmore also described over 189 new species and subspecies of birds. Dozens of previously unnamed animals were named in his honor, a collection he fondly called his "private zoo." During his tenure as secretary of the Smithsonian, Wetmore also oversaw a major expansion of the institution's research and museum facilities, opening in 1946 the National Air Museum (now the Air and Space Museum) in Washington and the Canal Zone Biological Area in Panama (now called the Smithsonian Tropical Research Institute). His achievements as a scientist, an administrator, and as a public figure were far-reaching.[33]

Both nature and travel fascinated Wetmore from an early age. The nature that he came to value as a professional scientist emerged from childhood experiences. He grew up in North Freedom, Wisconsin, but his first recorded field observation was at the age of eight, in 1894, while on a family vacation to Florida. "The pelican is a great big bird," he noted, "that eats fish."[34] He explained later to museum visitors that, as a young boy, "I was amazed at the Latin names applied to birds, entranced by accounts of the birds of Texas and other places that seemed equally remote, and fired with a desire to travel and to study the birds of distant places that has remained with me throughout my life."[35] As an adult, Wetmore loved to share this life-long passion for

FIGURE 14. Alexander Wetmore, sixth secretary of the Smithsonian Institution, pictured in his youth studying birds and dreaming of far-off lands, 1901. Smithsonian Institution Archives

nature and travel with the public. During a radio talk in 1939 titled "The Value of Travel," he told listeners:

> The absorbing interest of my life has been the study of biology, of all of the living things, plant and animal, that we find about us, and above

all, birds. While much of this work is done in the museum and in the laboratory, happily another part is only to be found outdoors. Since boyhood I have made studies of living creatures in the field, and regularly have had opportunity for travel in such pursuits.

Birds and nature, he emphasized, were the great joys of travel. He explained that "the urge to travel, to journey, is constant in the majority of individuals of the human race and happily many find it possible to satisfy this desire. There are few who are content to stay constantly in one locality." The best form of travel, he explained, was connected to the study of nature. This type of travel "is active and brings health." It "make[s] us better citizens, better trained for our own life problems, and better and happier people."[36] Wetmore, like many of his colleagues, was a strong believer that scientific exploration and international travel went hand in hand.

With what means, though, did Wetmore travel and explore? What relationships and practices did he embrace to finance his adventures? This in itself was a valuable lesson for aspiring naturalists. Wetmore's mode of tropical travel depended on geopolitical concerns. His fieldwork, from the beginning of his career, depended on US political and economic expansion in the circum-Caribbean. The Bureau of Biological Survey, part of the US Department of Agriculture, paid for his first overseas trip to Puerto Rico in 1911. His task, which also became his doctoral dissertation, was to study "bird life in connection with agriculture."[37] As the US government and corporations began to invest heavily in Puerto Rico in the decades after the Spanish-American War, scientific knowledge became crucial to the success of the colonial enterprise.[38]

The study of tropical flora and fauna, linked to economic necessity, encouraged scientific expeditions to develop along the lines of US empire-building.[39] When Wetmore traveled to the Caribbean—to Puerto Rico and then Haiti, Cuba, Guatemala, and Panama—he also relied on the financial and infrastructural support of the US government and military. During frequent research trips to Panama, for example, the US Army supplied Wetmore and his longtime assistant, Watson Perrygo, with a jeep. After World War II, US Caribbean Air Command also provided him with free helicopter and airplane transport to remote regions of the country. Wetmore wrote to Maj. Gen. Willis Hale, explaining that this "made it possible to cover a considerable area that would not otherwise have been available, and so added measurably to the results of the work. In fact, through this transportation the value of the data secured was more than doubled."[40] There, however, seemed to be strings attached to this reliance on the military. In correspondence with Caribbean

Air Command, Wetmore also offered useful environmental and geographic knowledge. After a collecting trip to the Darién, the border region between Colombia and Panama, for example, Wetmore wrote to Lt. Gen. Hubert R. Harmon. He began by thanking him for his support: "We reached Jaque expeditiously, thanks to your kindness in arranging transport for us in a C-47." Wetmore then proceeded to describe his journey and offer previously unknown information about trails "used regularly by the Indians" crisscrossing the Panama-Colombia border.[41]Unmapped details about local geography and transportation routes could prove useful for policing the often lawless border.

During his numerous visits to the isthmus, Wetmore also worked more directly for the US military. In the early 1940s, the army needed a biologist to undertake a survey of flora and fauna on San José Island in the Gulf of Panama before it tested phosgene, cyanogen chloride, mustard gas, sarin, and other potentially deadly chemicals. Wetmore was the lead biologist for the chemical weapons experiment, authorizing the testing and reporting to military officials that "the experiments in question may be carried forward on San Jose without too great disturbance of the animal and plant life found there if the area covered does not include more than one-third of the surface of the island."[42] He added that trained biologists, including himself and one of his assistants, should be allowed to observe and collect in the area before testing. Wetmore reported to the Smithsonian, "We took advantage of this [experiment] to make as complete collections as possible for the value that these would have to science."[43] US military chemical testing, it appeared, had created an opportunity for scientific collecting.

Science was not immune from the dynamics of state power; indeed, it depended on it. Scientists relied on and supported imperial expansion and geopolitical interests in their efforts to do research. In the nineteenth century, European scientists formed similar partnerships with the state. Charles Darwin, to offer a classic example, traveled to the Galapagos Islands on a British naval warship, HMS *Beagle*, which had been ordered to map the South American coastline. The ship's captain, Robert Fitzroy, wrote of the journey: "Never, I believe, did a vessel leave England better provided, or fitted for the service she was destined to perform, and for the health and comfort of her crew, than the Beagle. If we did want any thing which could have been carried, it was our own fault; for all that was asked for, from the Dockyard, Victualling Department, Navy Board, or Admiralty, was granted."[44] Wetmore's intimate relationship with the US military, in historical context, was part of an established scientific practice.

The close ties between science and empire influenced the directions and outcomes of naturalist research. But it also shaped the public's reception about what it meant to travel and explore. As early as 1919 the anthropologist Franz Boas warned about the dangers of mixing geopolitics with objective science. In a letter to *The Nation*, Boas protested US scientists engaging in military activities and even espionage. He wrote, "I wish to enter a vigorous protest [against] a number of men who follow science as their profession [and who] have prostituted science by using it as a cover for their activities as spies."[45] Boas claimed to have "incontrovertible proof" that at least four men who were representatives of scientific institutions in the United States were involved in espionage overseas. He did not name the men but strongly condemned their actions. The "service of truth" should be the very essence of a scientist's life, Boas argued, and yet secret state partnerships were threatening both the "results of their work" and "the development of international friendly cooperation."[46] His letter generated intense controversy in the US scientific community. The secretary of the Smithsonian, Charles Walcott, tried to get Boas fired from his teaching post at Columbia University. Although he was able to retain his job, Boas lost his prestigious position on the council of the American Anthropological Association and was forced to resign from the National Research Council.[47] The link between science and US foreign policy evidently was difficult to break.

The relationship between science and military interests can also be observed in the story of another ornithologist, whose name became associated with the most famous fictional spy. The real James Bond was an ornithologist working in the Caribbean in the first half of the twentieth century. He was a staff scientist at the Philadelphia Academy of Natural Sciences and in close contact with scientists at the Smithsonian. In 1936 Bond published a popular field guide, *Birds of the West Indies*.[48] The author Ian Fleming, who moved to Jamaica after serving in British intelligence during World War II, was a fan of Bond's work and decided to adopt the ornithologist's name for his famous spy novels. The real James Bond, the ornithologist, was not a spy.[49] But the synchronicity of names and experiences nevertheless is intriguing and perhaps metaphorically revealing. James Bond and Alexander Wetmore were also colleagues and good friends. In letters, Bond regularly referred to Wetmore as "my old friend." The two men corresponded throughout their lives, from the late 1920s to the early 1970s. "You oscillate between the north and south so rapidly," Bond wrote to Wetmore in 1941, "that it is a little difficult to catch up with you."[50] Later in life Wetmore also helped set up the James Bond Fund at the Smithsonian "for life-history studies of indigenous species of birds of the Antilles and other Caribbean islands and of the Bahamas."[51]

More than fiction, intelligence officers sometimes posed as naturalists and men of science to get access to "sensitive areas." The practice provoked both criticism and admiration. In August 1950 the *New Yorker* heralded the work of the Smithsonian ornithologist S. Dillon Ripley and his work at the Office of Strategic Services (OSS; predecessor to the Central Intelligence Agency). The magazine published a flattering eighteen-page profile of Ripley, describing him as a world traveler, explorer, ornithologist, and war hero.[52] The article detailed Ripley's activities with the OSS training and equipping Indonesian spies, all of whom were killed or disappeared during World War II. Ripley sent agents to Burma, Thailand, and Malaysia and worked closely with British intelligence. Maj. Gen. William J. Donovan, head of the OSS, claimed "Ripley's previous contacts and experience, and his imagination, resourcefulness, energy, and tenacity, made him very useful to us."[53] Although the public in the United States praised Ripley's involvement in espionage, it caused controversy abroad. "In one fell swoop, Ripley had alienated the new prime minister of India," according to the historian Michael Lewis, "and had confirmed the worst fears of those Indians suspicious of U.S. neo-imperialism."[54] Yet at home Dillon's reputation remained intact. In 1964 he was appointed the eighth secretary of the Smithsonian. He served twenty years in the position, and later was awarded the Presidential Medal of Freedom by President Ronald Reagan.

The point of bringing these historical observations together is not to join the club of conspiracy theorists but rather to show the very real links between science and imperial geopolitics, which merged and influenced the character of "the increase and diffusion of knowledge." One must seriously consider, what type of research and scientific knowledge emerged from within the confines of formal and informal military operations? What did it mean for objective men of science to arrive in remote communities and environments on military helicopters to document flora and fauna before the testing of chemical weapons? What type of science and adventure did these relationships justify and support in the minds of the public? Conclusions are more suggestive than definitive, but it should not be surprising that many exploring tourists would embody *empire as a way life* while on vacation. Why not? Who was there to guide them differently into nature?

Private Capital for Naturalist Expeditions

While scientists like Wetmore and Ripley traveled with the support of the US military and other federal agencies, some Smithsonian staff focused on fostering ties with the private sector. Another option available to naturalists seeking tropical adventure and research was to find a wealthy patron. Waldo Schmitt, a highly efficient collector and systematic zoologist studying marine crustaceans at the Smithsonian, made dozens of research trips to the Caribbean and the Pacific by courting and traveling with some of the richest families in the United States. In the early part of his career, in the 1910s and 1920s, Schmitt worked closely with the Department of Agriculture and the Bureau of Fisheries. But in the aftermath of the Great Depression, Schmitt began to look elsewhere for funding.[55] The expedition model he embraced became well known among Smithsonian colleagues: find a wealthy sponsor who wanted to cruise through the region where you wanted to collect and, with the Smithsonian stamp, allow the sponsor to get expenses written off by the federal government. The model was known as the "Bredin Format," named after John Bredin, a wealthy philanthropist and Florida real estate and hotel developer.[56] Schmitt met Bredin on a Smithsonian expedition to the Caribbean sponsored by another philanthropist and would be explorer Huntington Hartford.

In 1937 Schmitt organized a much-publicized expedition with one of the wealthiest families in the United States. Huntington Hartford, known as a young "playboy," wanted to explore the Caribbean and make his career as a writer of pirate lore and also as a naturalist. To carry out research, Hartford purchased a 111-foot, fully rigged sailing ship and renamed it after his favorite author, Joseph Conrad. "For years I had the hazily romantic notion," Hartford explained, "that I wanted to sail in a square-rigger. How grand it would be, I dreamed, to bowl over the seas in the wake of such swaggering adventurers as Morgan and Red Legs, Blackbeard and Dampier."[57] Money and fantasy merged into Smithsonian research.

Hartford was the heir to a family fortune, receiving an annual income of $1.5 million as early as the age of six. His grandfather had founded the Great Atlantic & Pacific Tea Company, which brought tea, coffee, and spices from the tropics to consumers, first in New York City and eventually throughout the United States. By 1930 A&P had become the country's largest grocery chain store. According to the *Wall Street Journal*, the company had more than sixteen thousand stores and generated more than $1 billion in revenue in the 1930s: "they were Wal-Mart before Wal-Mart."[58] But young Hartford, by his own account, detested the idea of running the family grocery business. "I had an income of over a million dollars a year," he told his biographer. "Can you imagine me sitting out with a bunch of clerks?"[59] While his father and uncle ran the family business, Hartford played the amateur explorer, writer, artist, and patron of science and creativity.

In the spring of 1937 Schmitt traveled from Washington, DC, to Palm Beach, Florida, to meet Hartford and the crew of the *Joseph Conrad*. Florida would be their point of departure for their expedition. "They have a most beautiful new home just recently acquired as sort of base of operations for Hartford's West Indian cruises," Schmitt wrote Wetmore, who oversaw the partnership. "Mr. Hartford," Schmitt added, "is not adverse [sic] to reasonable publicity and feels that the newspapers, if they ask for information, should be given something. It would not be amiss to send a note to *Science* and to the *Museums Journal*, and I would also like a copy sent to the Explorers Club for their little journal."[60] In addition to encouraging newspaper attention, Hartford would write his own article about the trip for *Esquire* magazine in October 1938, titled "Gone without the Wind."[61]

After a week of tuxedo dinner parties in Palm Beach, the expedition party sailed south. "We attracted a lot of attention [leaving port]," Schmitt recalled, "and a number of small motor boats came up close to get snaps of us and one indeed in movies."[62] The *Joseph Conrad* would sail to the Caribbean, "stopping at such islands," in the words of Schmitt, "as fancy may strike us." Over the course of three months, the expedition visited the Bahamas, Haiti, Puerto Rico, the US and British Virgin Islands, Saba, St. Eustatius, Dominica, Martinique, Barbados, Jamaica, and Cuba. "The cruise was a most successful one," Schmitt reported back to Wetmore in Washington, "covering about forty-five hundred miles and making nineteen stops." He noted that "a not inconsiderable collection of marine invertebrates was brought back, some algological material, two adult porpoises and embryo . . . and a few miscellaneous items."[63] During the trip Schmitt oversaw the collecting work, while Hartford was often busy with other matters. On shore, Hartford socialized with other wealthy travelers and white colonialists on the islands. Meanwhile, at sea he was often sick. "Every other wave," Hartford remembered, "was not a roller, but a steam roller. . . . My stomach, I regret to say, was not in a mood for extended arguments." Schmitt commented in his diary, "I do feel sorry for him, for he's a pleasant plucky chap."[64]

On the expedition Hartford also looked for land to develop. In between his naturalist field notes, Schmitt described that "Hunt wanted to see it [a small island] with viewing to buying. Has a wonderful sand beach and best flat reef for collecting this side of Tortugas."[65] Years later Hartford would return to the Caribbean to build his dream resort, purchasing a small island in the Bahamas for $11 million and spending an additional $20 million to construct a fifty-two-room luxury hotel with an expansive garden modeled after the Palace of Versailles. He called it "Paradise Island."[66]

These private partnerships also proved useful to the Smithsonian and its staff. Schmidt accumulated a huge collection of marine invertebrates. One colleague remembered, "He's a taskmaster as a collector. As soon as he got into the field he was a completely changed man. He was a demon. Thanks to him we got a lot of material."[67] Another colleague at the Smithsonian recalled, "I don't think the Institution would have the standing it does, if it hadn't been for Waldo."[68] In 1943 Schmitt was appointed head curator of the Department of Biology at the National Museum of Natural History. He owed his success, he believed, to his private patrons. After the new appointment, Schmidt wrote a letter to George Allan Hancock, owner of the Rancho La Brea Oil Company, describing how "down in the bottom of my heart, I know I owe it to my friends. The opportunities that you folks have extended me, making it possible for me to broaden my knowledge of zoology and extend my contacts in the scientific world, are in no small measure responsible for this good fortune. I am really truly grateful."[69] Schmitt had traveled with Hancock on a number of expeditions to the Caribbean and the West Coast of South America known as "the Smithsonian-Hancock Expeditions." Similar to the expeditions with Hartford and Bredin, Hancock's trips received scientific credibility by having an official Smithsonian curator aboard ship. Schmitt was also valuable in the field. His knowledge of marine invertebrates could point toward natural resources on the seabed. Oil companies such as Hancock's funded objective scientific studies with the hope that the discovery of invertebrate marine life would also identify undersea oil reserves. Scientific exploration could promise profits. Between the privately funded search for fossilized marine life and the tropical resort fantasies of Hartford, Schmitt also became a respected man of science and a model of adventure.

Adventure Tourism

When one reads about the history of US scientists and explorers abroad, one might think about Indiana Jones or Theodore Roosevelt–type individuals roughing it in the tropics to seek truth and knowledge. Their stories, though, were not feats of individual prowess. Instead, their overseas adventures, dependent on geopolitical interests, became sustaining beliefs for both popular culture and the tourism industry. "Once the province of elites," the anthropologists Robert Gordon and Luis Vivanco argued, adventure "has become accessible and fashionable among the middle classes, and is one of the fastest-growing segments of the tourism industry."[70] The rise of ecotourism, in particular, reflects this popularization of the naturalist's quest. Middle-class tourists can now act like explorers in search of pristine nature and beauty overseas. Although the history from exploration to ecotourism is not linear, a straight line from the early twentieth century to the present, old patterns of thought and action have nevertheless remained in use. Tourists to the Caribbean, and more broadly to the tropics, have followed in the cultural and geographic footsteps of earlier explorers. In the previous sections, this chapter offered thick and layered descriptions of naturalist experiences. While not everyone can work for the Smithsonian or explore like Roosevelt, they can on vacation still briefly feel the thrill, the illusion, of discovery.[71]

The tourism industry has cashed in on and packaged this desire to get close to, to experience, tropical nature. Adventure and exploration in nature, in this sense, are central to the tourism industry. Adventure, as the sociologist Georg Simmel theorized, promised participants "experiences that occur beyond the humdrum of everyday life."[72] The form, psychology, and environmental values of modern tourism grew out of this cultural desire to break from the humdrum of regular life. In the twentieth century, children playing explorers grew up to value vacation fantasies. Waldo Schmitt, who also had a Boy Scout troop named in his family's honor, remembered, "Young people have often come to me and have written more often to the Smithsonian Institution asking how they may get on trips to far-off places and how to prepare themselves for a life of exploring."[73] Adventure as expressed at the Smithsonian and other institutions of scientific research had a ubiquitous role in twentieth-century popular culture.

Built into the mimicked culture of exploration, however, were assumptions about the order of society and its relationship to nature. "In the field," as the historian Donna Haraway explained, the naturalist experience depended on "a complex social institution where race, sex, and class came together intensely."[74] The organization of the Smithsonian Tropical Research Institute in Panama, on Barro Colorado Island (BCI), offers a useful example for understanding this intersection between science, labor, and tourism. Today BCI is one of the most important research stations in the tropics and also a popular ecotourist attraction visited annually by more than five thousand visitors.[75] The research station, however, depended on social hierarchies and inequities. On the island, from the early 1920s to the mid-1960s, workers of color were assigned the most rigorous manual labor and segregated to the "Boys' House," apart from the main sleeping and dining quarters. Meanwhile, women of any racial background were prohibited from spending the night on the island. The station's administrators believed that women, and people of color, were incapable of and would get in the way of serious research. Scientific gatekeeping by men was a regular and frustrating occurrence. "Let us keep a place where real research men can find quiet, keen intellectual stimulation, freedom from any outside distraction," the scientist and patron David Fairchild wrote to fellow scientist and BCI founder Thomas Barbour.[76] The restful contemplation of the white male scientist at BCI in this sense foreshadowed the vacation escape of the privileged tourist.

The fascination with getting away, finding solitude in nature, fostered the belief that the tropics were somehow separate from the troubles of the industrialized and modern world—a refuge rather than a result of modernity. As the author and scholar Candace Slater argued, Western imaginations of the tropical environment created "a skewed and largely static approach toward a multilayered and decidedly fluid reality. The problem is not just that this vision is often false or exaggerated but that it obscures the people and places that actually exist there."[77] The naturalist experience worked to hide the layers of history leading visitors into the tropical environment.

Exploration depended on other's people labor. At BCI, people of color rowed the boats, constructed the houses, cut the trails, cooked the meals, and built and fixed the machines that allowed scientists and tourists to visit the island and imagine themselves alone in nature. Laborers obviously saw "adventure" and "exploration" from a dramatically different perspective. Fausto Bocanegra, a BCI employee in the 1940s and 1950s, explained: "When they got here, because of my knowledge, I was their teacher." Bocanegra and his supposedly "unskilled" colleagues who lived in the Boys' House knew as much or more about the tropical environment than their scientific guests. He remembered one time collecting specimens with a visiting scientist: "I worked here almost a month with a hunter. . . [but] I was the hunter and he was my helper, because I caught the animals and he took what he wanted."[78] Local people organized and made accessible the nature that scientists and tourists would discover. As the historian James Clifford described it, "a host of servants, helpers, companions, guides, and bearers have been excluded from the role of proper travelers because of their race and class, and because theirs seemed to be a dependent status in relation to the supposed independence of the individualist, bourgeois voyager."[79] Explorer culture reflected, reinforced, and often mobilized these prejudices and inequalities—even naturalized them. Back at the Cosmos Club in Washington and the Explorers Club in New York, where Alexander Wetmore, Waldo Schmitt, and other scientists gathered, socialized, and planned their adventures, women and people of color were prohibited from joining the adventure. If a woman entered the doors of those famous clubs, it was often as a servant, like the author Zora Neale Hurston did to pay her bills in the 1920s. [80] The Explorers

Club did not permit female members until 1981. The Cosmos Club did not open its doors to women until 1988.

The scientists of the past of course gave modern-day travelers important tools to think about and understand nature. In particular, they taught an appreciation for biodiversity and conservation. The dangerous perception of the old "jungle," as the historian Kelly Enright has documented, has been replaced by the diverse wonders of the rain forest in the twentieth century. Organisms and ecosystems, travelers are reminded, depend on interconnected relationships. Yet at the same time, the cultural legacy of naturalist exploration has left travelers with a less than ideal ideology and way of traveling to interact with those environments. As the poet and activist Alexis Pauline Grumbs discovered as she went in search of useful scientific studies, "the same language that fuels racism, gendered binaries and other forms of oppression shows up in 'scientific' descriptions. . . [and] most of these descriptions are also written by white western men."[81] The production of scientific knowledge emerged from within and depended on imperial and capitalist expansion and, in the process of doing science, promoted a culture of racial and gendered hierarchy and also a particularly powerful culture of possession and ownership over the natural world. The emerging tourism industry has followed that Western tradition. Tourists, whether aware of it or not, have carried that historical baggage of privileged and exclusionary practices of colonial explorer culture.

Scientific and nature travel are still often framed and marketed as highly gendered and racialized feats of adventure in untamed nature. They have become "crucial processes of Western identity formation."[82] Modern tourism has mimicked and packaged this adventure for mass consumption. Tourists are still encouraged to imagine themselves as explorers of undiscovered or threatened nature, while guides, trail cutters, maids, drivers, and a whole host of servants labor in the shadows to produce the sensation of discovery. We still live and travel with the effects of this truncated vision, where visitors can experience "pristine" rain forests without ever having to recognize the people and histories exiled from memory to make this ecological fantasy possible.

Tourism could mimic naturalist exploration, but it also embraced travel as an individualistic escape from the drudgery of home. In addition to socially constructed perceptions of individual prowess, scientific discovery, and tropical nature, the diffusion of travel culture for mass consumption also took on more existential and epicurean forms. The next chapter explores another aspect of the historical roots of modern tourist identity, examining the experiences of literary travelers who also motivated touristic behavior. Through the travel stories of literary authors, we can see both domestic motivations for leaving home (push) and also how dreams of tropical travel (pull) made their way into popular culture. Adventure promised escape from the everyday routine of life. There were myriad ways to experience this in the circum-Caribbean.

CHAPTER 5

Traveling Writers

Literary Dreams of Tropical Escape

> "Was it through books that you first thought of ships?"
>
> "Reading a book, sir, made me go abroad."
>
> —Wilfred Owen, "Navy Boy"

In the spring of 1933, David A. Smart, Henry L. Jackson, and Arnold Gingrich founded *Esquire* magazine. Their goal, they explained, was to publish a magazine that would "become the common denominator of masculine interests—to be all things to all men."[1] Immediately they began to search for authors who represented this particular masculine vision. Gingrich remembered, "We were going around New York with a checkbook calling on writers and artists trying to make them believe that we were actually going to come out with a luxury magazine, devoted to the art of living and the new leisure."[2]

The New York literary community and advertisers began to "believe" in *Esquire* when the author Ernest Hemingway agreed to write for the new magazine. Hemingway became, in the words of Gingrich, "one of the best friends this magazine ever had, and that at a time when its need of friends was the greatest. It is not too much to say that, at the very earliest point, he was its principal asset." Hemingway helped make *Esquire*. He even created inadvertently its name, addressing a letter to "Arnold Gingrich, Esq."[3] During the first seven years of the magazine's circulation, from 1933 to 1939, Hemingway contributed twenty-six articles, short stories, and "letters," which appeared as travel dispatches. He seemed to be the ideal writer for improving sales of a men's magazine dedicated to the "new leisure." After the publication of his novels *The Sun Also Rises* (1926) and *A Farewell to Arms*

(1929), Hemingway was a literary celebrity. Because of his name on the cover, according to the literary scholar Kevin Maier, *"Esquire*'s circulation skyrocketed from a modest 100,000 copies in 1933 to over 555,000 by 1936."[4]

Hemingway, the novelist of masculine adventure, was equally sought after for his nonfiction work. Some of his most popular travel writing about bullfights in Spain, hunting in sub-Saharan Africa, and offshore fishing in the Caribbean first appeared in *Esquire*. For the magazine's inaugural issue in the fall of 1933, Hemingway wrote an article about big-game fishing in Cuba. That summer the author traveled from Key West to Havana with Capt. Joe Russell. In his article "A Cuban Letter," Hemingway described his early-morning routine at the Hotel Ambos Mundos in Old Havana and his fishing adventures in the Gulf Stream. He reportedly caught fifty-two marlin and two sailfish that season. In the letter, he also offered fishing tips. "The main thing," he told readers, "is to loosen your drag quickly enough when he starts to jump and makes his run."[5] Leisure time and fishing on the island had become Hemingway's new writing material.

By the end of the 1930s, *Esquire* was the best-selling men's magazine in the United States. Its success also did something profound to Hemingway's role in popular culture. As readers looked to *Esquire* for fashion and adventure, the author became a key mediator of US imaginations of foreign travel. In his work and his daily life, Hemingway cultivated a traveler's identity rooted in white American ideals of masculinity, which he then wrote about for mass consumption. Travel, as the scholar Russ Pottle described, was "vital to supporting Hemingway's self-fashioned writer's lifestyle."[6] A sense of travel marked nearly all of his writing. He presented his stories as examples of strength and independence and often, at the same time, as glamorous and leisurely experiences. Many readers, and in particular white men, wanted to live and travel as Hemingway did; many still do. "He had his own poetic gift," the *New York Review of Books* said, "to make the reader feel it had happened to him."[7] The comedian, actor, and travel documentarian Michael Palin recalled that Hemingway "brought places to life, exotic places. . . . I just couldn't get him out my mind. When I read him, I was only a teenager, I never had left my hometown."[8] Another reader, who ended up traveling to Spain and being gored by a bull, remembered, "It felt like he was talking directly to me."[9] Whether to Europe or the Caribbean or sub-Saharan Africa, generations of readers followed in the literary and literal footsteps of Hemingway's travels.

Examining the journeys of creative writers, such as Hemingway, illustrates "the sequence of motion and fact which made the emotion" of foreign travel so appealing in the twentieth century.[10] Between the world wars, a new generation of writers began to articulate and practice leisure travel as the ultimate expression of "freedom." The era resounded with a literary call to go abroad. "Diaspora," the historian Paul Fussell argued, "seems one of the signals of literary modernism, as we can infer from virtually no modern writer's remaining where he's 'supposed' to be."[11] No one, apparently, wanted to stay home. All sorts of creative people—from writers to artists to musicians—embraced "the habit of flux."[12] In the interwar period, as the historian Emily Rosenberg explained, "the fascination with traveling around and describing foreign areas—long evident in human history—reached new heights."[13] Foreign travel became widespread desire.

The circum-Caribbean and its emerging tourism industry were fundamentally entangled with this new era of literature. The region—stretching from the southern shores of the United States to Mexico, Central America, the islands, and northern South America—was a crossroads where the dreams of writers and tourists met. However, admirers and scholars have often held up great works of modern literature as universal parables divorced from the social and environmental geographies, social inequalities, and racially charged encounters that writers actually experienced and wove into their stories. There seems to be a conscious or unconscious effort to exclude twentieth-century literature from transnational and imperial history. "Too often literature and culture," as the postcolonial literary scholar Edward Said put it, "are presumed to be politically, even historically innocent; it has regularly seemed otherwise to me . . . society and literary culture can only be understood and studied together."[14] Art, writing, and travel must be understood as relational. They have rarely if ever been closed off, geographically bound, or culturally coherent to one locale or one culture. Writing decontextualized from the mobile experiences of its authors, as the author and critic Toni Morrison put it, risks "lobotomizing" English-American literature from the fluid and often unjust world it was produced in.[15] Literature—for better, for worse—has shared responsibility for creating and reproducing the privileges and injustices of modern mobility.

Historians of European colonialism have been more open to examining the far-reaching and culturally influential journeys of creative writers. Travel writing, as scholar Mary Louise Pratt argued, was "one of the ideological apparatuses of empire."[16] During the era of European colonial exploration, writers described landscapes, natures, and people in vivid and often condescending language for readers back home. The rest of the world was, in their literary view, ripe for commercial expansion, new knowledge, and the fulfillment of fantasy. Travel writing helped justify European imperial control over distant people and places; and it also significantly reshaped society and culture in Europe. The influence of writers as travelers, though, did not stop with the slow decline of European imperialism. As Pratt explained, the visions of traveling writers have been "appropriated and commodified on an unprecedented scale by the tourist industry."[17] Their legacy has continued and evolved in the new era of tourism.

From the nineteenth century to the twentieth, though, there was a marked shift in travel culture. "Earlier travel writing," as the literary scholar Helen Carr explained, "often came out of travel undertaken for reasons of work, as soldier, trader, scientist . . . or perhaps for education or health; increasingly in the twentieth century it has come out of travel undertaken specifically for the sake of writing about it."[18] After exploration, there was travel, and after travel, there was tourism.[19] What historical and cultural processes, though, changed the motivations of international travel for US and Europeans writers in the twentieth century? Equally important, what characteristics defined their experiences? The generation of wanderlust writers who came of age between the two world wars, although a cog in a massive machine of change, played a crucial role in this transformation, helping to articulate, reproduce, and circulate a new modern ethos of travel: *to go for the sake of going.*

The journeys of a select group of writers reveals political and social changes intersecting with literary production and, in turn, shaping the perceptions and practices of tourism. Writers gave texture and meaning to societal dreams of being abroad. But to better understand this influence, we need to look more closely at how and why writers themselves valued foreign travel. We must, as Toni Morrison advised, refocus the critical gaze from the "described and imagined to the describers and imaginers."[20] The objective of this chapter therefore is not to analyze rhetoric or literary style but rather to study a hegemonic vision of the "writer's lifestyle" and critically understand how this persona shaped the experiences of modern tourism.

We begin by studying the writer's movement. The travel experiences of writers offer a window into the Caribbean's history of tourism, highlighting many of the escapist motivations encouraging tourists to leave home for a vacation. Literary experiences abroad also show how tropical destinations and ways of understanding cultural and geographic difference entered into mainstream thought. In their collective biography of mobility, we can see both push (domestic) and pull (international) forces coming together to create cultural routes of Caribbean tourism.

Away from home, writers translated their experiences into literature for public consumption, igniting travel imaginations. "One of realistic fiction's big jobs," according to the author and critic David Foster Wallace, "used to be to afford easements across borders to help readers leap over the walls of self and locale and show us unseen or dreamed-of people and cultures and ways to be."[21] Writers traveled, wrote about it, and then encouraged others to follow the path of their stories. Experiences abroad expressed in literature became part of the new culture of leisure travel.

Hemingway: Mixing Genres, Mixing Cultures

Traveling writers were not bound by literary genres. They could produce travel writing and distinctly, a novel, from the exact same experience. They blended ethnography, autobiography, and fiction to introduce readers to new worlds. Fiction and nonfiction often came from the same source and complemented one another in terms of their affect.[22] This cross-pollinating is seen clearly in the career of Hemingway.

From the early 1920s to the mid-1950s, Hemingway wrote about his travels in novels, nonfiction books, and in articles and short stories for magazines such as *Cosmopolitan*, *Life*, *Scribner's*, *Collier's*, and *Holiday*, in addition to *Esquire*.[23] His work and his way of being spoke to a social desire to find pleasure and self-affirmation in the act of traveling abroad. The best place to find real adventure and real experience, Hemingway articulated, existed beyond the rules and boundaries of home.

After his experiences in World War I and, for seven years, in Paris's expatriate scene, Hemingway moved to the Caribbean in the late 1920s—first to Key West and then to Havana. He had no desire to return home to Oak Park, Illinois, where he felt confined by the community's "wide lawns and narrow minds."[24] Instead, the islands became, for him, a new source of recreation and creative inspiration. Fishing the waters off Cuba, he explained, gave him a rush like no other and "a lot of time to think." Often narrating his tales in the second person, it was as if he was inviting "you," the reader, to join his escapades. For *Holiday Magazine* in 1949, Hemingway looked back at his years in Cuba, explaining:

> People ask you why you live in Cuba and you say it is because you like it. It is too complicated to explain about the early morning in the hills above Havana where every morning is cool and fresh on the hottest day in summer. There is no need to tell them that one reason you live there is because you can raise your own fighting cocks, train them on the place, and fight them anywhere that can match them and that this is all legal.[25]

He loved Cuba and the beauty of its sea, but more than anything he felt free—it was "all legal." He had escaped, in his mind, the oppressive rules of home. Here, he could drink, fight, fish, and live the way he wanted. Abroad, dreams could be actualized.

Traveling writers, whether telling their stories as fiction or nonfiction, could make fantasies of adventure feel possible. You read it and then dreamed of your own journey. One young man from rural Minnesota felt this sensation. Arnold Samuelson was twenty-two years old and an aspiring writer when he read a story by Hemingway called "One Trip Across," about a boat captain who fished the Gulf Stream between Havana and Key West. "Harry Morgan, the central figure," as described by Toni Morrison, "seems to represent the classic American hero: a solitary man battling a government that would limit his freedom and his individuality."[26] Samuelson was so enthralled by the story he decided to hitchhike from Minnesota to Key West. "That story," he explained later, "gave me the impulse to travel two thousand miles to the meet the writer."[27]

Samuelson arrived on Key West in the spring of 1934 after stowing away on the Florida East Coast Railroad. As soon as he got off the train, he went to look for Hemingway. "There seemed a good chance E. H. would show at his house in Key West," Samuelson remembered. "He was back from a hunting trip in Africa. I had seen a newspaper picture of his arrival on the boat in New York."[28] That afternoon Samuelson went to Hemingway's house and knocked on the door, where the encounter with the often boorish author went surprisingly well. The older man jotted down a reading list and lent him two books: a collection of short stories by Stephen Crane and a copy of A Farewell to Arms. The next day Hemingway offered Samuelson a job as night watchmen on his new fishing boat, the Pilar, recently purchased with an advance from Esquire.[29] Recounting their relationship for the magazine, Hemingway wrote, "Besides writing this young man had one other obsession. He had always wanted to go to sea. . . . To fulfill his desire . . . we promised to take him to Cuba."[30] Over the next year, Samuelson traveled with Hemingway back and forth between Key West and Havana. He lived on the boat, fished, and served drinks and also worked on his own writing material.

Arriving to Havana, Samuelson recalled, "we walked the narrow, shaded streets lined with buildings cemented together in a solid front against the sidewalks, which were just wide enough for us to walk in single file, with E. H. in the lead, taking long steps, Pauline [his second wife] behind him and me in the rear taking medium steps, walking on air. I was having that exhilaration, which only comes in full force during your first trip on foot in a foreign city."[31]

Samuelson had fulfilled his dream to travel overseas and improve his writing skills. But not long afterward, he stopped traveling and writing to find more stable income. Eventually he settled in rural Texas and started a small lumber business and raised a family. "I wanted to write," he wrote in a memoir posthumously published by his daughter, "not knowing there were thousands of others who wanted the same thing."[32] Hemingway's writing had inspired countless young authors. The short story of the boat captain that Samuelson loved, for example, would turn into the novel *To Have and Have Not* (1937) and would later become a Hollywood movie starring Humphrey Bogart. Authors who wrote of adventure in distant locales spoke to the desires of young people with dreams of travel and a literary career. But for every one traveler who made a career writing, there were hundreds, even thousands, who earned very little money and even less recognition as authors. Samuelson was one of many; so was Hemingway, though with literary and financial success. Everyone else it seemed was left reading and dreaming of foreign travel.

Forgotten Travelers, Forgotten Geographies

The history of Hemingway is just the tip of a societal iceberg of literary travel desire. Diverse authors engaged in and gave meaning to international travel for readers back home. Famous authors such as John Steinbeck, Aldous Huxley, and Graham Greene and less remembered writers such as Richard Halliburton, Harry Franck, and Harry Foster also traveled and wrote and shaped the imaginations of hopeful travelers. Less privileged writers of color such as Langston Hughes, Zora Neale Hurston, and Claude McKay were also part of this mobile network of literary production, although as discussed later in this chapter they were often highly discriminated against and typecast as representing the "other." In the first half of the twentieth century, English-reading peoples of the world were profoundly interested in reading about the rest of the world.

As international travel became more accessible, "national" authors and literature increasingly turned transnational.[33] Even authors traditionally associated with domestic literary subjects went abroad. John Steinbeck, for example, is remembered as a novelist of the Great Depression in the United States and life in Northern California. He began his career, though, writing about Panama and the Caribbean. In 1929, the same year Hemingway published his best seller *A Farewell to Arms*, Steinbeck published his first novel, *Cup of Gold*.[34] Steinbeck had traveled from California to New York via the Panama Canal a few years earlier, his first overseas trip. Inspired by the journey and the history around him, he wrote a novel about the legend of Henry Morgan and his attack on the Spanish colony of Panama in 1671.

His depiction of the famous English pirate, critics believe, was cut from his own fantasies of adventure. "They were starting for the Indies [Morgan and his crew]," Steinbeck wrote, "the fine far Indies where boys' dreams lived."[35] The highly romanticized book, published in August 1929, sold poorly. But as Steinbeck matured as an author, he continued to write about the people and places he visited in the Caribbean and Latin America. His novella *The Pearl*, about an impoverished family on the coast of Mexico that found a beautiful yet cursed pearl, drew on a story he had heard during his travels. The book is still read in school classrooms.[36] The firsthand account of a trip to Mexico with his friend, the marine biologist Ed Rickett, was also published as a book, *Log from the Sea of Cortez* (1941). Written as a rambling travelogue, the book was part adventure, part naturalist exploration, and part philosophical reflection. "It would be good to live in a perpetual state of leave-taking," Steinbeck considered, "never to go nor to stay, but to remain suspended in that golden emotion of love and longing; to be loved without satiety."[37] Steinbeck, the quintessential writer of the American experience, was quite transnational in his literary interests.

In the early 1920s, when Hemingway and Steinbeck were still relatively unknown, traveling writers such as Richard Halliburton had already established themselves as best-selling authors. In his book *The Royal Road to Romance* (1925), Halliburton explained his itinerant obsession, declaring, "Let those who wish have their respectability. I wanted freedom, freedom to indulge in whatever caprice struck my fancy, freedom to search in the farthermost corners of the earth for the beautiful, the joyous and the romantic."[38] In the 1920s and 1930s, Halliburton retraced Ulysses's journey in the Mediterranean, Cortez's conquest of Mexico, and Robinson Crusoe's fictional experience on the Caribbean island of Tobago. He even wrote about his own unusual journey swimming the length of the Panama Canal, paying the lowest toll in the canal's history. *Vanity Fair*, annoyed by his overwhelming success, profiled Halliburton in 1930, describing his books as "marvelously readable, transparently bogus, extremely popular." It critiqued that they "made their author a millionaire; because his invariable picture of himself (patent pending) is that of a diffident, romantic boy; because he is the most popular ladies club lecturer in America, and every knock *Vanity Fair* gives him is just a boost."[39] Romanticized travel writing was often viewed as a lesser art than fiction, but it was also lucrative. Over the years, however, as the editors at *Vanity Fair* hoped, the public did forget about Halliburton. Today, tour guides briefly mention his name as a quirky fact at the Panama Canal's visitors center. But during his lifetime, he was one of the most popular authors of his generation.[40] The broadcast journalist Walter Cronkite even credited Halliburton with his decision to become a news correspondent. He made travel glamorous, Cronkite remembered. The writer, philosopher, and activist Susan Sontag also read Halliburton in her youth and, looking back on her career, claimed that his books were "surely among the most important books of my life."[41]

While Halliburton traveled well beyond traditionally understood literary circles, he was not the only one. There is a long list of American and English authors who rarely lived at, or wrote about, "home." George Orwell, for example, also set his first book in Burma, and some critics believe that his best-known books *1984* and *Animal Farm* were actually based on his observations of colonialism in Southeast Asia.[42] Another twentieth-century British author, Aldous Huxley, spent more time abroad and wrote as much about the Americas—from the US Southwest to Mexico and Central America—than about his native England. He poked fun at an earlier generation of English writers, signaling out poet William Wordsworth (1770–1850), who chose to stay home:

> He chose, in a word, to be a philosopher, comfortably at home with a man-made and, therefore, thoroughly comprehensible system, rather than a poet adventuring for adventure's sake through the mysterious world revealed by his direct and undistorted intuitions. It is a pity that he never traveled beyond the boundaries of Europe. A voyage through the tropics would have cured him of his too easy and comfortable pantheism.[43]

Huxley, like so many authors of his generation, traveled to the tropics to write about it. Author Graham Greene also traveled to the Caribbean and Latin America and wrote books set in Cuba, Mexico, and Panama. "It was boredom," he told readers, that first sent him abroad.[44] Hart Crane, one of the most respected poets of the Lost Generation, the young people who came of age during World War I, also lived and wrote in Mexico and Cuba before committing suicide by jumping from a steamer in the Gulf of Mexico. Harlem Renaissance writers such as Langston Hughes, though faced with racism and restricted state travel measures, also found inspiration in Cuba and the Caribbean. "I am to go to Havana," Hughes wrote his literary patron, "for rest, new strength and contact with the song."[45] He later added in his memoir, *I Wonder as I Wander*, "I wanted to be lazy, lie on the beach as long as I liked, talk with whom I pleased, go to cockfights on Sundays, sail with fishermen, and never wear a coat."[46] During his travels Hughes also wrote enduring poetry. Claude McKay, the Jamaican-born writer, also wrote about life on the move in the Caribbean and the United States. "I was gripped by the lust to wander and wonder," he wrote. "The spirit of the vagabond, the demon of some poets, had got hold of me."[47] The African American author and ethnographer Zora Neale Hurston also spent more than two years traveling around the Caribbean. She wrote her most popular book, *Their Eyes Were Watching God* (1937), about an African American family in Florida while she was living in Haiti.

The transnational dimensions of literary production were culturally profound, despite retrospective navel-gazing in a few metropolitan hubs. The roots of twentieth-century literature extended well beyond New York, Paris, and London. Literature assumed to be produced distinctly in Europe or the United States was often created in a more global or, more precisely, transnational context. The Caribbean was part of that itinerary.

Lost Generation in the Paradox of Progress

Travel writing had for centuries portrayed the Caribbean, and travel to the tropics more broadly, as a mysterious and often magical region, albeit a historically dangerous one for Euro-American and European reading publics.[48] In the twentieth century, however, this colonial dream found itself in the context of rapid change. Escape to the south became even more enticing, medically safe, and technologically accessible and available. The rise of urban industrial capitalism, the expansion of transportation and communication technologies, and the fears of civilizational decline and world war made foreign travel one of the most popular literary subjects of the era. Whether one was a cynic or a believer in modern change, the story of travel had appeal.

To make sense of the social context fueling the desire to go abroad, we turn to the story of one forgotten traveling writer, Harry Foster. His life, and the lives of other writers on the move, exemplified a new era of transnational mobility emerging in the twentieth century. The disillusioned members of the Lost Generation became wandering leaders in an expanding and pleasure-based travel industry, helping circulate the message that going abroad had value when seemingly nothing else did.

In 1919, at the end of World War I, twenty-five-year-old Harry Foster began his travels as a freelance writer and a "tropical tramp." He was not the only young person, though, with the urge to go abroad after the war. "You're not the first one," the captain of a steamer lectured to him on the docks in Panama. "Every time I hit port a dozen fellows want to ship to South America. It's the war that did it. Those that didn't get over feel that they've been cheated out of something, and they're looking for it now."[49] As Foster admitted, he was tired of traditions and discipline, and he had no interest in returning home to a sedentary life. During the war he had served in the US Army's Seventy-Eighth Infantry Division. In the trenches of France, he was promoted to first lieutenant. Later he specialized as an instructor in modern warfare. Among rank-and-file soldiers, Foster was also considered well educated. Born in Brooklyn, in 1894, he had studied at an elite prep school in New Jersey and later at Lafayette College in Pennsylvania, this in an era when most students in the United States still did not complete secondary school.[50] All the early signs pointed toward a successful and comfortable future for Foster. His experience in the war, however, would change the direction of his life.

After the war Foster returned to the United States for his final deployment with the army, this time along the Mexican border. A few months later, after being honorably discharged, he crossed into Mexico and began to work his way south. "Seized by the same wanderlust that has led so many other ex-soldiers into foreign lands," he explained, "I had drifted down through Mexico and Central America." He wanted to explore, to be free, and he hoped to pay his way as a travel writer. He struggled, however, to find a publisher for his stories. By the time he reached Panama, it was obvious that writing on its own would not cover his expenses. Since magazines declined to publish his work, Foster decided "that the first requisite for a magazine writer of my particular species was a steady job of some sort." In Panama, he applied for work at the US government's Canal Zone commissary, where he was hired to be in charge of the shoe department. But he quickly grew dissatisfied. "The shoe department seemed to be no place for a would-be writer of romance."[51]

Foster walked the docks looking for a job shoveling coal on an outgoing tramp steamer but found no work. "Ain't you never heard of tropical tramps?" a friend asked him. "Lots of fellows—some of 'em college graduates—is doin' it regular. Big men, railroad superintendents an' everything—lots of 'em. . . . They just can't help the wanderlust." There was simply not enough work to support the influx of veterans and young people trying to travel their way through the tropics after the war. Foster decided to stay on at the Canal Zone's shoe department and save up for the trip. A month later he had the money needed. "Then I secured a map of South America, closed my eyes, and jabbed with a pin," he claimed. "The pin landed in Peru. When I collected my month's salary, minus deductions, I had just about enough for deck passage on a native coasting steamer to Callao, the seaport for the Peruvian capital."[52]

Between his days as a shoe clerk in the Canal Zone and his death by pneumonia twelve years later, Foster became a prolific writer. He wrote seven books about his travel experiences in the tropics of the Americas, Asia, and the South Pacific. His editors at Dodd, Mead & Company also published two guidebooks about the Caribbean, posthumously, under his name in 1935 and 1937.[53] Foster had found a measure of literary success. But unlike some of the more famous and enduring authors of his generation, he never earned enough from his publications to just be a writer. He was always running out of money. Often he resorted to playing ragtime piano in dive bars in the red-light districts of Panama, Singapore, and other tropical ports. To support his travels, he also worked as a tour guide. His fourth book, which was part guidebook and part jovial travel narrative, drew inspiration from his other career in the tourism industry. "Every day an adventure," he joked, "without trouble, danger, worry, or discomfort."[54]

Foster's story from soldier to writer and eventually tour guide highlights the massive wave of movement after World War I. Foster was clearly not the only veteran with the idea of becoming a traveling writer, a tropical tramp with stories to tell. The war became a catalyst for a new generation of disgruntled literary travelers.

Before World War I, it seemed as if progress was conquering time and space and nature for the benefit of humanity. In the first decades of the new century, there was tremendous optimism about the future. Medical professionals had defeated one disease after the next. Yellow fever and malaria were no longer the scourge of the tropics. Modern science and technology promised health and a wider world to explore in safety. The new networks of travel and communication—dependent on electricity, steel, and fossil fuel—made the world seem so much closer, more tangible. Although some people were suspicious of this highly rationalized and anthropocentric vision, the overwhelming majority, according to the historian Michael Adas, "held to the faith in progress, in the primacy of rationality, and in the unbounded potential of scientific inquiry and technological invention for human improvement which had been dominant throughout the nineteenth century."[55] The young and the old believed in the hope of progress—that is, until World War I.

In August 1914 the double-edged sword of technological mastery cut through the continents of Europe and the Americas. On the Isthmus of Panama, SS *Ancon* made the first official transit across the Panama Canal. After ten years of dynamiting and digging, the canal linking the Caribbean with the Pacific Ocean was open for commerce. For the United States, the canal symbolized humanity's conquest over nature and the infinite possibilities of technology in the twentieth century. The canal was celebrated as one of the greatest undertakings of the age.[56] Fear of nature's power had begun to erode. In that moment of confidence, however, it seemed that the leaders of Western Europe and the United States had also overlooked, perhaps forgotten, humankind's ability to destroy itself with technology. As the United States celebrated its canal—its symbol of world progress—Europe entered into a war that would cost over sixteen million lives.

Technology went from promising freedom to destroying it. "Human hordes, gases, electrical forces were unleashed in a free-for-all," the German philosopher Walter Benjamin recounted. "High-frequency shocks ripped through the landscape, new stars appeared in the sky, the airy heights and the ocean depths thrummed with propellers, and everywhere sacrificial shafts were sunk in the earth. This mighty struggle for the cosmos was for the first time fought out on a planetary scale, very much in the spirit of technology."[57] Millions of soldiers became the victims of the power of progress and the state leaders who controlled it. Technology could enrich life or take it away. The telegraphs, newspaper print, highly coordinated mail networks, and even the new technology of cinema also allowed civilians at home to witness the horror. No longer did loved ones have to wait months to hear tragic news from the front lines. Everyone could feel the consequences. "The world," as the historian Stephen Kern explained, "was alternately overwhelmed and inspired, horrified and enchanted" by the technological power that humanity unleashed on itself.[58]

The Great War, controlling technology and mobility for destructive purposes, also inspired a countercultural movement. Four million military personnel in the United States and many more civilians served the war machine. In Europe the numbers were greater: sixty million people mobilized for war. The hypocrisy of national leaders proclaiming the triumph of progress over the past and, at the same time, the need to preserve the traditional order became painfully apparent. Social reverence for technology and its patron, the nation-state, began to crack. The desire to live and move freely, rather than bow to the dictates of generals and bosses measuring every move, grew from a small circle of critics into a mass movement. The sentiments of one military veteran living in Panama expressed this rise in opposition to authority. "We civilians who fought in the late war have already forgotten many things," he wrote, "but there are some things which we ought not to forget. . . . Now, if by the word, soldier, one means a competent, reliable fighting man, then the trick of standing in a rigid, wooden attitude when a general passes by has absolutely nothing to do with the case . . . as long as our military pundits are unable to see this and decline to scrap all such obsolete hocus pocus, which has nothing to recommend it but tradition, their intelligence will be subject to question."[59] The brutality of modern violence, and the traditional indifference of its leaders, inspired an era of itinerant cynicism.

The war harnessed not only the destructive power of technology on battlefields but also solidified the rising power of the state over its citizenry at home. "I am positive the great war was fought," the stateless writer B. Traven criticized, "not for democracy or justice, but for no other reason than that a cop, or an immigration officer, may have the legal right to ask you, and be well paid for asking you, to show him your sailor's card, or what have you. Before the war nobody asked you for a passport. And were the people happy? Wars for liberty are to be suspected most of all."[60] Soldiers, who had been told they were fighting for freedom and sovereignty, returned to a highly regulated society. New rules took hold, just as young people returned home with a new set of eyes, a seasoned perspective, for understanding this societal shift.

In the United States, political authority emerged from the war more confidant. While Europe struggled to rebuild economically, many US industries boomed. Accompanying this economic growth was a renewed effort to maintain and spread progressive social mores and work ethic. For the supposed health of families and the productivity of factories, a coalition of progressives pushed through legislation to regulate civic morality. One of the most controversial of these laws was the ban on the sale and consumption of alcohol. Just as the war concluded, Congress passed the Volstead Act of 1919. What the nation's leaders called rational and necessary legislation looked to many like an effort at political and cultural domination. Young people, who had already begun to question the authority of their elders who led them into war, had yet another reason to feel rebellious.[61]

Within this culminating and volatile context—the transition from war to peace—travel for one's own pleasure and curiosities increased in popularity. Mobility came to represent a rejection of responsibility and authority, to set out one's own terms became an act of rebellion. "The notion began to spread among writers," according to the Lost Generation writer Malcolm Cowley, "that they were an oppressed minority, orphans and strangers in their own country, and that they had better leave it as soon as possible."[62] Foreign travel looked more and more appealing.

Writers, such as Hemingway, became spokesmen for postwar social discontent. They believed there was a generational breach between themselves and those in charge. In *The Sun Also Rises*, Hemingway popularized the notion of a "lost generation," which he adopted from the writer Gertrude Stein living in Paris.[63] The band of privileged expatriates he described spent their days drinking, traveling, fishing, and watching violent sports in northern Spain. Often his characters drank themselves into a hedonistic stupor. "Hemingway viewed drinking and getting drunk," according to the literary scholar Jeffrey Schwartz, "as an initiation rite and adventure." His writings expressed "both the communal enjoyment of life and its pleasures and a manner of rebelling against prohibition and its nationalist agendas."[64] Hemingway's mother, who wrote to him that his novel was "one of the filthiest books of the year," had earlier pleaded with him to return home and get a respectable job. Instead, he chose to continue living a bohemian life, traveling, drinking, and writing.[65]

Fellow Lost Generation author F. Scott Fitzgerald also wrote about his discontent with the cultural obsession with progressive mores and capitalist productivity. He, too, had an intense desire to escape. Fitzgerald's first novel, *This Side of Paradise* (1920), chronicled in a highly autobiographical style the misadventures and longings of a young man disillusioned with modern society. "I'm restless. My whole generation is restless," Amory Blaine, the main character, tells us. "I'm sick of a system where the richest man gets the most beautiful girl if he wants her, where the artist without an income has to sell his talents to a button manufacturer."[66] Although Amory was a privileged white American, a graduate of Princeton and a World War I veteran moving in elite circles, he sees nothing but superficial vice and false authority. He feels "beat-up" by and bitter at the rule-makers. "Progress," he slowly realized, "was a labyrinth . . . people plunging blindly in and then rushing wildly back, shouting that they had found it . . . the invisible king—the élan vital—the principle of evolution . . . writing a book, starting a war, founding a school." Amory was tired of it all. Disgusted by his social surroundings, Amory, and perhaps Fitzgerald, "wanted to creep out of his body and hide somewhere safe out of sight up in the corner of his mind." Or if he couldn't hide in himself, he would go abroad where he could indulge in whatever caprice:

> He felt an overwhelming desire to let himself go to the devil—not to go violently as a gentleman should, but to sink safely and sensuously out of sight. He pictured himself in an adobe house in Mexico, half-reclining on a rug-covered couch, his slender, artistic fingers closed on a cigarette while he listened to guitars strumming melancholy undertones to an age-old dirge of Castile and an olive-skinned, carmine-lipped girl caressed his hair. Here he might live a strange litany, delivered from right and wrong and from the hound of heaven and from every God (except the exotic Mexican one who was pretty slack himself and rather addicted to Oriental scents)—delivered from success and hope and poverty into that long chute of indulgence which led, after all, only to the artificial lake of death.[67]

Home, in his view, was terribly alienating. "Abroad," whether far away or right across the border, was an exotic alternative.

Lost Generation authors romanticized their alcoholic, sexual, and transnational freedom in opposition to Prohibition and the rules of home. Their books, even when fictionalized, were often biographical. "They tended," according to the literary critic and writer Kirk Curnutt, "to write about alienation, unstable mores (drinking), divorce, sex, and different varieties of unconventional identities."[68] Writers who were less biographical and exhibitionist in their publications also expressed frustration with Prohibition and increased state authority. Harry Franck, who wrote twenty-three books about his globe-trotting travels, regularly told of expatriates and foreign hosts ridiculing Prohibition. After serving as a lieutenant in the world war and writing an account of the war's aftermath in Germany, Franck returned to the Americas to tour the Caribbean. In his book *Roaming through the West Indies* (1920), he described "prohibition-abhorring visitors from the North" filling up hotels and of locals criticizing the United States for its lack of freedom. "From our point of view," one local journalist told Franck, "the United States is the greatest autocracy in the world; it has no real republican form of government, no real freedom of the people."[69] Foster chronicled encounters with travelers disillusioned with the US political system. In South America, he met one fellow tropical tramp who used to work in the United States until Prohibition encouraged him to go into self-exile. Over whiskey and singing in a gambling house, his new friend pronounced, "If the United States wants Frank Glamm back, they got to cut out prohibition."[70]

The writers of the Lost Generation gave voice to a new era of rebellion emerging in the 1920s that came to be characterized by outlaws, speakeasies, and "free" living. According to Malcolm Cowley, "the spokesmen for the new generation celebrated the value of simple experiences such as love, foreign travel, good food, and drunkenness."[71] These sentiments grew in popularity. The same values embraced by the Lost Generation also emerged as the consumer demands of the Caribbean's tourism industry, rooted in gambling, bars, and unrestricted pleasure.

The great paradox of the era, however, was that the changes the Lost Generation criticized were the same forces that created the opportunity for self-exile. Technological progress and national economic and political power gave writers the means to move faster and more freely. The alienating system they criticized also supplied the capital and the resources that carried them to distant locales to look back at and pick apart home. Progress and technology were, in their view, sources of modern slavery, chaos, inequality, and alienation. Yet at the same time they became the means of escaping the domestic consequences of urban industrial growth, war, and state power. Fast-moving steamships, the new technology of aviation dependent on oil, and the massive wealth that the United States acquired after the war produced a new era of social and economic privilege. With the power of their domestic economy behind them, writers could travel and live comfortably while the local population they visited often struggled. This paradox of progress seems to still define our contemporary era of travel. "Whether we happen personally to love technology, hate it, fear it, or all three," David Foster Wallace reflected, "we still look relentlessly to technology for solutions to the very problems technology seems to cause."[72] Modernity, which writers in the interwar era often described as "alienating," "bourgeois," "stressful," or "unexciting," assured their comfort abroad. The exiled writer of the interwar period was analogous to a dog trying to run away from its own tail.

Writers as Mediators

One of the most striking characteristics of the Lost Generation's countercultural movement was how popular it became in mainstream society. There seemed to be nothing more emblematic of modern "American identity" than wanting to leave the United States in search of new opportunity somewhere else. But by the mid-twentieth century, the notion of going abroad as an escape was depoliticized and packaged for mass consumption. International travel as cultural expression became part of the "culture industry." It morphed, in the words of critical theorists Theodor Adorno and Max Horkheimer, into "the freedom to choose what is always the same."[73] The wave of tourists, who followed the literary routes of traveling writers, were not nearly as critical of where they came from. Yet they have embraced, at least in part, the liberating sentiments of literary travelers. Writers like Hemingway, who expressed an almost hatred for banks and big government, ironically became heroes for people working for those very institutions. "I wanted to study Cuban cigars, Cuban rum and Hemingway, in that order," one bank president explained about his vacation.[74] Seemingly at odds, traveling writers, in search of authentic experience and liberating pleasure, and mass tourism, often ahistorically reproducing travel experiences over and over again, have in fact been mutually supportive of one another. As a social group, writers became literary conduits for aspiring readers bound to a regimented work regime but longing for new experiences.

Neither part of home nor fully incorporated into visiting communities, traveling writers operated between worlds, working as a bridge between hosts and guests. They became mediators. They participated, in the words of the historian Ricardo Salvatore, in "a representational machine."[75] Their writings and the stories of their own journeys pieced together representational practices for engaging in touristic behavior, helping tourists decide when and where to go, what to see, and how to treat the locals. And with the pool of potential tourists growing, writers found themselves in a privileged position. They could be literary guides for the masses.

Hemingway was one of the more iconic writers working as a tourist mediator. He helped popularize some of the most lucrative tourist economies in the Caribbean (in Key West and Havana) and in Europe (in Pamplona and Paris). Among friends, Hemingway would often say that if he ever gave up this "writing racket," he would become a sport fishing or hunting guide for rich tourists. "Hemingway," one Key West fishing guide claimed, "made this charter-boat business—he brought the fishermen down."[76] Through his writings, the author also influenced the tourism industries in Pamplona and Havana. Bronze statues of the author honor his career and his notable role in bringing tourists to those respective cities. "You might even say," as one journalist reported from the festival of San Fermín, "that he forged the modern idea of Pamplona and San Fermín, his celebratory words transforming what had been a provincial party into a global event."[77]

Hemingway legitimated and gave meaning to a hegemonic tourist identity. We could analyze any number of the behaviors he reproduced and sanctioned that have become part of the tourism industry—such as heavy drinking, cultural festivals, big-game fishing, and sexual exploits. But for the purposes of exemplification, let us focus on one crucial issue: the question of racial and gendered privilege embodied in his writing and coloring the tourism industry in the Caribbean. Perceptions of racial difference and interacting with "others," accepted forms of finding pleasure, and the meaning of the exotic were all enacted in his literature. Toni Morrison, in her book *Playing in the Dark: Whiteness and the Literary Imagination*, offered an insightful analysis of how Hemingway employed racist and racial privilege in his stories. Morrison argued that the "power" of Harry Morgan, the central character in the novel *To Have and Have Not*, was expressed in relation to the other—that is, dark skinned Afro-Cubans.[78] The white American protagonist, according to Morrison, "is virile, risk-taking, risk-loving, and so righteous and guiltless in his evaluation of himself that it seems a shame to question or challenge it." In Havana, Morgan and his wife have a privileged status as white American tourists. "The couple, Harry and Marie, is young and in love with obviously enough money to feel and be powerful in Cuba." But, as Morrison tells us, "into that Eden comes the violating black male making impertinent remarks."[79] Harry reacted to this seeming racial threat by quickly proving his dominance, hitting the man, knocking his straw hat off and into the street, where it gets run over by a taxi.

The more powerful and important characters in Hemingway's stories were almost always white men. Harry was the author's version of the white-male "Papa." This literary persona has also fed hegemonic expectations of foreign travel. To be a tourist was to be someone special. Meanwhile, people of color in Hemingway's writings, and in the dominant tourism industry, are depicted in servile positions. As Morrison summarized the affect, "cooperative or sullen, they are Tontos all, whose role is to do everything possible to serve the Lone Ranger without disturbing his indulgent delusion that he is indeed alone."[80] American and English literature has over and over again presented an archetypical identity for the tourism industry based on white male privilege. And racism has been at the center of this modern tourist experience. In racial inequality came the feeling of the visitor's individuality, of one's special worth.

It was common for writers to also see themselves as somehow superior to the camera-toting visitors. Nevertheless, they formed close relationships. Traveling writers, in addition to articulating an identity of privilege, provided more direct services. They sometimes worked as informal and formal guides. In the early 1930s, Hemingway and his second wife, Pauline Pfeiffer, complained that Key West was being ruined by the arrival of tourists. As Arnold Samuelson remembered, "Pauline worried about the WPA program turning Key West into a tourist town on account of what it would do to the cost of keeping servants. Tourists would be competing for servants and raising wages."[81] At their home in Key West, the Hemingways had at least five servants. The author also expressed his own critical opinions about tourism through his literary characters. "What they're trying to do is starve you Conchs [Key West locals] out of here so they can burn down the shacks and put up apartments and make this a tourist town," the narrator tells Harry Morgan while they drink at the bar. "That's what I hear. I hear they're buying up lots, and then after the poor people are starved out and gone somewhere else to starve some more they're going to come in and make it into a beauty spot for tourists."[82] But despite their criticisms, the Hemingways seemed to enjoy hosting visitors in Key West and Havana. Hemingway regularly invited friends and authors such as John Dos Passos. "Come on down and steal coconuts," he wrote to Dos Passos, who was in Mexico at the time. He joked about the two of them seceding from the Union and starting the Conch Republic in Key West. "We will be a free port," he wrote, and "set up gigantic liquor warehouses and be the most PROSPEROUS ISLAND IN THE WORLD. The PARIS OF THE SOUTH WEST."[83] When one tourist and fellow author arrived on Key West with her family for the Christmas holidays in 1936, Hemingway even fell in love. He began a tumultuous relationship with the writer Martha Gellhorn, eventually leaving his first wife Pauline. The boundaries separating tourist and writer were often fictitious.

While authors like Hemingway articulated what it meant to be a white American abroad, they did not necessarily share much with readers about the nuanced practices of local communities in the Caribbean. The reading and traveling public, however, was also curious to learn about the beliefs and cultures of communities they hoped to visit. Artists, writers, and increasingly tourists were fascinated with what they perceived to be "primitive" culture. In the early twentieth century, "negro" music, dance, art, and religion became fashionable in intellectual and artistic circles in the United States and Europe. As the Caribbean's tourism industry expanded, so did public interest in cultural practices and musical genres emerging from the region, such as jazz, calypso and samba.[84] All things "primitive" were in vogue.

Playing the Game as "Insiders"

The writings of Afro-Caribbean and African American authors also grew in popularity with the emerging tourism industry. Reading about African diasporic culture became particularly popular among white readers because it was "imagined as a form of close contact with 'the other' through the production of an illusion of hearing spoken creole or hints of the oral 'folk' culture."[85] Black writers and folkloric authors of diverse backgrounds found an eager readership. By harnessing white interest in the other, writers such as Zora Neale Hurston and Langston Hughes gained access to resources for their literary work and their travels.

There was a long tradition of privileged Europeans and Euro-Americans running away from the conditioned responsibilities of their home societies—often industrializing, hierarchal, and militarized—to look for a supposedly more pure or free way of life. It was a hope, a dream. People of African descent also shared these motivations for escaping the burdens of modern society, although often for different reasons than white writers. As the scholar of the African diaspora Paul Gilroy has argued, "whether their experience of exile is enforced or chosen, temporary or permanent, [black] intellectuals and activists, writers, speakers, poets, and artists repeatedly articulate a desire to escape the restrictive bonds of ethnicity, national identification, and sometimes even 'race' itself."[86] Black writers and artists wanted to get away. Zora Neale Hurston, for example, explained why she wanted to go abroad: "I do not wish to deny myself the expansion of seeking into individual capabilities and depths by living in a space whose boundaries are race and nation."[87]

It was white society, though—the very system traveling writers of color sought to get away from—that ironically, in its interests with the "exotic," often provided a material means for writers of color to travel abroad. "Two weeks before I graduated from Barnard," Hurston explained, "Dr. [Franz] Boas sent for me and told me that he had arranged a fellowship for me. I was to go south and collect Negro folk-lore." A few years later, Hurston would travel farther south for ethnographic fieldwork and document "folk" music and religious practices in the Caribbean. The trip also gave Hurston the chance to escape a painful romance. In the midst of failing love, Hurston received a Guggenheim fellowship to study voodoo and obeah culture and religion in Haiti and Jamaica. "This was my chance to release him," she recalled, "and fight myself free from my obsession, so I sailed off to Jamaica."[88] The book she produced from those travels, *Tell My Horse* (1938), offered a firsthand account, a travelogue, of the ceremonies and customs of African-descended people in the Caribbean. At times Hurston was rather over-the-top in her anthropological descriptions: "What with the music and the barbaric rituals, I became interested and took up around the place." And at other times, she was highly sympathetic to her research subjects: "They are drenched in kindliness and beaming out with charm."[89] Hurston's book, according to the literary scholar Ifeoma Kiddoe Nwankwo, "is a text written simultaneously from the perspective of an initiated insider and an observing anthropologist as well as from the perspective of a national outsider and a racial insider."[90] Although the book initially received mixed reviews in the *New York Times*, the *Saturday Review*, and the *New Yorker*, it nevertheless provided a sort of guide for travelers and tourists to consult. Occasionally Hurston even worked as an informal tour guide. During her travels she often set up musical performances for elite visitors from the US government and major US corporations such as Pan American Airways who wanted to hear African diasporic music.[91]

Hurston took on the role as mediator between curious white readers and tourists and the black communities she visited and observed. She embraced an identity as both an anthropologist (a cultural outsider) and as a black woman (an insider), gaining information inaccessible to white readers. Throughout her career, Hurston traveled as a research ethnographer and creative writer and interpreter of black culture, learning and then educating other researchers and also the public back in the United States.[92] Alan Lomax, for example, the well-known collector of folk music for the Library of Congress, first visited the Caribbean on the advice of Hurston and depended on her contacts. In 1936 she invited Lomax to do research with her in Jamaica and Haiti. "Boy," she enthusiastically wrote to him, "there are things here to see and hear! Already since yesterday when your letter came I have made an opening for you here."[93] The two collectors eventually agreed to do a trip together through Florida and coastal Georgia. But soon afterward, Lomax, at the insistence of Hurston and using her list of contacts, made a trip farther south. Lomax recalled that Hurston was an invaluable guide.

Hurston spent several years in the circum-Caribbean traveling, collecting, and writing. Back in New York and Florida, she also turned her research into popular performances. "I introduced," she explained, "West Indian songs and dances and they have come to take an important place in America." They "aroused a tremendous interest in primitive Negro dancing."[94] In the 1920s and 1930s, Hurston and other traveling writers of color associated with the Harlem Renaissance such as Claude McKay, Eric Walrond, and Langston Hughes influenced US understandings of "local" Caribbean culture.

If there was any doubt about the influence of writers of color on the Caribbean's tourism industry, the critiques of prominent African American leaders such as W. E. B. Du Bois seem to affirm the contested significance of their reception. Du Bois claimed that McKay's work appealed to the "prurient demand" of white readers.[95] A reviewer for the African American newspaper *Pittsburgh Courier* likewise claimed that Walrond's writings pedaled "the bizarre, the exotic, the sexy, the cabaret side of Negro life for white readers."[96] Du Bois and his peers held up a rather elite standard of African American and Afro-Caribbean respectability. Nevertheless, their critiques highlight the imaginative ways white and black readers interpreted black literary work. Traveling writers of color offered a supposedly insider and sometimes troubling look at the "exotic."

The financial and literary rewards for writers of color, however, did not match the touristic influence and financial success of white-male traveling writers. Hurston, for instance, never earned more $900 during her life for any of her books. She died penniless after spending the end of her life working as a maid for white families in South Florida. Hemingway, on the other hand, earned $500 to $1,000 for each of his thousand-word travel "letters" to *Esquire*. Tourists, magazine editors, and advertisers more readily supported the stories of traveling writers who affirmed their own social, racial, and gendered privileges.[97]

The early Caribbean tourism industry appeared to be a white man's fantasy, and it paid authors who embodied that ideal. The role of writers introducing the public to foreign lands and cultures has had a long tradition in the history of Western expansion and colonialism. In the nineteenth century, before the closing of the western frontier, writers brought home tales of indigenous communities and wild rivers and mountains. With those territories conquered, writers ventured farther afield. Mark Twain, the classic storyteller of the Mississippi River, was first brought to public attention as a writer and lecturer of the Sandwich Islands—that is, Hawaii. According to the American studies scholar Amy Kaplan, "Twain's career, writing, and reception as a national author were shaped by a third realm beyond national boundaries: the routes of transnational travel, enabling and enabled by the changing borders of imperial expansion."[98] Writers traveling in the twentieth century clearly did not invent a new literary tradition by focusing on foreign travel experiences. What they brought to readers, though, was an updated set of reasons for going abroad. In the past, foreign travel was seen to be a risky endeavor for those in search of God, glory, or gold—that is, to save souls, be a hero, get rich, and explore unknown lands. The Lost Generation of traveling writers coming of age between world wars forsook those traditional motivations.

In the twentieth century, pleasure in itself emerged as a guiding force for tropical travel. Several generations of traveling writers and tourists in the United States have since followed this reason to move. After the Lost Generation, members of the Beat Generation of the 1950s and 1960s, after wandering around the United States, also went abroad in search of pleasure and, in their words, spiritual growth. Jack Kerouac and his friends on the road crossed into Mexico looking for debauched leisure and self-discovery. Kerouac claimed that his time in Mexico "was one of the great mystic rippling moments of my life."[99] His writings convinced many other young people that foreign travel promised them the same freedom for revelry and revelation. "It's a great feeling entering the Pure Land," he told readers. "You can find it, this feeling, this fellaheen feeling about life, that timeless gayety of people not involved in great cultural and civilization issues—you can find it almost anywhere else, in Morocco, in Latin America entire, in Dakar, in Kurd land."[100] The Lost Generation had provided an inspirational spark for the Beats and their readers. Millions of tourists would also be inspired by their stories of wanderlust and stereotyped fantasy. Packaged versions of epicurean pursuit have become a standard expectation of the Caribbean and tropical vacation experience for a range of tourists—from backpackers in search of the authentic, to spring breakers looking for trouble, to bourgeois tourists in need of temporary respite, to retirees acting out pent-up fantasies.

By the middle of the twentieth century, however, the convergence of imperial routes and hegemonic tourist identity was spiraling out of control.

The consolidation of US empire in the Caribbean and the willingness of regional elites to build their national economies around foreign desires opened the door to hundreds of thousands of tourists seeking to act out dreams of adventure—whether in tropical nature as explorers or in dark alleys and streets as adventurous pleasure junkies. But the hotels and bars and nightclubs where travelers and tourists thought they had escaped to soon would turn into scenes of protest, violent street battles, and revolution against the "gringos." The privileged culture of tourism that took shape in the first half of the twentieth century became a central target in the fight against imperialism and racism in the 1960s, and beyond.

Chapter 6

Burning Privilege

Luxury in the Age of Decolonization

> One day, to everyone's astonishment, someone drops a match in the powder keg and everything blows up. Before the dust has settled or the blood congealed, editorials, speeches, and civil-rights commissions are loud in the land, demanding to know what happened.
>
> —James Baldwin, "The Northern Protestant"

On January 11, 1964, two young Panamanians launched an attack against the Hotel Tivoli, a US-owned hotel overlooking the Panama Canal. That evening Raúl Chan and Manuel Allonca snuck into the Patilla Airport in Panama City and stole a small commercial airplane (with no passengers aboard). Chan and Allonca, their lawyer explained later, "intended to fly the aircraft, under the cover of darkness, and drop homemade bombs onto the hotel."[1] In the air, however, their plan went awry. Three minutes into the flight the plane mysteriously plummeted into the Bay of Panama. The young men survived the watery crash—"attracting a great deal of spectators"—but were quickly arrested by the Panamanian National Guard. From the perspective of Panamanian state officials and their US allies, the plane crash was a failed terrorist attempt. Protesters gathered in the streets, though, heralded the two men as "patriots."[2]

If one were to open a more traditional book on the history of US–Latin American relations, you would find little evidence that a hotel such as this was of life-and-death importance. Historians occasionally might reference a famous speech given on a hotel veranda, chronicle the visit of a famous dignitary or celebrity who stayed there, or perhaps discuss a local disturbance outside, on the nearby streets, seemingly unrelated to the bread-and-butter activities inside the hotel. "Aside from the work of antiquarians," as the historian Daniel Levinson Wilk summarized, there has been "no sustained interest in the topic [of hotels]."[3] In the history of US foreign relations, hotels and their guests most often appear as superfluous backdrop to grander historical events. "Skeptics," as the historian Dennis Merrill explained, "have long discounted the intellectual and cultural depth of the tourist experience, a critique that implicitly dismisses the significance of tourists to international relations." However, this perspective of international relations, following Merrill and fellow historians such as Christopher Endy, is slowly changing.[4]

As more scholars chronicle the history of tourism, the role of hotels is also being revisited. Much more, it turns out, has happened around luxurious spaces than frivolous leisure and comfort. For historians rooted in one particular discipline or geographic region, examining this serious history requires both interdisciplinary and transboundary thinking. Historians, in a sense, must also travel afield. There are, for instance, innovative studies by scholars of international relations such as Lisa Smirl and Kenneth Morrison, who respectively analyzed a Holiday Inn's role as a geopolitical hub during the Bosnian War of the early 1990s. Located on Sarajevo's "sniper alley," the hotel was ground zero for that terrible war and the journalists who covered it and thus loaded with cultural and political significance.[5] Urban studies scholars such as Sarah Fregonese and Adam Ramadan have also outlined new research possibilities moving beyond "hotels as neutral sites," instead arguing that "hotel spaces . . . are connected to broader architectures of security and insecurity, war- and peace-making."[6] Although these multidisciplinary scholars are more the exception than the norm, they remind us that there are many historical entanglements connected to hotels in need of further investigation. On hotel grounds and just outside their gates, the boundaries of transnational social privilege have been solidified and sometimes challenged.

Events leading up to the attack on the Hotel Tivoli in 1964, as this chapter shows, reveal a great deal about the contentious relationship between tourism, social inequality, and anticolonialism. Hotels like the Tivoli functioned as places of luxury and escape but also as spaces of resistance. Beginning in 1906, the Tivoli served privileged travelers from the United States and Europe eager to experience the tropics of Central America and the Caribbean. No trip to Panama, tour guides claimed, was complete without staying at or visiting the hotel. Visitors could eat fresh lobster or native corbina at the hotel's upscale restaurant or sip drinks at its Roosevelt Bar, appropriately named and located in the Empire Lounge.[7] "The hotel's register," the *New York Times* reported in the 1950s, "read like an index to a World Atlas or a Who's Who of the last half-century." Guests included kings, presidents, scientists, artists, and soldiers—not to mention thousands of middle- and upper-class tourists.[8] In the first half of the twentieth century, few hotels in

Latin America and the Caribbean were as widely known. The Tivoli, as the *Saturday Evening Post* put it, had "a great deal of perverse charm."[9]

January 1964, however, would mark the end of the hotel's celebrated era. Chan and Allonca, in their quixotic air raid, were not alone in their effort to destroy the Tivoli. Two days earlier, thousands of protesters had actually begun to gather outside the hotel. In the preceding years, in fact decades, Panamanian politicians had also tried to shut down the hotel. This chapter describes this multipronged opposition. It also positions that history within a wider international context linking tourism and decolonization. In their own struggles against foreign rule in Egypt and Cuba, for example, similar types of attacks occurred.[10] The how and why of these hotel attacks in the mid-twentieth century have much to tell not only about the past but also about contemporary issues, where protesters and sometimes terrorists continue to target sites of leisure. There was nothing apolitical, one realizes, about the historic spaces of tourist consumption, and there was nothing random about the resistance that mobilized around them. Tourism's history is wrapped up in some of the most significant political battles of the modern era.

In the 1950s and 1960s, in the words of the historian Robin Kelley, "revolt was in the air."[11] Famous tourist hotels were swept into the maelstrom. This is an aspect of twentieth-century history not often recognized by historians but one crucial to understanding the cross-cultural clash at the heart of decolonization. Anticolonialism in the mid-twentieth century, to express it mildly, was more personal than diplomatic or geopolitical disagreement. Witnessing a group of foreign visitors on one's street in search of pleasure could be just as revolutionarily mobilizing as suffering from an unjust trade deal. The tourism industry brought people from different classes, races, and nationalities into intimate contact. In many ways, it structured quotidian and often exploitative encounters between residents of the developing world and residents from the metropole, whether from the United States or Europe. Luxury hotels and their surrounding bars, restaurants, and streets were crucial zones of interaction. They operated as nodes of connection—as, more precisely, "contact zones."[12] Organized around racial and national inequalities, however, they were also vulnerable to becoming "conflict zones." By the mid-twentieth century, the expansion of US power and the growth of tourism in Latin America and the Caribbean had produced a powerful wave of anti-Americanism. "The North American presence," as the gonzo journalist Hunter S. Thompson reported from Colombia in 1963, "is one of the most emotional political questions on the continent."[13] This "presence," of course, included soldiers and government officials, but it also included civilian tourists—drinking, hitting golf balls, fishing, swimming in fancy pools, visiting cabarets, and residing in luxury accommodations, all in the midst of the poverty and uncertainty of Latin American and Caribbean underdevelopment.

Modern power congealed in the means, or lack thereof, to travel and the accommodations offered or denied. The anthropologist Claude Lévi-Strauss observed this dynamic during his own travels. He viewed mobility and its infrastructure as an early sign of the troubles of twentieth-century modernity. Arriving in Goiania, Brazil, in the 1930s, Levi-Strauss visited the main hotel, the biggest building in town. It looked, he wrote, like "a bastion of civilization." But it was a "clumsy and unlovely" structure, in his view, because it was "a place of transit not of residence."[14] To be able to travel as a tourist and stay in the luxurious hotels of the world signified one's social, indeed international, status—one's wealth, comfort, and freedom. Since at least the nineteenth century, as the sociologist John Urry has documented, hotels "were very much public places open to all with money, for wealthy men and women, to see and be seen in."[15] Who could, and likewise who could not, enter these spaces represented the order of society. Tourist hotels, in this way, helped define desirable "insiders" and undesirable "outsiders," those who have and have not.

Hotels were crucial nodes in networks of mobility. They became microcosms of larger societal trends. Throughout the colonial and decolonizing world, as the historian Maurizio Peleggi put it, hotels created spaces "for

FIGURE 15. The Hotel Tivoli, built during the canal construction era, became a target for Panamanian protests in the 1960s. Doug Allen Postcard Collection.

the localization of modernity in the colonial milieu."[16] Inside, guests wined and dined enjoying modern comforts, while sharply uniformed and dark-skinned locals catered to their travel desires. From the outside looking in, this exclusive system was a sign of what was wrong with the colonial world. As bastions of privilege, yet dependent on racialized and exploited labor, hotels evolved into battlegrounds between the colonial past and an undecided future. They were, in the words of the scholar James Clifford, "crucial sites for an unfinished modernity.'"[17] That was, it seems, what the Hotel Tivoli meant in the expanding era of decolonization—a site not only for luxury but also protest and struggle.

Tivoli in the Midst of Revolt

On January 9, protesters first began to throw rocks at the Hotel Tivoli. Tensions quickly escalated. Witnesses staying at the hotel reported that "rioters were attempting to put a torch to the building."[18] Guests could also see overturned cars "burning fiercely" on Fourth of July Avenue, the main thoroughfare passing by the hotel and the de facto border separating the Republic of Panama from the US-controlled Canal Zone. The Tivoli and its guests were in the middle of a populist uprising against the US presence on the isthmus. On the south side of the street, there was Panama City and a growing crowd of protesters; on the north side was the Hotel Tivoli and the Canal Zone. Fourth of July Avenue, a street named in honor of US Independence, had ironically become a battleground between Panamanian independence fighters and Canal Zone police and then US armed forces.[19]

In front of the hotel, Canal Zone police officers attempted to push back protesters with tear gas and gunfire. The Panamanian press claimed police fired directly into the crowd, killing a number of civilians. US authorities, however, disputed the charge, arguing that the police only fired warning shots above the heads of protesters. "I have never seen men act with more restraint and composure," Canal Zone district judge Guthrie Crowe told the press.[20] Despite these competing narratives, it was clear that police and later US military efforts to control the protests actually had the opposite effect. "The criminal actions" of US officials, Panamanian nationalists argued, "only made the situation more desperate."[21] The crowd outside the hotel continued to grow. Between seven and eight o'clock on the evening of January 9, it more than doubled.

David S. Parker, the acting governor of the Canal Zone, arrived on the scene to investigate. Immediately he ran into trouble. "My car was stoned twice in the vicinity of the Tivoli," he reported, "and by that time a crowd estimated between 5 and 6 thousand was gathering along 4th of July Avenue." Canal Zone police, he assessed, would not be able to hold back the "mob," and protesters would overrun the Tivoli within minutes. "Accordingly," Parker explained, "I reported in person to General [Andrew P.] O'Meara that as Acting Governor I was unable to maintain law and order . . . and I therefore requested General O'Meara to assume command of the Canal Zone and to seal off the Canal Zone border." As commander in chief of US Southern Command, General O'Meara declared martial law and ordered army units with tanks and armored cars to move into the area.[22] Soldiers took over the defense of the hotel. "Hundreds of sandbags," according to eyewitnesses, were "carried to the third floor to fortify the [hotel's] wooden structure."[23]

The Tivoli's management and staff attempted, initially, to ignore the protest and go about business as usual. Full-course meals were served to guests on both Thursday and Friday, January 9 and 10. A few precautions, though, were taken. "All the Louvre doors were closed and the lights were [made] very dim in the Pergola Bar, the only protected area in the hotel's public rooms." From Panama's side of Fourth of July Avenue, however, snipers fired at the hotel's windows and open corridors. Zone officials reported that "most of the sniper action was directed against the south end of the building, but there was no serious concentration at dinner time." Yet after the evening meal, the shooting intensified. "Civilians as well as Army personnel ran rapidly past openings and constantly ducked from the zing of sniper bullets." One man was shot in the lobby; dozens more were injured. The hotel's manager at that point announced the evacuation of the hotel. "The guests were," reportedly, "led through the barbershop and out the back door."[24]

Over the course of three days, rioters shot at and attempted to burn and aerial-bomb the hotel. More than two thousand bullet holes were later found in the Tivoli's structure.[25] The hotel attracted the first protesters and the largest number, but it was not the only target. "Rioters," according to State Department officials, were "attacking symbols of America."[26] In Panama City, the offices of the US Information Agency (USIA) and the US embassy, along with the offices of such US corporations as Goodyear, Firestone, Pan American World Airlines, and Braniff International Airlines, were attacked next. Demonstrators also stoned the Chase Manhattan Bank and the National City Bank. Devastating fires caused by Molotov cocktails occurred at the USIA and Pan Am offices. Rioters also attempted to storm the US embassy. "They smashed all our windows," officials reported, "and had us surrounded at times."[27] Embassy staff destroyed important documents and then evacuated the building. The Hotel Tivoli, in context, was part of a milieu of anticolonialism on the isthmus—part of a constellation of symbols of oppression and injustice.

In other parts of Panama City, rioters attacked the US-owned Tropical Radio office and the All America Cables office. Cars suspected of carrying US citizens were also stoned and set on fire. "My cars, they are lying all over town, burned and wrecked," a Hertz rental agent told journalists. Mobs chased anyone who "looked American" off the streets. The journalist Hank Suydam, reporting on the protests/riots for *Life* magazine, claimed "it was necessary to improvise official stickers for our cars and outrageously fraudulent press credentials for ourselves—anything that would identify us as correspondents of any nationality other than American."[28] In that moment, to be a suspected official, civilian resident, or visitor from the United States had become a dangerous identity.

Protests occurred simultaneously at the Caribbean terminal of the Panama Canal. In Colón, property damage was worse than in Panama City. Sears, the Chase Manhattan Bank, and the YMCA were looted. US government supply stores, known as commissaries, burned to the ground. The most sustained attack in Colón concentrated on the Sojourners Lodge of the Masonic Order, an exclusive club for white American men. US Army troops defended the building. A journalist reported from the scene, "Occasionally we could hear the soft sounds of sniper fire, then the louder report of a gas grenade being launched in return from an M-1."[29] Rioting also broke out in the Panamanian province of Chiriquí, near the Costa Rican border. A spokesman for the Chiriquí Land Company, a subsidiary of the United Fruit Company, described protesters surrounding the homes of US employees, "threatening violence, shouting anti-American slogans, attempting to burn cars, and smearing cars and buildings with paint."[30] Violence continued for several days across the country. The popular phrase "burn, baby, burn," which became an anthem in major US cities the following summer, seemed to have a cousin to the south.[31] White American privilege at home and abroad was under siege.

Like many social movements around the world in the 1960s, the match that sparked the powder keg came from students. On the afternoon of January 9 at around four thirty, two hundred students from the National Institute, Panama's most prestigious public school, had marched into the Canal Zone carrying the Panamanian national flag. Along the way, they sang the republic's national anthem and intermittently shouted "Yankee, go home!" Some students also carried banners that read, "Panama is sovereign in the Canal Zone." The protesters were attempting to enforce a diplomatic agreement signed in 1963 by President John F. Kennedy and Panama's president, Roberto Chiari. The agreement stated that "the Panamanian flag would be flown alongside the U.S. flag on civilian land areas in the Canal Zone wherever the latter flag was flown by civilian authorities."[32] Beginning on January 7, however, a group of students and their parents in the Zone decided to ignore the directive and fly the US flag at Balboa High School, without the presence of the Panamanian flag. Balboa High School was attended largely by white Zonians who were US citizens and whose parents worked in the US Canal Zone. For three days, Zonian students stood vigil, singing patriotic songs and guarding the US flag from removal. "We students," one Balboa alumna remembered, "had simply stood up for what was right and had been recognized. I don't think that anyone realized then that we had actually given the enemies of the United States just the reason they were looking for to cause trouble."[33] The flag controversy became front-page news in the Republic of Panama, provoking a rising sense that action needed to be taken.

The protests, which culminated at the hotel and became known as the "flag riots," resulted in the deaths of three US soldiers and twenty-three Panamanian protesters, along with injuries to more than five hundred people.[34] The violence also turned into an economic crisis. Panama had been a hub of US political and economic interests in Latin America and the Caribbean since 1904. That stability, however, was shaken with the riots. Business and foreign investment slowed to a halt. "The most directly affected area of the economy," according to observers, was "the tourist trade."[35] Commercial flights from the United States to Panama were suspended. Nine cruise ships carrying an estimated five thousand tourists canceled their January visits.[36] Hotels were left empty. Taxi drivers could find few, if any, foreign customers. "The once-lush tourist business," the *Miami Herald* reported, "is dead for the present. This is a blow to the businessmen and the government treasury alike."[37] Tourism and the transit-service economy, which accounted for nearly one-third of Panama's gross national product, disappeared almost overnight. For months after the riots, Panama City and Colón resembled burnt-out urban war zones. One local journalist reported in June 1964, nearly six months after the riots, that Panama's two main cities still looked like "something between a jungle and a cesspool, with all the garbage."[38] Buildings were left in ruin, and international visitors stopped coming. The tourist economy's entanglement with this violence, however, was not a mere side effect of anarchy in the streets. Instead, it was, along with other "symbols of America," at the center of local anger. The situation at the Tivoli was far from an isolated incident of a hotel getting caught up in a revolutionary moment. Tension had been building for decades.

From the Hotel Veranda, the History of US-Panamanian Relations

The arc of the Hotel Tivoli's history paralleled the rise and demise of US influence in Panama and more broadly the circum-Caribbean. The Isthmian Canal Commission, which oversaw the canal construction project (1904–14), had begun construction of the hotel in 1905 to serve the influx of tourists expected to visit the new "path between the seas."[39] The Tivoli's first official guest was President Theodore Roosevelt in 1906. After the president's much-publicized tour, the hotel grew in popularity.[40]

The combination of imperial boosterism, along with advancements in tropical medicine, made the tourist trade a lucrative industry on the isthmus and around the Caribbean. The US government's health campaign against malaria and yellow fever during the canal project encouraged tourists to reimagine the tropics—from that of a diseased and dangerous landscape (a tropical frontier) to that of a conquered land ideal for a safe and comfortable vacation. As canal construction came to a close, the number of international tourists visiting Panama increased to roughly twenty thousand people annually—a substantial number, considering Panama City was home to only an estimated twenty-five thousand residents during those same years.[41]

By the 1920s the economic importance of international tourism in Panama was comparable to Cuba's, and even South Florida's, tourism industry. In 1926 the *Panama Times*, an English-language newspaper, claimed:

> The second greatest resource of Panama [City] and Colon is the ever-present tourists, some 70,000 of whom pass through our narrow streets and peer longingly into our unique shop doorways every year. . . . Many a dollar is exchanged here annually for Panama hats, rum, and coach fares, and every fakir, coach driver, and rum vender knows that as soon as one shipload of tourists is gone another will arrive. They always have and they always will.[42]

The Hotel Tivoli was the crown jewel of this burgeoning tourist economy. As travel writer Harry Foster, returning to the isthmus in the mid-1920s, observed, "Every tourist stops at the Tivoli at least for dinner, which consists usually of about twelve courses of chinaware and cutlery, wiped, flourished, and served with much ceremony by a score of negro waiters."[43] The hotel, with its white guests and black staff, had exported a racialized-class system of privilege similar to Jim Crow in the US South. This, though, seemed unproblematic to most guests.[44]

From the hotel's big veranda on Ancon Hill, visitors could look across Fourth of July Avenue and down at Panama City below. It became a sort of "right of passage" for tourists to stay and dine at the Tivoli and in the evening cross the border into Panama to pursue evening activities. The red-light district of bars and brothels was located just a few blocks from the hotel and the Canal Zone border.[45] "The tourist in Panama," as Foster noted, "will be troubled mainly by an upset sense of direction. He's never quite sure whether he's in the Canal Zone or in Panama, and can't decide whether he ought to disapprove or have a good time himself."[46] Guests could thus walk, or take a short taxi ride, from the Canal Zone to Panama City. As early as 1913, Willis Abbot reported that "the tourist, who abides in the intensely modern and purely United States hotel, the Tivoli, has but to give a dime to a Panama Hackman to be transported into an atmosphere as foreign as though he had suddenly been wafted to Madrid."[47] The Tivoli served as the comfortable residency for tourists in search of travel fantasies. It marked a border, a frontier, between US comforts and foreign excitement. The hotel, in this way, was part of a growing network of tourist accommodations in the first half of the twentieth century linking tourists with the tropics. As the historian Dennis Merrill argued, these "expensive North Americanized hotels served as the tourist's equivalent to forward military bases, bastions of comfort and security to which empire-exploring gringos could safely retire at the end of the day."[48]

For Panamanians struggling to survive on the other side of the road, however, the hotel represented dreams of prosperity and comfort thwarted by racism and injustice. "It was the American dream to cross the street," wrote the Panamanian novelist and journalist Joaquín Beleño. "This dream remained intact despite the fact that the Zone represented the land of hate, of black and white, of insult and sin."[49] Panamanians, especially of color, looked across the street and up at the hotel with envy and, increasingly, hate. They could work as bellboys or bartenders or entertainers at the hotel but were barred from being paid guests. The Tivoli remained an exclusive white establishment. According to the Panamanian historian Patricia Pizzurno, "*Los estadounidenses* [US citizens], with their strong commitment to racism and segregation, created the perfect climate for the emergence of painful preoccupations and sorrow among Panamanians, which only exacerbated over time."[50] At the hotel and throughout the Canal Zone, racism was part of daily life. As Afro-Panamanian activists such as George Westerman lamented, "the colored people on the Isthmus of Panama find themselves hemmed in on the Canal Zone by racial bigots who operate a high-geared machinery of discrimination and segregation."[51] White Americans and people of color had separate public facilities in the Canal Zone—drinking fountains, swimming pools, neighborhoods, shops, housing, clubs, and so on. The US government called these distinctions the Gold and Silver rolls. But in practice, it was no different than Jim Crow segregation, and it remained unchanged into 1964.[52]

The small community of Panamanian elites, who had closer racial and economic ties with white Americans, also grew to resent the hotel's presence. The Tivoli was unwanted economic competition, a US-owned hotel "stealing" tourist dollars. From the early 1900s into the late 1940s, international visitors arriving by sea had to pass through the Canal Zone before venturing into Panamanian-controlled territory. The US government, which already ruled over five hundred square miles in the middle of Panama (i.e., the Canal Zone), also controlled the main ports where passenger steamships docked. The Zone, as a result, became the republic's main tourism competitor. Canal Zone commissaries and hotels, owned by the US government, lured visitors away from businesses privately owned by Panamanians, who were on the other side of the Zone border. Early elite hopes of economic collaboration with the United States, as Panamanian president Ricardo Alfaro wrote, appeared to be "a grand illusion."[53]

The tourist trade emerged as a diplomatic point of contention. In the Hull-Alfaro Treaty of 1936, popularly known as the "Beer and Meat Treaty," the Panamanian government pushed back against economic competition from the Canal Zone. As the treaty's informal title suggests, Panamanian businessmen wanted to sell basic commodities, such as beer and meat, in the Zone. Part of the negotiations also included the operation of the Hotel Tivoli and the Hotel Washington, located on the Colón side of the canal. Despite early promises that the US government would not operate for-profit businesses in the Zone, the Tivoli and the Washington continued to serve tourists and bring in profits. The treaty, however, did not resolve the underlying issue. "If the United States of America only would open a race track, a lottery and a few more bars in the Canal Zone," one Panamanian politician claimed, "they could put Panama out of business entirely!"[54] In the early 1950s Panamanian officials again negotiated over issues related to the tourism industry, forcing US authorities to change the official name of the Tivoli from the "Hotel Tivoli" to the "Tivoli Guest House." The hope was that tourists would instead stay in the republic's new luxury hotel, the Hotel Panama, built via a government partnership with the Hilton Hotel chain.[55] The shift in nomenclature and the opening of the Hilton, though, did little to appease Panamanian discontent in the streets.

US citizens who lived and worked in the Canal Zone seemed baffled by Panamanian frustrations. "I've been down here for 24 years," one Zonian woman told the press after the events of 1964, "and this is the worst thing that's ever happened. I've just got into an argument with our maid over this. . . . We've been so generous—we treat our children and the maid's family just the same. I can't see how this country can be aroused to hate when we've been so generous. After all, we've paid our rent."[56] A few US residents on the isthmus, though, understood the cause of the trouble. "Truly," Mrs. Fairchild wrote to her friend, Mrs. Wetmore, back in the United States, "were I a well educated Panamanian with a slightly dark skin, or even without one . . . I would resent Americans." Fairchild, who was now looking to sell her home in Panama, added, "Always there has been a feeling of envy and dislike for Americans here."[57]

While white Americans lived comfortably on the isthmus, the majority of Panamanians struggled to get basic services. The average income for a Panamanian was less than $500 a year in 1964, almost a tenth of the average US salary at the time. Health care and public education through high school was also inaccessible to the majority of the population. Dozens of patients were reportedly turned away daily from Panama City's main hospital because of lack of beds.[58] Yet the "gringos" lived a country club, vacation lifestyle. "The 'American set' in the Canal Zone live much like the British did in India and other colonies when they were in power," according to the union leader Joseph Curran. "They erected a sort of fenced-in compound where they lived in luxury while the natives lived in squalor outside. Even without fences to mark off the area, the effect was the same. The Americans enjoy the best of conditions—swimming pools, tennis courts, gardens; while just across the street, in the Republic, the people live in dilapidated shacks."[59] The Canal Zone represented exclusive leisure. The system, though, reflected how white Americans traveled and lived across Latin America and the Caribbean, in de facto colonies and enclaves, whether serving in the military, working for a private corporation, or on vacation.[60]

The Zonian way of life was not unique. The feelings of superiority and the material privileges associated with Canal Zone life also applied to the hundreds of thousands of visitors who annually traveled in the Caribbean and to the isthmus—as soldiers, officials, and civilian tourists. "The ugly American," which William J. Lederer and Eugene Burdick fictionalized in their best-selling novel in 1958, had a real-life equivalent for many Panamanians and Latin American nationalists. "Something happens," in the words of Lederer and Burdick, "to most Americans when they go abroad."[61] They lose their inhibitions and their manners. Soldiers, Zonians, and other US residents visiting the isthmus, from the Panamanian perspective, were not separate social groups. "They were thirty-year tourists," as one Panamanian described Zone residents. "Most people are tourists two weeks. They visit a country, they buy the hats and T-shirts, and take pictures. And then they go back to the cruise ship and it's over. But a Zonian was here for thirty years—until he got his pension. But they were still just tourists in Panama."[62] The culture of colonial privilege that Zonians enjoyed year around on the isthmus was the same culture enacted by tourists who visited the region for shorter stays. The archetypical Zonian—in the words of historian Michael Donoghue, "hunting, drinking, and whoring"—eerily resembled the white American dream of a tropical vacation.[63] For everyday Panamanians, they, the "gringos," all looked the same; they were all tourists.

US political leaders seemed unwilling to recognize the extent of the US role in creating Panamanian discontent. There had to be someone else to blame. The trouble was the communists and especially Fidel Castro. The Panamanians could not really hate us, the logic went. After all, the United States had built the canal, paved streets, conquered malaria and yellow fever, and brought new economic opportunities to the isthmus. Former CIA director Allen Dulles (1953–61) claimed that "Castro-itis" was spreading across the region.[64] According to one US representative from West Virginia, the riots in Panama were actually "a carefully calculated move of communism against Americanism."[65] The United States had to get tough and hold on. The communists, Undersecretary of State George W. Ball told the press, "were taking advantage of the situation, I don't have the slightest doubt."[66] The argument turned into a heated and enduring political debate, from the mid-1960s into the Ronald Reagan era of the 1980s.

A handful of US leaders tried to heed the warning and awaken the public, but few listened. "There is an inevitable divergence," Sen. William J. Fulbright lectured in March 1964, "between the world as it is and the world as men perceive it. . . . When our perceptions fail to keep pace with events, when we refuse to believe something because it displeases or frightens us, or because it is simply startlingly unfamiliar, then the gap between fact and perception becomes a chasm, and action becomes irrelevant and irrational." The people of the United States, Fulbright warned, were "clinging to old myths in the face of new realities."[67] US culture abroad clung to many myths, but one of the greatest and most pervasive was that the Caribbean region could continue to serve, in the same way, as a playground for white American vacation fantasies in the era of decolonization.

An International Wave

Panama in the 1960s was part of a larger wave of revolution sweeping across the developing world. At the beginning of the twentieth century, the United States and European powers governed people and territory in Asia, Africa, the Middle East, and the Americas. It was, in essence, white rule over the rest of the world. Following World War II, however, the contradictions of this colonial and racist system became increasingly obvious. Third World nationalists and antiracist activists began to interpret Western progress as analogous to the culture that had given rise to Fascism and Nazism. "I knew," W. E. B. Du Bois wrote, "that Hitler and Mussolini were fighting communism, and using race prejudice to make some white people rich and all colored people poor. But it was not until later that I realized that the colonialism of Great Britain and France had exactly the same object and methods as the fascists."[68] The fight for freedom did not end with the fall of Hitler and the Nazis. After 1945 revolt spread. The United States and its possessions in Latin America and the Caribbean were not exempt from this expanding revolutionary commitment to liberty and justice. "The winds of change that have been sweeping through Non-Self-Governing Territories in other parts of the world," George Westerman explained, "are reaching this Continent."[69] Panamanians joined in the anticolonial movement. The isthmus, according to journalists writing for *The Nation* magazine in 1960, contained "all the conditions for a nationalist revolution which will rival the recent upheavals in Cuba and Egypt."[70]

International tourism and its hotels found themselves in the middle of this transnational struggle. An early and foreboding event, for example, occurred in Egypt in January 1952. Like Panama and its canal for the United States, Egypt and the Suez Canal were of geopolitical and commercial value to the British Empire.[71] Twelve years before the Panamanian riots, Egyptians took to the streets in protests-turned-riots against British colonial rule. One of the main targets for these protesters was the famous Shepheard's Hotel, a favorite destination for metropolitan visitors since the mid-nineteenth century. By the end of the riots, which collectively became known as the "Cairo fire," the Shepheard was gutted and totally destroyed. Although the hotel was rebuilt five years later outside of downtown Cairo, its colonial prestige nevertheless had been taken away. Accompanying the triumph of the Egyptian revolution and the nationalization of the Suez Canal, the destruction of the historic Shepheard's Hotel represented the end of British decadence in Egypt.[72]

Six years later, across the Atlantic Ocean, another revolution was triumphing and reshaping geopolitics. Again the tourism industry was at the forefront of events. In Cuba tourism had become one of the most lucrative industries and also one of the most controversial. In 1958, the year before the Cuban revolution, over two hundred thousand tourists visited the island, the majority from the United States.[73] Cuba's elite politicians and businessmen, led by dictator Fulgencio Batista, had aligned with the Mafia and US corporations to convert Havana into a tourist's paradise of hotels, casinos, and cabarets. The development of the city's seedy and corrupt tourist economy, in turn, fueled revolutionary sentiments against oligarchic rule. As Merrill has shown, "modern tourism so misrepresented Cuban culture and diluted local identity that it helped destabilize the country's social order and contributed to the rise of Fidel Castro's communist regime."[74] Revolutionaries on the island had long criticized touristic vice at home and throughout the Caribbean. As early as 1948, according to one of his revolutionary compatriots, young Fidel Castro visited Panama and witnessed a "depressing and unforgettable sight": an "endless succession of brothels, nightclubs, and other lurid amusements." The same type of activities were happening in his native Cuba, which Castro concluded was "the only reason that Cuba was so well-liked and well-known beyond its frontiers."[75] Tellingly, when the revolutionary *barbudos* (bearded ones) entered Havana on January 8, 1959, they took over the Havana Hilton Hotel. Castro made the hotel his headquarters, and for the first three months of the new regime he lived in Continental Suite, room 2324. The imperial era of tourism, Castro argued, would end with the triumph of the revolution. Hotel casinos were shut down, and the flow of US tourists to the island came to an end (because of both Castro's anti-imperialist policies and the US embargo).[76]

Ninety miles farther south, on the island of Jamaica, the future of the tourism industry was also in serious doubt in the 1960s. For nationalists in Jamaica, tourism represented a pillar of white colonial rule. The nation was divided about the industry's future. In 1963 the popular broadcast journalist Peter Abrahams discussed "how ambivalent we all are about the whole business of tourism." One listener, he reported, "wanted to know why we should be friendly towards these North Americans. Another listener felt that, all the money notwithstanding, tourism is a corrupting thing and the sooner we packed it up, the better, and yet another listener was of the opinion that until we see tourism as a straightforward business, we would get nowhere, and, he went on to say, in business the customer is always right." The problem, Abrahams explained, was that the majority of tourists to the island were racially white, "and it is a plain fact that because of America's racial picture there are many Jamaicans who do not want to be friendly to [white] Americans."[77] Following independence in August 1962, tourism operators such Abe Issa, owner of Hedonism Resort, claimed that Jamaicans were engaging in "anti-social behaviour" toward tourists and therefore hurting the business. Issa worried about the increase in crime, disrespect, and hustling in Jamaica's tourist zones. Colonial reverence had disappeared. Although Jamaicans never engaged in direct and organized attacks on the tourism industry like protesters and revolutionaries did in Cuba and Panama, Jamaicans singled out the island's industry nonetheless as a means for showing one's anger and frustration with racism, social privilege, and inequality. Jamaica's tourism industry continued to grow in the postcolonial era, but many observers believed that the rise of all-inclusive resorts and the abandonment of the tourism industry in urban areas such as Kingston was in direct response to changes in Jamaican attitudes.[78]

Mobilizing against the social inequities of tourism, however, extended beyond the Third World. The tourism industry was also entangled with the civil rights movement in the United States. Tourism inequalities at the time were as much about race as they were about national and class privileges. African American activists, in their effort to challenge the institutions of white privilege, also focused their collective energy on the travel and tourism industry.[79] In June 1964, for example, Dr. Martin Luther King Jr. and thousands of protesters gathered in the tourist town of St. Augustine, Florida. Outside the "big posh lily-white motels" of the oldest town in the United States, protesters marched and sang freedom songs. As an act of civil disobedience, Dr. King and his chief aide Ralph D. Abernathy were arrested in front of the Monson Motor Lodge. King and Abernathy had attempted to dine at the hotel and were charged with violating Florida's unwanted guest law. The general manager, who was also the president of the Florida Hotel and Motel Association, told King and his supporters, "You realize it would be detrimental to my business to serve you here." The manager then reportedly turned to the television cameras documenting the scene and said, "I would like to invite my many friends throughout the country to come to Monson's. We expect to remain segregated."[80] The attention that civil rights protesters brought to St. Augustine, however, kept visitors away. "The tourist trade," according to one reporter at the scene, "is already off at least 50 per cent . . . and many a motel owner is threatened by bankruptcy and foreclosure."[81]

Three weeks after his arrest in Florida, Dr. King traveled to Washington, DC, to witness the signing of the Civil Rights Act of 1964, which formally banned discrimination based on race, color, religion, sex, or national origin. Dr. King's dream, as expressed during the March on Washington the year before, was being actualized. Singling out the issue of travel, he had lectured:

> We can never be satisfied as long as our bodies, heavy with the fatigue of travel, cannot gain lodging in the motels of the highways and the hotels of the cities. We cannot be satisfied as long as the Negro's basic mobility is from a small ghetto to a larger one. We can never

be satisfied as long as our children are stripped of their selfhood and robbed of their dignity by signs stating: "For Whites Only."[82]

Civil rights leaders recognized that the injustices of mobility were as transnational as they were national. As early as 1941, the president of the NAACP, Arthur B. Spingarn, visited Panama to assess racial conditions on the isthmus. He subsequently wrote to President Franklin Roosevelt, "I was extremely shocked by the racial segregation practiced there, which appeared to me to be substantially the same as that existing in the lower south."[83] In the postwar years, *Crisis Magazine*, the official publication of the NAACP, also covered racial issues in Panama and the Caribbean. Reporting from Panama, George Westerman offered a critical assessment for the magazine in 1951 and again in 1953. His article "America-Panamanian Relations" appeared alongside the writing of Ralph Ellison, author of the widely acclaimed novel *The Invisible Man* (1952). In his article, Westerman explained:

> In analysis the Canal Zone becomes a paradise for the North Americans and the chosen few, while most Panamanians and the West Indian Negroes (the latter elements brought to the Isthmus by the United States Government by the thousands to give their blood and brawn to help build the Canal) are considered inferior in aptitude, ability and initiative to white American citizens, as well as ignorant, inefficient, and indolent in comparison to the average Caucasian worker.
>
> This condition of "Yankee superiority" almost in the center of the Western Hemisphere, has led many a Latin American diplomat to look suspiciously at Washington's advocacy of democracy and equality the world over.
>
> The past few years have brought a strong anti-U.S. movement among young Panamanians, especially those of the middle and lower classes, based on an intense and sometimes justified nationalism, which manifests itself with increasing strength in the politics of the country.[84]

Resentment toward white American cultural and racial attitudes had converted into mass demonstrations in 1947 and mass strikes again in 1958 and 1959. There was even a small armed rebellion in the Panamanian interior in the style of the Cuban revolutionaries of the Sierra Maestra (which was quickly defeated). All of these nonviolent and violent actions fed into the much more widespread protests of 1964.[85]

Panamanian nationalists saw their struggle allied not only with black activists in the United States but also with protesters and revolutionaries throughout the colonial world. Unfolding anticolonial and antiracist movements in

Africa, Asia, and the Middle East awoke Panamanians to the global stretch of imperialism. The Egyptian revolution, for example, and its battle for the Suez Canal was heavily reported in the Panamanian press, inspiring similar calls for action on the isthmus. Journalists such as Westerman chronicled this rising tide of anticolonial sentiment. Westerman described to Panamanian readers in one notable article that there were only four independent African nations in 1945, but that by 1962 there were thirty-two. He concluded:

> These events, like so many others which the world has been witnessing of recent times, is a reflection of the profound changes that character-ize our era; the era of disintegration of the old colonial system, and the formation of new national personalities; the era of the right of peoples to the service of constructive achievements in which former colonies and dependent territories are progressing towards freedom and inde-pendence at a tempo no one would have thought possible some ten years ago.[86]

In the era of global revolt, it was clear that racialized colonial privileges were being challenged. And whether colonial authorities or the metropolitan pub-lic recognized it or not, the networks and luxuries of the tourism industry were understood as part of this unjust system and thus also targets of the rebellion.

From Anticolonial Activism to International Development

In the aftermath of anticolonialism, in the 1960s and 1970s, the future of international tourism in the Caribbean was at first uncertain. Would the for-eigners and their dollars return to their once favorite destinations after the violence and protests subsided?

The Caribbean's tourism industry, besides in revolutionary Cuba, re-bounded remarkably fast. The drive for political self-determination and eco-nomic resources would encourage political leaders to promote what activists had previously fought against: a transnational economy dependent on privi-lege and luxury. To make sense of what happened after a revolt, we have to, as the historian E. P. Thompson advised, "try to understand both things—the continuing traditions and the context that has changed."[87]

In the postcolonial era, policymakers, government planners, and develop-ment organizations such as the World Bank and the International Monetary Fund pushed tourism "as among the best solutions to the problems faced by the 'developing' world."[88] The postcolonial development of tourism fol-lowed the pattern of postcolonial development more generally. The tourism industry survived political decolonization, but no longer did imperial powers, or white businessmen, exclusively control the industry. "Countries once treated as colonial underdogs," the development scholar Wolfgang Sachs explained, "now measure up to their masters, and people of color take over from the white man."[89] The owners and promoters of international tourism, and the politicians and businessmen who profited, became more racially and nationally diverse.

The postcolonial career of George Westerman exemplifies this transition in power. Westerman was a committed anticolonial and antiracist activist for nearly four decades, from the late 1920s into the 1970s. He spoke out against racism and inequality in the circum-Caribbean, the United States, and also on the African continent. Westerman was an advocate for the liberation of colonial-controlled people, and for his efforts he was recognized as a national hero in Panama and awarded prestigious diplomatic posts.[90] As his colleagues remembered, Westerman's voice "was constantly raised in support of the aspirations of the West Indies whenever the opportunity arose. His penetrating observations were the source of great concern to the metropolitan powers involved."[91]

In addition to his career as a journalist, activist, and diplomat, he was also an aspiring businessman. Westerman believed that his insights and his political connections could also be financially lucrative. In the 1960s and 1970s he partnered with developers from the United States and Canada. For the Canadian construction firm Dalite Corporation, Westerman traveled the Caribbean as its regional representative. He negotiated construction deals on behalf of Dalite to build hotels, tourist infrastructure, and housing developments in Panama, Barbados, the Bahamas, and the US Virgin Islands, among other nations and island territories. In Trinidad, Westerman also negotiated on behalf of Dalite to build a new international airport for the government of Prime Minister Eric Williams. His business plans were numerous.[92]

While engaging in transnational business, Westerman also continued to embrace his role as a diplomat and social justice advocate. After a visit to the Bahamas to inspect Dalite's "fashionable Lucayan Beach Hotel," he traveled directly to Philadelphia where he lectured about issues of national sovereignty to the American Friends Service Committee. Discussing the trip with a business associate, he wrote, "They enjoyed my talk about US-RP [Republic of Panama] problems and want to have me do a lecture tour for them in California."[93] Westerman was a key spokesman for anticolonial causes and, at the same time, represented a new era of circum-Caribbean development. He carried within him the postcolonial combination of old and new. His business connections, he anticipated, would bring him the financial success and wealth he had been unable to achieve as a member of an oppressed racial group. He hoped to promote regional development determined by political leaders of color in the Caribbean, with the use of foreign capital.

As Westerman's experience highlights, tourism and foreign investment continued to be a primary vehicle for attracting capital in the postcolonial era. Development efforts—from Panama to Mexico, Colombia, the Bahamas, and across the circum-Caribbean and Latin America—continued to encourage international tourism. Development strategies traditionally associated with the privatization of public utilities, the promotion of massive infrastructure projects, and institutional modernization also paired with tourism development. The binary and revolutionary view of white people against the oppressed peoples of the world, with this historical hindsight in mind, appears like a simplified view of a complex social and economic relationship. Although there was territorial and administrative decolonization, following the revolts of the 1960s there was far from decolonization of economic and development values. Anyone in this newly decolonized context could aspire to be, in theory, a tourist or a tourist developer. The hotels and ships and attractions of the Caribbean would open to travelers and consumers of all backgrounds. The protests of the 1960s paved the way. However, they did little to relieve the economic and social strains faced by the majority of people. The question remained, what good was "access" if one did not have enough money or power to enjoy it? The lines of inequality shifted from legal racism and national restrictions to more informal and economic forms of inequality. As Westerman pursued his new role as a transnational businessmen and tourism developer, he realized: "Unless one has lots of money to move around one does not impress most favorably. I have found that the North American business operator likes to feel that he is dealing with someone of rank or influence if he is non-white and from a 'dependent' country. This being so I am perforce obliged to make my moves accordingly."[94] Tourist privileges based exclusively on the intersection of race, class, and nationality had been replaced by a new geometry of transnational power and wealth. In this sense, we can begin to understand how tourism survived the anticolonial movements of the 1960s and found renewed life under nationalist governments in the second half of the twentieth century. "The only privilege of the President," the writer Graham Greene claimed to see during his visit with revolutionary leader Omar Torrijos, "was to have a reserved parking place for his car at the Panama Hotel."[95]

Conclusion

Perilously Cruising into the Future

> To listen to and tell a rush of stories is a method.
>
> —Anna Lowenhaupt Tsing, *The Mushroom at the End of the World*

In March 1995 the author David Foster Wallace embarked on a seven-night Caribbean cruise. In an essay for *Harper's Magazine*, Wallace described the pleasures and discomforts of his vacation experience. His essay, titled "Shipping Out: On the (Nearly Lethal) Comforts of a Luxury Cruise," begins with a strange collage of observations:

> I have now seen sucrose beaches and water a very bright blue. I have seen an all-red leisure suit with flared lapels. I have smelled suntan lotion spread over 2,100 pounds of hot flesh. I have been addressed as "Mon" in three different nations. I have seen 500 upscale Americans dance the Electric Slide. I have seen sunsets that looked computer-enhanced. I have (very briefly) joined a conga line.[1]

Wallace's editor at *Harper's* claimed that the writing was so addictively readable that it was like "pure cocaine on our hands." "Literally everybody," according to the author and biographer David Lipsky, "seemed to be talking about it."[2] The cocaine analogy, though rather crude, captures the power of Wallace's prose. It also captures the gilded experience of Caribbean tourism. Cocaine and its ability to detach consumers from reality is a fitting metaphor for modern travel culture. Both illusions—drug and tourism—also demand a great deal of behind-the-scenes work to deliver their product to consumers.

Below the surface of pleasure, historical layers of production and transportation link consumers and their fantasies with underpaid workers and exploited environments.

In his essay "Shipping Out," Wallace assumed the role of a sober and perplexed narrator. "I have heard," he noted, "upscale adult U.S. citizens ask the ship's Guest Relations Desk whether snorkeling necessitates getting wet, whether the trapshooting will be held outside, whether the crew sleeps on board, and what time the Midnight Buffet is." These observations drove the sensitive author, in his words, to "despair." Between meals and awkward small talk, Wallace spent his time hiding in his room writing in his Mead notebooks, trying not to mentally break down from what he perceived to be the absurdity of the cruise experience. "There's something about a mass-market Luxury Cruise," he realized, "that's unbearably sad. Like most unbearably sad things, it seems incredibly elusive and complex in its causes yet simple in its effect."[3] Witnessing fellow US citizens indulging in their luxury vacation was difficult for him to handle. There was something "symbolically microcosmic," he believed, about adult tourists enacting vivid fantasies that they did not even recognize as fantasies.

Wallace's sense of gloom in the midst of comfort and luxury is arguably a symptom of tourism's complicated relationship to history.[4] By the time he vacationed to the Caribbean in 1995, the past had disappeared into a timeless package. The tourism industry—from cruise ships to all-inclusive resorts—had remade history into something presently pleasurable: a vacation. The brochure for Wallace's cruise ship explained: "INDULGENCE BECOMES EASY and RELAXATION BECOMES SECOND NATURE and STRESS BECOMES A FAINT MEMORY."[5] The emotional complexity of history flattened into a simple image. From the viewpoint of the present and the privileged, the Caribbean had always been a tropical paradise awaiting one's leisurely arrival. But what if these things had not always been what they are imagined to be?

As we have seen throughout this book, the Caribbean's modern tourism industry has its roots in the early twentieth century. Its structure (of infrastructure, policies, and interconnected destinations) and its social practices (of privilege and adventure) were born in the crucible of empire building. Although contemporary tourists have seemingly forgotten this process of historical assemblage, this collective and selective forgetting does not undercut the fact that history has shaped their vacation experience. Tourists do not need to know where their ideas and behavior come from in order to be guided by them.

The experience of being on a Caribbean vacation is analogous to Plato's Cave, retrofitted for modern dwellers willing to confuse the shadowy performance for reality. The terms of confinement have been upgraded, from a crude fire to a fully stocked bar with air conditioning.[6] One can dream and travel without ever having to be aware of the historical and contemporary relations that produced one's mobile fun. Wallace, though, began to question this vacation experience:

> All of the Megalines offer the same basic product—not a service or a set of services, but more like a feeling: a blend of relaxation and stimulation, stressless indulgence and frantic tourism, that special mix of servility and condescension that's marketed under configurations of the verb "to pamper."[7]

Something, he recognized, was wrong. He kept asking himself—how and why did the crew keep smiling through this all? This can't be fun or pleasurable for them, repeating over and over again, thousands of times, the same thankless tasks and cheerful greetings. "There's something crucially key about Luxury Cruises in evidence here," he suspected, "being entertained by someone who clearly dislikes you, and feeling that you deserve that dislike at the same time that you resent it."[8] Making sense of this uncomfortable social dynamic that Wallace and so many tourists have experienced requires historical analysis of underlying and often hidden resentments. What is the story—the history—behind all those service smiles and all those tourist fantasies?

Yes, those waiters and hosts are smiling at you. Yes, you are important to them. Yes, they chose to be here working on this massive cruise ship traveling the Caribbean. But do they *like* you, and do they like their job? The novelist Jamaica Kincaid, as if talking directly to Wallace and his fellow tourists, offers sharp criticisms about the history of this tourist-service dynamic in her book *A Small Place.* "That the native does not like the tourist," she wrote, "is not hard to explain. . . [because] every native would like to find a way out, every native would like a rest, every native would like a tour. But some natives—most natives in the world—cannot go anywhere. They are too poor."[9] The meaning behind a professional smile, when contextualized by history and contemporary political-economic relations, is clear: the service smile is a survival tool in the face of centuries of historic inequalities. Whether on a cruise ship or at port in the Caribbean, whether smiling or not, service workers are reminded of their place, and it doesn't look like a vacation.[10] Yet, in the twenty-first century, the number of global "natives" working in the tourism industry has increased dramatically. In 2019 the industry accounted for one out of every ten jobs in the world. The tourism industry has become one of the most profitable and global industries, alongside modern counterparts such as fossil fuels, the arms business, and drugs.[11] Tourists and their demand for leisure and luxurious experiences are at the crux of modernity. The contradictory combination—to travel in luxury / to pamper in poverty—is thoroughly and unfortunately representative of the privileges and injustices of the modern world.

Postcolonial Tourism

In the postcolonial and neoliberal era, mobile inequalities have only exacerbated. The democratization of the vacation experience, the standardization and privatization of development models, and increasingly cheap and efficient transportation technology have made many sunny and beautiful places potential tourist destinations. It's as if everyone now wants to be a tourist or a tourist entrepreneur, enjoying the fruits of capitalist consumption. The Caribbean's history of tourism, born from colonialism, has been repackaged as a template for regional and perhaps global development. Governments across the Caribbean and the developing world have adopted generous economic and political policies to attract tourists and foreign investors to their respective countries. In Panama, for example, tourists—if they want to stay for the long term—can get fast-track approval for national residency and major tax breaks for home and small business construction. Law 481 offers a twenty-year tax exemption for construction materials used in tourism development, no import tax for vehicles used for "ecotourism," and a twenty-year exemption for real estate purchased for tourism, among other incentives.[12] One investment firm, responding to the new law, explained, "South Florida faces a rising rival in tourism. . . . Investors are pouring hundreds of millions of dollars in hotels into the small Central American country."[13] Even revolutionary Cuba, which was supposed to end the historical inequities separating locals and foreigners, has returned to a tourist economy. In the face of material and existential uncertainty, with no clear oppressor, former revolutionaries and anticolonial activists have turned to one of their original enemies: luxury tourism. Tourism development in nations like revolutionary Cuba may seem exceptional but in fact is emblematic of a broader phenomenon. In search of foreign capital, postcolonial leaders—whether socialist or capitalist—have allied themselves with an industry and way of travel that emerged from social practices, privileges, and inequities born in an earlier era that they originally fought to overthrow.

This extensification and intensification of tourism confirms some of the worst fears of anticolonial activists. Mahatma Gandhi's warnings of the dangers of industrialism and Western development are particularly insightful when also considering the growth of tourism. As early as 1928, Gandhi critiqued the unsustainability of Western patterns of consumption that were beginning to be embraced and spread in the developing world. He explained, "The economic imperialism of a single tiny island Kingdom (England) is today keeping the world in chains. If an entire nation of 300 million took to similar economic exploitation, it would strip the world bare like locusts."[14] Extending Gandhi's warning—what would happen if not millions, but billions, of people tried to travel and consume like the hegemonic version of a twentieth-century tourist? It's already happening. In 2018 the UN's World Tourism Organization estimated that 1.4 billion people traveled internationally as tourists. Consider the billions of tons of materials and waste and the number of people who received low wages and faked smiles to serve that global mass of visitors.[15]

Royal Caribbean, one of the largest cruise ship operators in the world, tells guests, "The Sea is calling. Answer it Royally." To be treated royally, however, requires an immense amount of effort and labor from other people. Visualize for a minute, a cruise ship with thousands of people aboard consuming like ancient kings and queens. What would the social, economic, and ecological impacts be of an endless repetition of supposedly divinely chosen elites visiting Caribbean shores? In his cruise essay, Wallace described this scene when their ship arrived in port:

> I cannot convey to you the sheer and surreal scale of everything: the towering ship, the ropes, the anchor, the pier, the *vast lapis lazuli dome of the sky*. Looking down from a great height at your countrymen waddling into poverty-stricken ports in expensive sandals is not one of the funner moments of a 7NC Luxury Cruise, however. There is something inescapably *bovine* about a herd of American tourists in motion, a certain greedy placidity.[16]

Technologically driven leisure mobility has depended on the same kinetic convergence that historically fed empire: the accumulation of resources and energy for the few. The towering ships, ropes, piers, dredged ports, and the low-paid workers of color served the same master: the world's privileged consumer.[17]

The history of Caribbean tourism reveals the historical roots of this problem. At the beginning of the twentieth century, when the United States government and business expanded southward, "conquering the tropics" through military campaigns, massive engineering projects, and chemically infused wars against tropical disease, tourists began to reimagine the tropics as a vacation playground. This legacy still matters; it has only spread and become more pervasive and desired. Yet most contemporary travelers and tourists have never heard of this history of the present.

Why Do They Smile?

During my research I also participated in and observed the historical milieu of modern tourism. My time abroad, like most historians, was not exclusively in dusty archives and libraries. On one research trip, for example, I traveled by cruise ship from South Florida to Colón, Panama, to experience and study the vacation package. For one week I was both tourist and researcher, experiencing the fun along with the frustrations that Wallace and Kincaid expressed. What follows are some notes from that trip, which considers history's effect on contemporary experience:

> The culture of service begins as soon as we arrive at Port Everglades in Fort Lauderdale, Florida. Police, security, and parking attendants with bright traffic wands guide us to the cruise entrance. At the terminal, porters smile and help with our bags. Waiting for a tip, there is an outpouring of hospitality. "Enjoy your cruise, sir; have a wonderful trip!" Inside the terminal, which resembles a giant aircraft hangar, another round of service workers come by smiling, dressed in all white, passing out lemonade and cookies. As we wait in a very long line to board the ship, I reread sections of Wallace's essay, "trying to summon up," in his words, "a kind of hypnotic sensuous collage of all the stuff I've seen and heard and done."
>
> There is a cacophony of movement in port: of jet planes, forklifts, plates clattering against forks and knives on deck, boat horns, a slight breeze, muddled chatter and laughter from multiple directions. Three other mega–cruise ships surround the ship—one port side, the other starboard, a third at our stern. In the port, there are six giant, white cruise ships, each capable of carrying thousands of passengers. Small boats motor by. Outside the barrier island protecting the port, sailboats and more recreational vessels in the waves. From the top deck of our cruiseship, a forty-foot sailboat looks like a raft belonging to a group of nomadic ants. The mangroves, or what's left of them, also border the port. Two worlds: one ecological and the other made of steel and plastic. As we head out to sea, two mega–cruise ships flank our ship. It's a race to vacation, an armada of tourism, the modern Great White Fleet heading to the Caribbean.

Aboard ship, there are approximately one thousand crew members to three thousand passengers—a 3:1 tourist-to-service ratio.[18] *Labor in the tourism industry, I learn, is abundant and cheap. Royal Caribbean waiters and cabin attendants receive a remarkable $50-a-month base salary; the rest of their income depends on tips. Meanwhile, "utility cleaners" work twelve hours a day and earn $550 a month, with no tips. Thanks to the ship's foreign flag of convenience, from Panama, US labor and environmental laws are easily brushed aside.*[19] *No wonder this vacation is so affordable. Cruise competitors search the world for the cheapest labor.*

The crew members of our ship come from the Dominican Republic, Turkey, Bulgaria, Chile, China, Colombia, the Czech Republic, Ghana, Honduras, India, Italy, Jamaica, Latvia, Macedonia, Nepal, Nicaragua, Peru, the Philippines, Poland, Romania, Panama, Serbia, South Africa, Spain, St. Lucia, Sweden, Ukraine, the United Kingdom, Venezuela, and Uzbekistan. Of the one thousand employees, twenty-four are from the United States and mostly work in the ship's officer class or as professional entertainers. There is a rhythm-and-blues band on board from Memphis, Tennessee. Meanwhile, crew members from northern European countries—tall, blue-eyed, and blond men dressed in white uniforms—represent the ship's officers. Everyone else on the ship works in the galley, belowdecks, cleaning, or serving food and drinks, entertaining, and making us tourists feel special.

The majority of the crew has traveled from the so-called developing world to work on this floating luxury resort. Wendell, our waiter who serves dinner in the Great Gatsby Dining Hall, has been at sea for six months, away from his wife and children on the island of St. Lucia. In a brief moment of conversation, he shares, "I've been doing this quite a while now. I rather be home, but there's no work there." He has worked on cruise ships for thirteen years. Another crew member we meet, José, folded countless towels by lunchtime, which may not sound too difficult, except for the fact that he shaped each of them into a variety of cute animals, such as swans, elephants, and turtles—that special touch for guests. He explains that he's been away from his wife and young child in Colombia for five months. At port, he stays on the ship. It's too expensive to go ashore, he explains; he's working for his family. This is a sacrifice rather than an adventure for him. How many workers share the same fate?

Meanwhile, we the tourists are thoroughly entertained. The buffet never ends, ice cream is bottomless, performances go late into the evening, and the casino never closes.[20] *Every day we are given a list of activities to choose from. On the fifth day of the trip, the ship's newsletter,* Cruise Compass *informs us that "the most exciting place to be in all of the Caribbean at this very moment is right here. As a citizen of our nation, you're free to roam from deck to deck and ask yourself, why not?" Activities for the day include:*

- *International Parade of Flags. It's like a floating United Nations.*
- *World's Sexiest Man Competition. Ouh, la, la . . .*
- *Pool Volleyball Guests vs. Staff. Let's get a game started . . .*
- *Royal Cash Prize Bingo. Join a thrilling game of B-I-N-G-O today . . .*
- *70s Disco Inferno. Join your Cruise Director Rico and the Cruise Director's Staff as we take a journey back to the days when the leisure suit reigned supreme and the big afros were in style.*
- *70s After Party. Enjoy the best 70s music. Go Out With A Bang!*

"A vacation," Wallace noted, "is a respite from unpleasantness." By paying close attention to the intersection between the past and the present, however, one becomes aware of its exact opposite. The tourist's pleasure depends on the historical accumulation of low wages and discomfort for people from the rest of the world.

Making the Fragments Whole

Historical narrative and thick description offer clues for understanding the seemingly elusive and complex causes shaping contemporary tourist behavior and service-labor relations. "History," as the popular aphorism goes, "is what the present wants or needs to know about the past." To study tourism's history, therefore, is to commit to more conscious travel.

The Caribbean, we are told, used to be a hotbed of colonialism. Those days are supposedly over. Slavery and the era of empire have passed into history. The tourism industry tells us so. Critical and postcolonial scholars, though, have challenged this packaged "Mickey Mouse" version of history. As the historian Robin Kelley has argued, "we are hardly in a 'postcolonial' moment. The official apparatus might have been removed, but the political, economic, and cultural links established by colonial domination still remain with some alterations."[21] Although much of the Caribbean has experienced the political end of colonialism, the decolonization of everyday life has yet to happen.[22] As the writer and social critic James Baldwin observed, history "does not refer merely, or even principally, to the past. On the contrary, the great force of history comes from the fact that we carry it within us, are unconsciously controlled by it in many ways, and history is literally present in all that we do. It could scarcely be otherwise, since it is to history that we owe our frames of reference, our identities, and our aspirations."[23] How we travel, or don't travel, as tourists is part of this history.

As I have argued in this book, Caribbean tourism is the historical successor of economic and social relationships, which enabled the West and especially the United States to profit from the region in the twentieth century. The modern ethics and habits of Caribbean tourism are rooted in the history of empire. Imperial networks of production and consumption, scientific research and technology, and social conflicts linking the tourist's home with distant communities have created socioeconomic boundaries of mobility still difficult to overcome.[24] This often-forgotten legacy goes beyond the organization of labor relations and access to mobility and transportation technology.

Contemporary cultural fantasies have their origins in the colonial past. Literary and visual representations packaged and consumed by tourists still mimic old beliefs and practices. There is the enduring popularity, for example, of J. M. Barrie's Peter Pan fighting pirates and making friends with Indians on an exotic island where he never has to grow old, Robinson Crusoe and his man Friday on a tropical isle, Indiana Jones and his quest for lost treasure, and Johnny Depp and his pirates of the Caribbean living for pleasure. Stories and images, copied from past tales, continue to guide contemporary vacationers.

Tourists can dine luxuriously in the Great Gatsby Dining Hall, drink bottomless Coca-Cola, eat vast amounts of food, dance and gamble, and lounge aboard ship late into the evening, or morning. Meanwhile, on shore, they can tour an old fort or an old plantation or go on an ecotour into the rain forest to find nature and meet authentic "natives." These experiences are formed historically. This formation, though, gets whitewashed, and what is left is a seemingly innocent international experience of the interesting and luxurious. Pirates plundering and pillaging become childhood heroes, slaveowners and racists become dignified planters and merchants, explorers and writers in the service of empire become role models of adventure. "Today we see such images from an historical distance," Mimi Sheller tells us—if we see them at all—"thinking we are free of their condescension, yet much within them is still sculpted into the living landscape of Caribbean resorts."[25] To be a tourist is still to be part of history.

Old travel patterns have overdetermined contemporary tourist culture, maintaining and reactivating old elements. Stereotypes continue to be actualized in the twenty-first century. Back at home historically guided tourists may be respectable citizens with well-paid jobs, caring spouses, beloved members of families and local communities. But on vacation, responsibilities disappear. As tourists, they feel liberated. A vacation for them is an escape from the rules and mundaneness of home, an adventure, a chance for fantasies to be enacted, with impunity. All the while, family and friends wait for their return, to learn of their cleaned-up vacation. Safely at home, hedonism is reinterpreted into a fishing trip, beach time, a relaxing vacation, a necessary break to "blow off steam."

The tourist's metamorphosis from prudent citizen to freed vacationer is eerily reminiscent of one of colonialism's most infamous literary characters. In Joseph Conrad's novella *Heart of Darkness*, Kurtz was a respected company official, with an adoring wife at home who worshipped his every move. But abroad he embraced another, "wild" side. Upriver in the untamed colony, working as an ivory trader, he experienced a metamorphosis. Conrad's sympathetic narrator Marlowe tells us, though, that this behavior was not geographically or culturally predetermined by the place visited but really something that Kurtz carried hidden within him on the journey from the metropole to the colonial outpost, released in the moment of encounter.[26] Like his fellow colonialists, the darkness was within looking for a means of escape.

The heart of colonialism, as expressed by Conrad, relates to the heart of tropical tourism. The hegemonic identity of a modern tourist has embraced an upgraded version of the colonial ability to project and naturalize one's repressed desires onto an "other" nature, an "other" culture. The tourist drinks because that is what one does on vacation. The tourist philanders because that is *their* "other" way of being. The tourist gambles because *their* "other" morality says so. The tourist treks through the muddy forest because *their* nature is supposedly more pristine. Like Kurtz, the tourist is supposedly adapting to a foreign locality. This behavior, however, is more reflective of the sending culture than the receiving one.[27]

Examining the Past to Reimagine the Future

Whether by sea or air, a profound social transformation occurs when tourists arrive at their vacation destination. This change is *rooted in* and *routed by* history. The ideas and experiences of past travelers have *prescripted* many of the expectations, perceptions, and travel itineraries of modern-day tourists. While not all tourists and travelers follow the dominant paths of history, nevertheless a significant number—an overwhelming majority—have acted and continue to engage in a hegemonic culture of Caribbean tourism.

As historians Will and Ariel Durant put it, "the present is the past rolled up for action." Social practices and values of tourism have been passed down from one generation to the next—from political leaders, writers, naturalists and explorers, southern frontiersmen, businessmen, service workers, family members and friends, and a host of forgotten historical travelers. Tourism is in this way the past rolled up for leisurely action. Following this line of historical reasoning is the second half of the Durants' statement "the past [when examined closely] is [also] the present unrolled for understanding."[28] But sometimes past experiences, once understood, must be left behind, buried with those who came before. As F. Scott Fitzgerald, in an interview with himself in 1920, declared, "the wise literary son kills his own father."[29] Creative destruction, Fitzgerald reasoned, was the only way to make something new.

Historical reflection requires looking deeply, remembering, in order to avoid making the same journey. It demands an intense and often uncomfortable analysis of the legacy within. By looking to history, future travelers may be able to leave behind some of the guiding experiences of those who toured before: all the romance and exoticism and vacation excess of international travel mimicked and reproduced in magazine stories and glossy advertisements. Millions of travelers have fallen for illusory tales and believed them true: the Caribbean is a paradise, waiting to be discovered. Cultural tropes, invented in an era of imperial folly, twisted into modern vacation dreams. Many good people have gone off to experience these fantasies only to hurt body and soul and to perpetuate a system of injustice. Illusions are dangerous not only to the people and places visited but also to oneself. The dream of a Caribbean vacation enacted is a microcosm of the cockeyed world we live in, where desires of pleasure and relief depend on and spread their opposite. Very few people dreaming of a vacation, however, seem to recognize this modern predicament. Reality can be too cruel and weird for those who like happy endings.

Historical consciousness, though, does not mean we should stay home, returning to our small towns and cities to never travel again. As scholars and philosophers have argued for millennia, knowledge begins with experience, and travel is one of the most intimate and experiential ways to understand the diversity and possibilities of the world. As the Caribbean scholar Aimé Césaire explained, "It is a good thing to place different civilizations in contact with each other; that it is an excellent thing to blend different worlds; that whatever its own particular genius may be, a civilization that withdraws into itself atrophies; that for civilizations, exchange is oxygen." But Césaire also asked, have the people of the Caribbean really been in "contact" with Europe and North America, "or, if you prefer, of all the ways of establishing contact, was it the best?"[30] That is the key philosophical and ethical question guiding us in the twenty-first century.

Travel, cross-cultural contact, and exchange produce the creative "oxygen" of modern life. We must seriously consider, however, whether the rules and norms of mobility and immobility in their current form are the way we want to facilitate this contact, to support exchange. I am far from alone in raising that critical question. Many people are trying to imagine and live an alternative way of mobility—from no-fly movements to solidarity travel to zero-waste movements. Yet, on an international scale, an ideal and just mode of travel has yet to be put into practice or fully imagined. The privileges of modern life should not and cannot remain a one-way and singular path of mobility—from the Global North to the Global South.

The Caribbean's history of tourism, with all its historic problems and challenges, offers clues for reimagining the present and future of international travel. In conclusion, tourism is simple in its contemporary effects but complex in its historical causes. But by recognizing and reflecting on this underlying history of the present, perhaps the next generation will be set free to wander and wonder in new ways, neither bound nor blind to the history within.

Notes

Abbreviations Used in the Notes

ABP   Archivo Belisario Porras, Panama City
ABRA   Archivo y la Biblioteca Ricardo J. Alfaro, Panama City
AMRE   Archivo del Ministerio de Relaciones Exteriores, Panama City
ANC   Archivo Nacional de la República de Cuba, Havana
ANP   Archivo Nacional de Panamá, Panama City
FEUF   Florida Ephemera Collection, University of Florida
GPO   Government Printing Office
JARD   Jamaica Archives and Records Department, Spanish Town
LOC   Manuscript Division, Library of Congress, Washington, DC
NARA   US National Archives and Records Administration, College Park, MD
PAW   Pan American World Airways Records, University of Miami
PCUF   Panama and the Canal Collection, University of Florida
RG   record group
RU   record unit
SCRBC   Schomburg Center for Research in Black Culture, New York
SIA   Smithsonian Institution Archives, Washington, DC

Foreword

1. Christopher Hibbert, *The Grand Tour* (New York: G. P. Putnam's Sons, 1969), 24–25.

2. Brian Dolan, *Ladies of the Grand Tour* (New York: HarperCollins, 2001). See also Rosemary Sweet, "British Perceptions of Florence in the Long Eighteenth Century," *Historical Journal* 50, no. 4 (2007): 837–59.

3. Jack Simmons, "Railways, Hotels, and Tourism in Great Britain, 1839–1914," *Journal of Contemporary History* 19, no. 2 (April 1984): 201–22; John Armstrong and David M. Williams, "The Steamboat in Popular Tourism," *Journal of Transport History* 26, no. 1 (March 2005): 61–77; Susan Barton, *Working-Class Organisations and Popular Tourism, 1840–1970* (Manchester: Manchester University Press, 2005).

4. John K. Walton, "The Demand for Working-Class Seaside Holidays in Victorian England," *Economic History Review* 34, no. 2 (May 1981): 249–65.

5. John K. Walton. "Thomas Cook: Image and Reality," in *Giants of Tourism*, ed. Richard W. Butler and Roslyn A. Russell, 81–92 (Wallingford, UK: CABI International, 2010), 87.

6. John F. Sears, *Sacred Places: American Tourist Attractions in the Nineteenth Century* (Amherst: University of Massachusetts Press, 1989); Marguerite S. Shaffer, *See*

America First: Tourism and National Identity, 1880–1940 (Washington, DC: Smithsonian Institution Press, 2001).

7. See, e.g., Diane P. Koenker, *Club Red: Vacation Travel and the Soviet Dream* (Ithaca, NY: Cornell University Press, 2013), and Shelley Baranowski, *Strength through Joy: Consumerism and Mass Tourism in the Third Reich* (Cambridge: Cambridge University Press, 2004)

8. Eric G. E. Zuelow, *A History of Modern Tourism* (London: Palgrave, 2016), 112–33, 165–79.

9. Daniel Hiernaux-Nicolas, "Cancún Bliss," in *The Tourist City*, ed. Dennis R. Judd and Susan S. Fainstein, 124–42 (New Haven, CT: Yale University Press, 1999).

10. Gethin Chamberlain, "Tourists in India Told to Avoid 'Human Safaris' as Row Widens," *The Observer*, January 22, 2012.

11. Thomas R. Metcalf, *Ideologies of the Raj* (Cambridge: Cambridge University Press, 1995). See also Edward W. Said, *Orientalism* (New York: Vintage Books, 1978), and Mary Louise Pratt, *Imperial Eyes: Travel Writing and Transculturalism* (Abingdon, UK: Routledge, 1992).

12. M. S. S. Pandian, "Gendered Negotiations: Hunting and Colonialism in Late Nineteenth Century Nilgiris," *Contributions to Indian Sociology* 20, nos. 1–2 (1995): 239–64.

13. See, e.g., Kara Godfrey, "Lands of No Return," *U.S. Sun*, August 8, 2021; "No Heads in the Clouds," *The Economist*, February 13, 2021; Becca Milfeld, "Simple and Close to Home: Pandemic Vacations Embrace the Travel Norms of Earlier Eras," *Washington Post*, September 18, 2020; Sarah Firshein, "To Many Travelers, 2020 Was the Summer of 1965," *New York Times*, September 4, 2020; and Lionel Laurent, "Does Venice Hold the Key to Saving Cities from Mass Tourism?," BloombergQuint, August 5, 2021, https://www.bloombergquint.com/gadfly/what-amsterdam-paris-barcelona-can-learn-from-venice-cruise-ship-ban.

Preface

1. Donna Olshan, "Coronavirus Has New Yorkers Fleeing the City and Hunting for Second Homes," *Forbes*, May 10, 2020.

2. Mimi Sheller, *Mobility Justice: The Politics of Movement in an Age of Extremes* (New York: Verso, 2018), 1.

3. C. L. R. James, *Beyond a Boundary* (1963; repr., Durham, NC: Duke University Press, 1993), 113.

4. "Tourism and Jobs: A Better for Future for All," UNWTO, September 27, 2019, https://www.unwto.org/world-tourism-day-2019.

5. Nicholas Kulish, "What It Costs to Be Smuggled across the U.S. Border," *New York Times*, June 30, 2018.

6. Emily Williams, "Coronavirus Crisis Will Cost Charleston Tourism More than $1B in 2 Months," *Post and Courier*, April 17, 2020.

Introduction

1. Cornelia Scott (my paternal grandmother) in discussion with the author, May 2009. The small vacation house my family rented in Florida was originally built for a "coast watcher" on the lookout for German submarines cruising the Florida

coast and the Caribbean during World War II. The repurposing of that house, from military to civilian use, is exemplary of an established historical pattern: the infrastructure of war becoming the backbone of future tourism.

2. On the history of Florida's demographic growth in the twentieth century, see Gary R. Mormino, *Land of Sunshine, State of Dreams: A Social History of Modern Florida* (Gainesville: University Press of Florida, 2008).

3. For Jerry Seinfeld's jokes about Florida, see, e.g., his appearance on *The Tonight Show* on *Johnny Carson: King of Late Night*, directed by Mark Catalena and Peter Jones (Arlington, VA: Public Broadcasting Service American Masters Series, 2012), DVD.

4. Although the tropics are geographically delimited in latitude by the Tropic of Cancer at N 23°26′11.1″ and the Tropic of Capricorn at S 23°26′11.1″, the terms "tropics" and "tropical" have often been culturally and linguistically employed beyond those geographic boundaries. Throughout this book, I use the terms as they were used by historical figures and actors in the early to mid-twentieth century, which in the Western Hemisphere often referred to spaces from South Florida to the Caribbean islands to Central and South America. The tropics historically have been as much a cultural construct as a physically coherent space on earth. For a related argument, in relation to tourism and the tropics, see Catherine Cocks, *Tropical Whites: The Rise of the Tourist South in the Americas* (Philadelphia: University of Pennsylvania Press, 2013).

5. For critical analyses of contemporary tourism in the Caribbean, see Angelique V. Nixon, *Resisting Paradise: Tourism, Diaspora, and Sexuality in Caribbean Culture* (Jackson: University of Mississippi Press, 2015); Martha Honey, ed., *Cruise Tourism in the Caribbean: Selling Sunshine* (London: Routledge, 2019); George Gmelch, *Behind the Smile: The Working Lives of Caribbean Tourism* (Bloomington: Indiana University Press, 2003); and Polly Pattullo, *Last Resorts: The Cost of Tourism in the Caribbean* (Kingston, Jamaica: Ian Randle, 1996).

6. For historical monographs focused on the history of tourism in one particular country or territory in the Caribbean region, see Rosalie Schwartz, *Pleasure Island: Tourism and Temptation in Cuba* (Lincoln: University of Nebraska Press, 1997), and Frank Fonda Taylor, *To Hell with Paradise: A History of the Jamaican Tourist Industry* (Pittsburgh: University of Pittsburgh Press, 1993).

7. For tourism development in the Caribbean in the post–World War II era, see Dennis Merrill, *Negotiating Paradise: U.S. Tourism and Empire in Twentieth-Century Latin America* (Chapel Hill: University of North Carolina Press, 2009), chap. 3–5, and Evan R. Ward, *Packaged Vacations: Tourism Development in the Spanish Caribbean* (Gainesville: University Press of Florida, 2008).

8. For recent historical studies of tourism in Latin America and the Caribbean, see Lisa Pinley Covert, *San Miguel de Allende: Mexicans, Foreigners, and the Making of a World Heritage Site* (Lincoln: University of Nebraska Press, 2017); Mark Rice, *Making Machu Picchu: The Politics of Tourism in Twentieth-Century Peru* (Chapel Hill: University of North Carolina Press, 2018); and Andrew Wood, ed., *The Business of Leisure: Tourism History in Latin America and the Caribbean* (Lincoln: University of Nebraska Press, 2021).

9. Richard Grove, *Green Imperialism: Colonial Expansion, Tropical Island Edens, and the Origins of Environmentalism, 1600–1800* (New York: Cambridge University Press, 1996), 3.

10. Cocks, *Tropical Whites*, 2, 7–27. There is a long-running debate about the use of the term "American" to exclusively represent people from the United States, especially when writing about US-Latin Americans. People throughout the Americas often consider themselves "Americans." To avoid confusion, I have tried to be a specific as possible when identifying travelers, officials, and tourists from the United States. However, if I am quoting or paraphrasing an historical source, I follow their choice in language, which may include "North American," "Americans," or sometimes "white Americans."

11. David Foster Wallace, "Shipping Out: On the (Nearly Lethal) Comforts of a Luxury Cruise," *Harper's Magazine*, January 1996, 34.

12. For tourism's historical relationship to imperial expansion in North Africa and the Middle East, see Waleed Hazbun, "The East as an Exhibit: Thomas Cook & Son and the Origins of the International Tourism Industry in Egypt," and Kenneth J. Perkins, "The Compagnie Générale Transatlantique and the Development of Saharan Tourism in North Africa," in *The Business of Tourism: Place, Faith, and History*, ed. Philip Scranton and Janet F. Davidson (Philadelphia: University of Pennsylvania Press, 2021), chap. 1–2. On the role of the Mediterranean in British travel imaginations, see John Pemble, *The Mediterranean Passion: Victorians and Edwardians in the South* (Oxford: Oxford University Press 1987), and Robert Holland, *The Warm South: How the Mediterranean Shaped the British Imagination* (New Haven, CT: Yale University Press, 2018).

13. William Cronon, "The Trouble with Wilderness; or, Getting Back to the Wrong Nature," in *Uncommon Ground: Rethinking the Human Place in Nature*, ed. William Cronon (New York: W. W. Norton, 1995), 69–90. For more on the American West, the frontier, and tourism, see Hal K. Rothman, *Devil's Bargains: Tourism in the Twentieth-Century American West* (Lawrence: University Press of Kansas, 1998); David Wrobel and Patrick Long, eds., *Seeing and Being Seen: Tourism in the American West* (Lawrence: University Press of Kansas, 2001); and Thomas Andrews, "'Made by Toile': Tourism, Labor, and the Construction of the Colorado Landscape, 1858–1917," *Journal of American History* 92, no. 3 (December 2005): 837–63. For later tourism developments, with the automobile, see Paul S. Sutter, *Driven Wild: How the Fight against Automobiles Launched the Modern Wilderness Movement* (Seattle: University of Washington Press, 2002).

14. Clifford Geertz, "The Wet and the Dry: Traditional Irrigation in Bali and Morocco," *Human Ecology* 1, no. 1 (March 1972): 38.

15. Jorge Luis Borges, "The Argentine Writer and Tradition," in *Labyrinths: Selected Stories and Other Writings*, ed. Donald A. Yates and James E. Irby (New York: New Directions, 1964), 181.

16. Nixon, *Resisting Paradise*, 17. On the ways power has selectively silenced the past, see Michel-Rolph Trouillot, *Silencing the Past: Power and the Production of History* (Boston: Beacon Press, 1995).

17. John Urry and Jonas Larsen, *The Tourist Gaze 3.0* (London: SAGE Publications, 2011), 1–30.

18. My methodological approach is genealogical, following the insights of Michel Foucault, who explained, "If the genealogist refuses to extend his faith in metaphysics, if he listens to history, he finds that there is something altogether different behind things: not a timeless and essential secret, but the secret that they have no

essence or that their essence was fabricated in a piecemeal fashion from alien forms." Michel Foucault, "Nietzsche, Genealogy, History," in *Language, Counter-Memory, Practice: Selected Essays and Interviews*, ed. D. F. Bouchard (Ithaca, NY: Cornell University Press, 1977), 142.

19. Neil Leiper, "An Etymology of 'Tourism,'" *Annals of Tourism Research* 10, no. 2 (1983): 277–81.

20. Zuelow, *History of Modern Tourism*, 9.

21. Ascem Anand, *Advance Dictionary of Tourism* (New Delhi: Sarup & Sons, 1997), 41.

22. Urry and Larsen, *Tourist Gaze 3.0*, 4–5.

23. Quoted in Zuelow, *History of Modern Tourism*, 15. For more on tourism's long history in Europe, see Maxine Feifer, *Tourism in History: From Imperial Rome to the Present* (New York: Stein & Day, 1986).

24. On tourists from the United States traveling to Europe and particularly Paris in the nineteenth century, see Harvey Levenstein, *The Seductive Journey: American Tourists in France from Jefferson to the Jazz Age* (Chicago: University of Chicago Press, 2000), and David McCullough, *The Greater Journey: Americans in Paris* (New York: Simon & Schuster, 2011). On Latin American elites traveling in Europe, see Meri L. Clark, "From the Andes to the Alps: Colombian Writers on Travels in Europe," in Wood, *Business of Leisure*, 23–48. On tourism history across Europe, see Eric G. E. Zuelow, ed., *Touring beyond the Nation: A Transnational Approach to European Tourism History* (New York: Routledge, 2011).

25. Mark Twain, *The Innocents Abroad, or The New Pilgrims' Progress* (Hartford, CT: American Publishing, 1869), 19.

26. On the nineteenth-century history of tourism in the United States, see Cindy Aron, *Working at Play: A History of Vacations in the United States* (New York: Oxford University Press, 1999); Dona Brown, *Inventing New England: Regional Tourism in the Nineteenth Century* (Washington, DC: Smithsonian Institution Press, 1995); and Sears, *Sacred Places*.

27. On the early growth of tourism to the tropics of the Americas, see Cocks, *Tropical Whites*.

28. "City Officials to Dine on 475 Lbs. of Bass [sic]," *Waukegan News-Sun*, September 18, 1961.

29. Cornelia Scott in discussion with the author, May 2009.

30. "Tropical Bay Estates: In the Famed Florida Keys," flyer, Big Pine Key, Florida, Scott Family Papers.

31. On the history of Florida retirement and vacation development projects, see Jason Vuic, *The Swamp Peddlers: How Lot Sellers, Land Scammers, and Retirees Built Modern Florida and Transformed the American Dream* (Chapel Hill: University of North Carolina Press, 2021).

32. On Florida's tourism history, see Tracy Revels, *Sunshine Paradise: A History of Florida Tourism* (Gainesville: University Press of Florida, 2011), and Julio Capó, *Welcome to Fairyland: Queer Miami before 1940* (Chapel Hill: University of North Carolina Press, 2017).

33. Brochure, "Florida Cuba," RUs 4601–20, FEUF.

34. Brochure, "Florida East Coast Railroad, Hotels, and Tour Books," RUs 2521–30, FEUF.

35. On the history of Flagler in Florida, see Edward N. Akin, *Flagler: Rockefeller Partner and Florida Baron* (Gainesville: University Press of Florida, 1991), and Pat Parks, *The Railroad That Died at Sea: The Florida East Coast's Key West Extension* (Key West, FL: Langley, 1968).

36. Les Standiford, *Last Train to Paradise: Henry Flagler and the Spectacular Rise and Fall of the Railroad That Crossed an Ocean* (New York: Crown, 2002). To develop the area surrounding the Miami rail line, Flagler dredged a channel, built streets, and instituted the first water and power systems in the city.

37. On early tourism development in Florida, see Christopher Knowlton, *Bubble in the Sun: The Florida Boom of the 1920s and How It Brought on the Great Depression* (New York: Simon & Schuster, 2020).

38. On tourism privileges and racial inequality in Miami, see Chanelle Nyree Rose, *The Struggle for Black Freedom in Miami: Civil Rights and America's Tourist Paradise, 1896–1968* (Baton Rouge: Louisiana State University Press, 2019).

39. My argument about the generational and class transfer of tourist consumer patterns follows Sidney Mintz's analysis of consumer patterns concerning sugar. People of lower social status, he argued, have historically tried to emulate higher classes in their consumption choices. Mintz introduces two terms to explain this social process in his classic book *Sweetness and Power*: "intensification" and "extensification." Intensification refers to the mimicking of upper-class consumption to show one's improving status—the transfer of the uses and meanings of those of higher position to lower ranks. Extensification, meanwhile, refers to the use of old materials in new contexts and "with new or modified meanings—an extensification of previous usages." Sidney Mintz, *Sweetness and Power: The Place of Sugar in Modern History* (New York: Viking, 1985), 140.

40. Chanelle N. Rose, "Tourism and the Hispanicization of Race in Jim Crow Miami, 1945–1965," *Journal of Social History* 45, no. 3 (Spring 2012): 735–56.

41. Mike Wallace, *Mickey Mouse History and Other Essays on American Memory* (Philadelphia: Temple University Press, 1996); Richard E. Foglesong, *Married to the Mouse: Walt Disney and Orlando* (New Haven, CT: Yale University Press, 2001).

42. William Appleman Williams, *The Shaping of American Diplomacy: Readings and Documents in American Foreign Relations, 1750–1955* (Chicago: Rand McNally, 1956), xx.

43. My narrative approach is influenced by microhistorical scholarship. See Lara Putnam, "To Study the Fragments/Whole: Microhistory and the Atlantic World," *Journal of Social History* 39, no. 3 (2006), 615–30; Jill Lepore, "Historians Who Love Too Much: Reflections on Microhistory and Biography," *Journal of American History* 88, no. 1 (2001), 129–44; and Sigurður Gylfi Magnússon and István M. Szíjártó, *What Is Microhistory? Theory and Practice* (Milton Park, UK: Routledge, 2013). For classic microhistory, Carlo Ginzburg, *The Cheese and the Worms: The Cosmos of a Sixteenth Century Miller* (Baltimore: Johns Hopkins University Press, 1992).

44. Ralph Waldo Emerson, "History," in *Essays: First and Second Series* (New York: Vintage Books, 1990), 240.

45. Stuart Hall, "Minimal Selves," in *Identity: The Real Me*, ed. Homi Bhabha and Lisa Appignasesi (London: Institute of Contemporary Arts, 1987), 45.

46. Kimberlé Crenshaw, "Mapping the Margins: Intersectionality, Identity Politics, and Violence against Women of Color," *Stanford Law Review* 43, no. 6 (1991), 1241–99.

47. Doreen Massey, "A Global Sense of Place," in *Space, Place, and Gender* (Minneapolis: University of Minnesota Press, 1994), 154.

48. Putnam, "To Study the Fragments/Whole," 617.

49. "Tourism Statistics: The Bigger Picture," Caribbean Council, accessed July 2020, https://www.caribbean-council.org/tourism-statistics-bigger-picture/.

50. My use of the term "transnational" follows a line of reasoning developed by Laura Briggs, Gladys McCormick, and J. T. Way in "Transnationalism: A Category of Analysis," *American Quarterly* 60, no. 3 (2008), 625–48.

51. "Florida Is the World's Port of Call," *Florida Trend*, April 15, 2015, https://www.floridatrend.com/article/18344/florida-is-the-worlds-port-of-call?page=1; "Florida Home to 3 of the World's Most-Visited Cruise Terminals," *Orlando Business Journal*, April 21, 2015, http://www.bizjournals.com/orlando/morning_call/2015/04/florida-home-to-3-of-the-worlds-most-visited.html; "Cruise Industry Overview—2013: State of the Cruise Industry," Florida-Caribbean Cruise Association, accessed July 15, 2015, http://www.f-cca.com/downloads/2013-cruise-industry-overview.pdf.

52. For excellent overviews of Caribbean history from precolonial to contemporary times, see Stephan Palmié and Francisco A. Scarano, eds, *The Caribbean: A History of the Region and Its Peoples* (Chicago: University of Chicago, 2011); O. Nigel Bolland, ed., *The Birth of Caribbean Civilization: A Century of Ideas about Culture and Identity, Nation and Society* (Kingston, Jamaica: Ian Randle, 2004); and Sidney Mintz, *Three Ancient Colonies: Caribbean Themes and Variations* (Cambridge, MA: Harvard University Press, 2010).

53. For a classic text on Florida and the Spanish conquest, see Herbert E. Bolton, *The Spanish Borderlands: A Chronicle of Old Florida and the Southwest* (New Haven, CT: Yale University Press, 1921).

54. On the Caribbean's transnational and colonial history, see Carrie Gibson, *Empire's Crossroads: A History of the Caribbean from Columbus to the Present Day* (New York: Grove Atlantic, 2015).

55. Deborah Cullen and Elvis Fuentes, eds, *Caribbean: Art at the Crossroads of the World* (New Haven, CT: Yale University Press, 2012).

56. On Panama's transit history, see Aims McGuinness, *Path of Empire: Panama and the California Gold Rush* (Ithaca, NY: Cornell University Press, 2008), and Ashley Carse, *Beyond the Big Ditch: Politics, Ecology, and Infrastructure at the Panama Canal* (Cambridge, MA: MIT Press, 2014).

57. Glenda A. Walters, *Panama City* (Charleston, SC: Arcadia, 2008).

58. Derek Walcott, *The Antilles: Fragments of Epic Memory; The Nobel Lecture* (New York: Farrar, Straus & Giroux, 1993).

59. On European colonial fantasies of the Caribbean, see Peter Hulme, *Colonial Encounters: Europe and the Native Caribbean, 1492–1797* (London: Methuen, 1986).

60. Bob Friel, "8 Dream Beaches of the Caribbean: Sand, Sea and Palm Trees: Fantasies Come True Here," NBC News, May 11, 2005, http://www.nbcnews.com/id/7818136/ns/travel-romantic_getaways/t/dream-beaches-caribbean/#.VfhTbUuJlg0.

61. John S. Hogue, "Cheeseburger in Paradise: Tourism and Empire at the Edges of Vacationland," *American Quarterly* 63, no. 1 (March 2011): 203–14.

62. Wallace, *Mickey Mouse History*, 133–58.

63. Eduardo Galeano, *Open Veins of Latin America: Five Centuries of the Pillage of a Continent* (New York: Monthly Review Press, 1997), 2.

64. Mintz, *Sweetness and Power*. For more on sugar and Caribbean history, see Reinaldo Funes Monzote, *From Rainforest to Cane Field in Cuba: An Environmental History*

since 1492, trans. Alex Martin (Chapel Hill: University of North Carolina Press, 2008), and Frank Moya Pons, *History of the Caribbean: Plantations, Trade, and War in the Atlantic World* (Princeton, NJ: Markus Wiener, 2007).

65. On the history of export commodities from Latin America and Caribbean, see Stephen Topik, Carlos Marichal, and Zephyr Frank, eds., *From Silver to Cocaine: Latin American Commodity Chains and the Building of the World Economy, 1500–2000* (Durham, NC: Duke University Press, 2006), and Richard P. Tucker, *Insatiable Appetite: The United States and the Ecological Degradation of the Tropical World* (Berkeley: University of California Press, 2000).

66. John Soluri, *Banana Cultures: Agriculture, Consumption, and Environmental Change in Honduras and the United States* (Austin: University of Texas Press, 2005).

67. Mintz, *Sweetness and Power*, xxv.

68. Mimi Sheller, *Consuming the Caribbean: From Arawaks to Zombies* (London: Routledge, 2003), 14.

69. Walter Benjamin, "Theses on the Philosophy of History," in *Illuminations*, ed. Hannah Arendt, trans. Henry Zohn (New York: Schocken Books, 1968), 253–64.

70. Paul Gilroy, *The Black Atlantic: Modernity and Double Consciousness* (Cambridge, MA: Harvard University Press, 1993), 4.

71. On the metaphor of a ship at sea, see Hans Blumenberg, *Shipwreck with Spectator: Paradigm of a Metaphor for Existence*, trans. Steven Rendall (Cambridge: MIT Press, 1997).

72. United Fruit Company steamships, officially known as the Great White Fleet, echoed the US Navy's famous around-the-world expedition from December 16, 1907, to February 22, 1909, which was also popularly nicknamed the Great White Fleet. In both instances, the fleet of ships (military and civilian) represented the expansion of US power abroad.

73. John Soluri, "Empire's Footprint: The Ecological Dimensions of a Consumers' Republic," *OAH Magazine of History* 25, no. 4 (2011): 17.

74. On the history of the United Fruit Company in Central America and the Caribbean, see Aviva Chomsky, *West Indian Workers and the United Fruit Company in Costa Rica, 1870–1940* (Baton Rouge: Louisiana State University Press, 1996); Marcelo Bucheli, *Bananas and Business: The United Fruit Company in Colombia, 1899–2000* (New York: New York University Press, 2005); and Soluri, *Banana Cultures*.

75. Harry Foster, *A Tropical Tramp with the Tourists* (New York: Dodd, Mead, 1925), 305.

76. Eric Walrond, "Wharf Rats," in *Tropic Death* (New York: Collier Books, 1972), 72–73.

77. Marcus Garvey, "Autobiography: Articles from the Pittsburgh Courier," in *Marcus Garvey: Life and Lessons*, ed. Robert A. Hill and Barbara Bair (Berkeley: University of California Press, 1987), 88.

78. On the history of UNIA and Garvey, see Tony Martin, *Race First: The Ideological and Organizational Struggles of Marcus Garvey* (Dover, MA: Majority Press, 1986).

79. On Garveyism and its influence on the history of black travel in the Caribbean, see Frank A. Guridy, *Forging Diaspora: Afro-Cubans and African Americans in a World of Empire and Jim Crow* (Chapel Hill: University of North Carolina Press, 2010).

80. Claude Lévi-Strauss, *The Savage Mind* (Chicago: University of Chicago Press, 1966).

81. Tom Miller, *The Panama Hat Trail: A Journey from South America* (New York: Morrow, 1986).

82. Walter Benjamin, "Doctrine of the Similar," *New German Critique* 17, Special Walter Benjamin Issue (1979): 65–69. On mimesis, see Michael Taussig, *Mimesis and Alterity: A Particular History of the Senses* (New York: Routledge, 1993).

1. Empire's Lake

1. Winifred James, *The Mulberry Tree* (London: Chapman & Hall, 1913), 225.

2. "Tales of the Great White Fleet," *UNIFRUITCO* (August 1929): 24–25.

3. See Ashley Carse, Christine Keiner, Pamela M. Henson, Marixa Lasso, Paul S. Sutter, Megan Raby, and Blake Scott, "Panama Canal Forum: From the Conquest of Nature to the Construction of New Ecologies," *Environmental History* 21, no. 2 (2016): 206–87.

4. On the history of the Panama Canal construction project, ranging from triumphal to critical, see David G. McCullough, *The Path between the Seas: The Creation of the Panama Canal, 1870–1914* (New York: Simon & Schuster, 1977); Matthew Parker, *Panama Fever: The Epic Story of One of the Greatest Achievements of All Time—the Building of the Panama Canal* (New York: Doubleday, 2007); Alexander Missal, *Seaway to the Future: American Social Visions and the Construction of the Panama Canal* (Madison: University of Wisconsin Press, 2008); and Julie Greene, *The Canal Builders: Making America's Empire at the Panama Canal* (New York: Penguin, 2009).

5. Carse, *Beyond the Big Ditch*, 40.

6. Stephen Graham, *In Quest of El Dorado* (London: Macmillan, 1924), 167.

7. For the history of tropical disease and its relationship to mobility, see Mark Carey, "Inventing Caribbean Climates: How Science, Medicine, and Tourism Changed Tropical Weather from Deadly to Healthy," *Osiris* 26, no. 1 (2011): 129–41; Philip D. Curtin, *Death by Migration: Europe's Encounter with the Tropical World in the Nineteenth Century* (New York, 1989); and John Robert McNeill, *Mosquito Empires: Ecology and War in the Greater Caribbean* (New York: Cambridge University Press, 2010).

8. Richard Harding Davis, *Three Gringos in Venezuela and Central America* (New York: Harper & Brothers, 1896), 193. According to Theodore Roosevelt, the writings of Richard Harding Davis provided "a textbook of Americanism." See Beatriz Urraca, "A Textbook of Americanism: Richard Harding Davis's Soldiers of Fortune," in *Tropicalizations: Transcultural Representations of Latinidad*, ed. Frances R. Aparicio and Susana Chávez-Silverman (Hanover, NH: University Press of New England, 1997), 21–50.

9. Krista Thompson, *An Eye for the Tropics: Tourism, Photography, and Framing the Caribbean Picturesque* (Durham, NC: Duke University Press, 2007), 4–5.

10. Curtin, *Death by Migration*, 62.

11. On the historical relationship between tourism and transportation infrastructure but in the context of the American West, see Andrews, "Made by Toile," 837–63. On infrastructure and tourism mobility in Europe, see Andrew Denning, "From Sublime Landscapes to 'White Gold': How Skiing Transformed the Alps after 1930," *Environmental History* 19, no. 1 (2014): 78–108.

12. James, *Mulberry Tree*, 226.

13. Quoted in Missal, *Seaway to the Future*, 127.

14. Address of Theodore Roosevelt to the employees of the Isthmian Canal Commission, Colón, Panama, November 11, 1906, uncataloged, PCUF.

15. James, *Mulberry Tree*, 241.

16. The narrative of Haskins's journey comes from a series of newspaper clippings: W. C. Haskins, "Early Day Reminiscences," Richard W. Pat Beall Collection, PCUF. Haskins ended up staying in Panama and getting a job with the Isthmian Canal Commission but explained, "I was making some sacrifices."

17. On European and Euro-American perceptions of the tropics as dangerous and diseased, see Nancy Leys Stepan, *Picturing Tropical Nature* (London: Reaktion Books, 2001); specific to Panama, Stephen Frenkel, "Jungle Stories: North American Representations of Tropical Panama," *Geographical Review* 86, no. 3 (July 1996): 327. For the white's man grave narrative more generally, see Phillip D. Curtin, "'The White Man's Grave': Image and Reality, 1780–1850," *Journal of British Studies* 1, no. 1 (November 1961): 94–110.

18. In 1855 a railroad connecting Colón with Panama City was completed, making the trip much faster across the isthmus. See McGuinness, *Path of Empire*, and Robert D. Aguirre, *Mobility and Modernity: Panama in the Nineteenth Century Anglo-American Imagination* (Columbus: Ohio State University Press, 2017).

19. James Clark Diary (1851–1852), box 1, Canal Zone Library-Museum Panama Collection, LOC. From the records, it is unclear if Clark survived the illness he reported in his 1852 journal.

20. Alfredo Castillero Calvo, *Historia general de Panamá* (Panama City: Comisión Nacional del Centenario, 2004); Christopher Ward, *Imperial Panama: Commerce and Conflict in Isthmian America, 1550–1800* (Albuquerque: University of New Mexico Press, 1993).

21. During the colonial era, the dangers of the Caribbean tropics also worked as a natural defense against intrusions from other European colonial powers and settlers. Disease wiped out invading armies and adventurers coming from more temperate zones. See McNeill, *Mosquito Empires*.

22. McCullough, *Path between the Seas*, 124–203.

23. Mariola Espinosa, *Epidemic Invasions: Yellow Fever and the Limits of Cuban Independence, 1878–1930* (Chicago: University of Chicago Press, 2009).

24. Timothy C. Winegard, *The Mosquito: A Human History of Our Deadliest Predator* (Melbourne, Australia: Text Publishing, 2019), 354.

25. William Crawford Gorgas, *Sanitation in Panama* (New York: D. Appleton, 1915), 6–7.

26. Quoted in McCullough, *Path Between the Seas*, 451.

27. Mariola Espinosa, "The Question of Racial Immunity to Yellow Fever in History and Historiography," *Social Science History* 38, nos. 3–4 (Fall/Winter 2014): 437–53.

28. Michael L. Conniff, *Black Labor on a White Canal: Panama, 1904–1981* (Pittsburgh: University of Pittsburgh Press, 1985). Conniff estimated that the total number of deaths in the West Indian community approached fifteen thousand—one out of every ten migrants.

29. For the canal's influence in Afro-Caribbean diaspora literature, see Rhonda Frederick, *Colón Man a Come: Mythographies of Panama Canal Migration* (Lanham, MD: Lexington Books, 2005), and Lara Putnam, *Radical Moves: Caribbean Migrants and the Politics of Race in the Jazz Age* (Chapel Hill: University of North Carolina Press, 2013).

30. Letter from Albert Peters, box 25, Canal Zone Library-Museum Panama Collection, LOC.

31. For critical reads of race and the canal, see Conniff, *Black Labor on a White Canal*, and Marixa Lasso, *Erased: The Untold Story of the Panama Canal* (Cambridge, MA: Harvard University Press, 2019).

32. Farnham Bishop, *Panama, Past and Present* (New York: Century, 1916), 203.

33. See Natalie J. Ring, "Mapping Regional and Imperial Geographies: Tropical Disease in the U.S. South," in *Colonial Crucible: Empire in the Making of the Modern American State*, ed. Alfred W. McCoy and Francisco A. Scarano (Madison: University of Wisconsin Press, 2009), 299.

34. See Greene, *Canal Builders*, and Conniff, *Black Labor on a White Canal*.

35. Haskins, "Early Day Reminiscences."

36. Alfred Kimball Hills, ed., "Hygiene at Panama," *Medical Times: A Monthly Journal of Medicine* 36 (April 1908): 114. Another famous visitor to the isthmus, quoted by the journal, reasoned that "nowhere else on earth was there concentrated in a single spot so much foul disease, such a hideous dungheap of moral and physical abomination."

37. Marie D. Gorgas and Burton J. Hendrick, *William Crawford Gorgas: His Life and Work* (Garden City, NY: Doubleday, 1924).

38. For the history of yellow fever in Cuba, see Espinosa, *Epidemic Invasions*.

39. Gorgas and Hendrick, *William Crawford Gorgas*, 201.

40. McCullough, *Path between the Seas*, 405–26.

41. At the turn of the century, the British developed similar health campaigns to deal with malaria in West Africa and India. See Ronald Ross, *Mosquito Brigades and How to Organize Them* (London: George Philip, 1902).

42. Paul S. Sutter, "Nature's Agents or Agents of Empire? Entomological Workers and Environmental Change during the Construction of the Panama Canal," *Isis* 98, no. 4 (December 2007): 724–54.

43. William Crawford Gorgas, "The Conquest of the Tropics for the White Race," president's address at the Sixtieth Annual Session of the American Medical Association, Atlantic City, NJ, June 9, 1909, *Journal of the American Medical Association* 52, no. 25 (1909): 1967–69.

44. Joseph Pennell, *Pictures of the Panama Canal* (Philadelphia: J. B. Lippincott, 1912), 10.

45. Frenkel, "Jungle Stories," 327.

46. Lasso, *Erased*, 154–90.

47. Quoted in Michael Adas, *Dominance by Design: Technological Imperatives and America's Civilizing Mission* (Cambridge, MA: Belknap Press of Harvard University Press, 2006), 186.

48. Address of Roosevelt to employees of the Isthmian Canal Commission, Colón, Panama, November 11, 1906.

49. Arthur Bullard, *Panama: The Canal, the Country, and the People* (New York: Macmillan, 1914), 66. For a sampling of canal triumphal literature, see Willis J. Abbot, *Panama and the Canal in Picture and Prose* (New York: Syndicate Publishing, 1913); Emory Adams Allen, *Our Canal in Panama: The Greatest Achievement in the World's History* (Cincinnati: United States Publishing, 1913); and Ralph Emmett Avery, *America's Triumph at Panama* (Chicago: L. W. Walter, 1913).

50. Bullard, *Panama*, 66–67.

51. Gorgas, "Conquest of the Tropics for the White Race," 1967–69.

52. Letter from President Theodore Roosevelt, August 21, 1908, *Canal Record*, September 9, 1908.

53. "The Great White Fleet," advertisement in *Scribner's Magazine*, 1916, from Wikimedia Commons, accessed December 10, 2014, https://commons.wikimedia.org/wiki/File:United_Fruit_Ad_1916.jpg.

54. Quoted in Cocks, *Tropical Whites*, 91.

55. Quoted in Paul S. Sutter, "Tropical Conquest and the Rise of the Environmental Management State," in McCoy and Scarano, *Colonial Crucible*, 317.

56. Erastus Howard Scott, *Panama, Yosemite, Yellowstone* (Chicago: Scott, Foresman, 1925), 13.

57. Sutter, "Tropical Conquest," 318.

58. Quoted in Missal, *Seaway to the Future*, 69.

59. Sutter, "Nature's Agents or Agents of Empire?," 724–54.

60. On the history of disease and mosquitoes in the US South, see Margaret Humphreys, *Yellow Fever and the South* (New Brunswick, NJ: Rutgers University Press, 1992), and Gordon Patterson, *The Mosquito Crusades: A History of the American Anti-Mosquito Movement from the Reed Commission to the First Earth Day* (New Brunswick, NJ: Rutgers University Press, 2009).

61. On Cuba's long-running fight for independence, see Ada Ferrer, *Insurgent Cuba: Race, Nation, and Revolution, 1868–1898* (Chapel Hill: University of North Carolina Press, 1999), and Louis A. Pérez, *The War of 1898: The United States and Cuba in History and Historiography* (Chapel Hill: University of North Carolina Press, 1998).

62. On the 1903 treaty between the United States and Panama, see Ovidio Diaz Espino, *How Wall Street Created a Nation: J. P. Morgan, Teddy Roosevelt, and the Panama Canal* (New York: Basic Books, 2003), and Walter LaFeber, *The Panama Canal: The Crisis in Historical Perspective* (New York: Oxford University Press, 1978).

63. Brooks Adams, "The Spanish War and the Equilibrium of the World," *The Forum* 25, no. 6 (March–August 1898): 648.

64. Alfred T. Mahan, "The United States Looking Outward," *Atlantic Monthly*, December 1890, 816–24. See also Alfred T. Mahan, *The Interest of America in Sea Power, Present and Future* (London: Sampson Low, Marston, 1897).

65. On the history of US imperial expansion, see Matthew Frye Jacobson, *Barbarian Virtues: The United States Encounters Foreign Peoples at Home and Abroad, 1876–1917* (New York: Hill & Wang, 2000); Daniel Immerwahr, *How to Hide an Empire: A History of the Greater United States* (New York: Farrar, Straus & Giroux, 2019); and Greg Grandin, *The End of the Myth: From the Frontier to the Border Wall in the Mind of America* (New York: Metropolitan Books, 2019).

66. David Healy, *Drive to Hegemony: The United States in the Caribbean, 1898–1917* (Madison: University of Wisconsin Press, 1988).

67. Abbot, *Panama and the Canal*, 8.

68. Jefferson B. Browne, *Key West: The Old and the New* (St. Augustine, FL: Record, 1912), 114. For more on Key West's historical role in the Spanish-American War, see Wright Langley and Joan Langley, *Key West and the Spanish American War* (Key West: Langley, 1998).

69. Brochure, "Florida East Coast Railway Guide, 1911," RUs 2521–30, FEUF.

70. Quoted in Louis A. Pérez, *Cuba under the Platt Amendment, 1902–1934* (Pittsburgh: University of Pennsylvania Press, 1986), 44.

71. Abbot, *Panama and the Canal*, 360.

72. *Canal Record*, March 18, 1908.

73. Frederick Haskins, *The Panama Canal* (Garden City, NY: Doubleday, 1914), 170.

74. "Chairman and Chief Engineer, George W. Goethals to Secretary of War, Washington D.C., 5 November, 1910," box 112, file 13-K-15, RG 185, Records of the Panama Canal, NARA.

75. Rosa Luxemburg, "The Idea of May Day on the March," in *Selected Political Writings of Rosa Luxemburg*, ed. Dick Howard (New York: Monthly Review Press, 1971), 317.

76. Bishop, *Panama, Past and Present*, 241.

77. See McGuinness, *Path of Empire*, 12. McGuinness argues that "rather than separate stages or competing processes, the making of the United States as a transcontinental nation and U.S. expansion overseas in Panama were coincident with one another and intertwined."

78. Bullard, *Panama*, 45.

79. Gorgas and Hendrick, *William Crawford Gorgas*, 1–68.

80. Clifford Foust, *John Frank Stevens: Civil Engineer* (Bloomington: University Press of Indiana, 2013).

81. "Biographical Notes," *Yearbook: Society of the Chagres*, 1911–17, PCUF.

82. Frederick Jackson Turner, "The Significance of the Frontier in American History," presented at the meeting of the American Historical Association, Chicago, July 12, 1893, http://nationalhumanitiescenter.org/pds/gilded/empire/text1/turner.pdf.

83. William Appleman Williams, "The Frontier Thesis and American Foreign Policy," *Pacific Historical Review* 24, no. 4 (November 1955): 379–95.

84. On the meaning of the frontier in US history, see Kerwin L. Klein, *Frontiers of Historical Imagination: Narrating the European Conquest of Native America, 1890–1990* (Berkeley: University of California Press, 1997).

85. For an early and now classic critique of the culture of manifest destiny, see Albert Weinberg, *Manifest Destiny: A Study of Nationalist Expansionism in American History* (Baltimore: Johns Hopkins University Press, 1935). On the relationship between the western frontier and tourism, see Anne Farrar Hyde, *An American Vision: Far Western Landscape and National Culture, 1820–1920* (New York: New York University Press, 1990).

86. On US imperialism in the Pacific, see Rebecca McKenna, *American Imperial Pastoral: The Architecture of US Colonialism in the Philippines* (Chicago: University of Chicago Press, 2017).

87. *Yearbook: Society of the Chagres*, 1915, PCUF.

88. On the history of US military activities and illicit nightlife in Panama, see Jeffrey Wayne Parker, "Empire's Angst: The Politics of Race, Migration, and Sex Work in Panama, 1903–1945" (PhD diss., University of Texas at Austin, 2013), and Matthew Scalena, "Illicit Nation: State, Empire, and Illegality on the Isthmus of Panama" (PhD diss., Stony Brook University, 2013).

89. *Yearbook: Society of the Chagres*, 1915, PCUF.

90. William Appleman Williams, *Empire as a Way of Life: An Essay on the Causes and Character of America's Present Predicament, along with a Few Thoughts about an Alternative* (New York: Oxford University Press, 1980).

91. On the conquest of the American West and popular entertainers, see Louis S. Warren, *Buffalo Bill's America: William Cody and the Wild West Show* (New York: Alfred A. Knopf, 2005).

92. *Annual Report of the Board of Regents of the Smithsonian Institution, Showing the Operations, Expenditures, and Condition of the Institution for the Year Ending June 30 1924* (Washington, DC: GPO, 1925), 358–62, SIA.

93. *Panama Times*, March 19, 1927.

94. "Biographical Notes," *Yearbook: Society of the Chagres*, 1911, PCUF.

95. The *Panama Times* can be accessed at National Library of Panama, Ernesto J. Castillero R., Panama City.

96. John O. Collins, *The Panama Guide* (Mount Hope, Canal Zone: ICC Press, 1912); John O. Collins, *Recreation in Panama* (Culebra, Canal Zone: self-pub., 1914).

97. *Canal Record*, December 18, 1912.

98. *Yearbook: Society of the Chagres*, 1913, PCUF. W. M. Baxter seemed to like making fun of himself and the tourists he had to show around: "My wife admits that I am naturally mean, but I will not. At least it was not meanness that made me act so badly in the case of the man with the umbrella," who was a tourist.

99. Harry A. Franck, *Zone Policeman 88: A Close Range Study of the Panama Canal and Its Workers* (New York: Century, 1913), 312.

2. Service Sector Republics

1. On UFCO's fleet of ships, see Mark H. Goldberg, *"Going Bananas": 100 Years of American Fruit Ships in the Caribbean* (Kings Point, NY: American Merchant Marine Museum, 1993).

2. Correspondence between Panamanian president Florencio Harmodio Arosemena and Cuban president Gerardo Machado y Morales, November 1928, Legación de Panamá en Cuba, 1928, AMRE.

3. Quoted in George Roberts, *Economic Survey of the Republic of Panama*, 1929, ABRA, printed in Spanish, *Investigación económica de la República de Panamá* (Panama City: Imprenta Nacional, 1930).

4. Guillermo Andreve, *Cómo atraer el turismo a Panamá* (Panama City: Edición oficial, 1929).

5. On the history of tourism in Cuba and state legislation supporting the industry, see Schwartz, *Pleasure Island*; Evaristo Villalba Garrido, *Cuba y el turismo* (Havana: Editorial de Ciencias Sociales, 1993); and Andrea Colantonio and Robert B. Potter, *Urban Tourism and Development in the Socialist State: Havana during the "Special Period"* (Burlington, VT: Ashgate, 2006), 91.

6. Andreve, *Cómo atraer el turismo a Panamá*.

7. Rodrigo Miró, "Don Guillermo Andreve y su labor literaria," *Epocas* (July 2000): 3; Guillermo Andreve, "Escritos de Andreve," *Revista Lotería*, nos. 282–84 (August–October 1979). In addition to his own writing, Andreve founded and directed *El Heraldo del Istmo*, *El Cosmos*, and the literary journal *La Biblioteca de Cultura Nacional*.

8. Peter A. Szok, *La última gaviota: Liberalism and Nostalgia in Early Twentieth-Century Panama* (Westport, CT: Greenwood, 2001).

9. Michael Gobat, *Empire by Invitation: William Walker and Manifest Destiny in Central America* (Cambridge, MA: Harvard University Press, 2018).

10. On the history of liberalism in Latin America and the Caribbean, see E. Bradford Burns, *The Poverty of Progress: Latin America in the Nineteenth Century* (Berkeley: University of California Press, 1983). For more country specific studies, see, for Panama, Szok, *La última gaviota*, and, for Cuba, Louis A. Pérez, *Cuba: Between Reform and Revolution* (Oxford: Oxford University Press, 2010).

11. Roberts, *Economic Survey of the Republic of Panama*, 190. Cocks notes a similar relationship between tourism and land development in her book *Tropical Whites*, 46: "Tourism for all of these entities remained intimately tied to colonization, and nearly all the publicity materials extant from the turn of the twentieth century reflect the same assumption that visitors were essentially prospective citizens."

12. Arturo Escobar, *Encountering Development: The Making and Unmaking of the Third World* (Princeton, NJ: Princeton University Press, 1995), 47.

13. Szok, *La última gaviota*, 7.

14. Legación de Panamá en Cuba, 1928, AMRE.

15. Mintz, *Sweetness and Power*, xxix.

16. Amanda Stronza, "Anthropology of Tourism: Forging New Ground for Ecotourism and Other Alternatives," *Annual Review of Anthropology* 30 (2001): 269.

17. Frederick Cooper and Jane Burbank, *Empires in World History: Power and the Politics of Difference* (Princeton, NJ: Princeton University Press, 2010), 4.

18. Patricia Pizzurno Gelós and Celestino Andrés Araúz, eds., *La modernización del estado panameño bajo las administraciones de Belisario Porras y Arnulfo Arias Madrid* (Panama City: Editorial Mariano Arosemena del Instituto Nacional de Cultura, 1992).

19. On José Martí and his writings, see Jeffrey Belnap and Raúl Fernández, eds., *José Martí's "Our America": From National to Hemispheric Cultural Studies* (Durham, NC: Duke University Press, 1998).

20. Belisario Porras, *Trozos de la vida* (San José, Costa Rica: Imprenta Alsina, Sauter, Arias, 1931). For more on Porras's life, see Manuel Octavio Sisnett, *Belisario Porras o la vocación de la nacionalidad* (Panama City: Imprenta Universitaria, 1972).

21. See Belisario Porras, *La venta del istmo: Manifesto a la nación* (Panama City: Editorial Portobelo, 1996).

22. Ernesto J. Castillero Reyes, *La causa inmediata de la emancipación de Panamá: Historia de los orígenes, la formación y el rechazo por el senado colombiano, del tratado Herrán-Hay* (Panama City: Imprenta Nacional, 1933), 108.

23. Porras, *Trozos de la vida*, 107–8.

24. See Patricia Pizzurno Gelós and Celestino Andrés Araúz, *Estudios sobre el Panamá Republicano, 1903–1999* (Cali, Colombia: Manfer, 1996), 207–55.

25. "La flota llega el 18, con que la espera usted?," *El Diario Nuevo*, February 2, 1923; "Tourists Should Follow Example of U.S. Sailors," *Star and Herald*, February 27, 1931.

26. Parker, "Empire's Angst," 217.

27. Porras, *Trozos de la vida*, vii.

28. On the San Francisco exposition celebrating the Panama Canal, see Robert W. Rydell, *All the World's Fair: Visions of Empire at American International Expositions, 1876–1916* (Chicago: University of Chicago Press, 1987), 208–33.

29. Exposición Nacional de Panamá: Commemorativa al Descubrimiento del Océano Pacífico Porras, vol. 24, ABP. The *Pan-American Magazine* is available online at the Hathi Trust Digital Library, http://catalog.hathitrust.org/Record/000636937.

30. *Canal Record*, March 24, 1915.

31. Exposición Nacional de Panamá, vol. 24.

32. John O. Collins, "The Panama Canal and Its Jonah," *Pan-American Magazine* 22, no. 2 (November 1915): 111.

33. *Memoria que el secretario de estado en el despacho de fomento presenta a la Asambela Nacional de 1914* (Panama City: Diario de Panamá, 1914). Note that all *memorias* (government reports) cited in this chapter are housed at the Biblioteca Nacional de Panamá, Ernesto J. Castillero R., Panama City.

34. Correspondence between James Zetek and President Porras, June 1915, Exposición Nacional de Panamá, vol. 24.

35. On the relationship between tourism and development projects in Cuba, see Armando Maribona, *Turismo y ciudadania* (Havana: Grafica Moderna, 1943).

36. "Ideas del presidente sobre agricultura e inmigración," *El Diario de Panama*, January 2, 1923.

37. Benjamin Kidd, *Social Evolution* (New York: Macmillan, 1894), 316. For a critical analysis of racist political thinking in Latin America, see Nancy Leys Stepan, *The Hour of Eugenics: Race, Gender, and Nation in Latin America* (Ithaca, NY: Cornell University Press, 1991).

38. Aviva Chomsky, "'Barbados or Canada?' Race, Immigration, and Nation in Early-Twentieth-Century Cuba," *Hispanic American Historical Review* 80, no. 3 (August 2000): 420.

39. Fernando Ortiz, "La inmigración desde el punto de vista criminológico," *Derecho y Sociología* 1, no. 5 (May 1906): 55.

40. On tourism and lifestyle migration, see Ana K. Spalding, "Lifestyle Migration to Bocas del Toro, Panama: Exploring Migration Strategies and Introducing Local Implications of the Search for Paradise," *International Review of Social Research* 3, no. 1 (February 2013): 67–86.

41. Alfredo Castillero Calvo, "Transitismo y dependencia: El caso del istmo de Panamá," *Nueva Sociedad*, no. 5 (1973): 35–50.

42. Hernán F. Porras, *Papel histórico de los grupos humanos en Panamá* (Panama City: Editorial Portobelo, 1998).

43. Marco A. Gandásegui, ed., *Las clases sociales en Panamá: Grupos humanos, clases medias, elites y oligarquía* (Panama City: Centro de Estudio Latinoamericanos, 2008).

44. "Comunicaciones y telegramas de diversas entidades comerciales, apoyando las gestiones que realizaba el comité acción turística para que se sometan a la consideración de las clases económicas las modificaciones que se vaya hacer en la legislación sobre turismo," Havana, February 21–July 18, 1934, box 85, Secretaria de Presidencia, ANC, Havana.

45. "First Airmail Miami-Cristobal-Miami, Charles A. Lindbergh, 2/4/29–2/13/29," collection 341, box 250, folder 6, PAW.

46. See Andreve, *Cómo atraer el turismo a Panamá*, and Maribona, *Turismo y ciudadania*.

47. Interview with Luis Machado, Oral History Program, World Bank / IFC Archives, July 18, 1961, http://oralhistory.worldbank.org/transcript/machado/transcript-oral-history-interview-luis-machado-held-july-18-1961; "Luis Machado, 79, Ex-Envoy of Cuba," *Washington Post*, February 10, 1979.

48. Luis Machado y Ortega, *Informe*, June 14, 1941, Presidencia de Arnulfo A. Madrid, box 6, ANP.

49. Ora E. Chapin, "Across Boundary Lines: Rotarians of Cuba and Florida Adopt Rotary's Good-Will Formula," *The Rotarian* 36 (January 1930): 26–27, 48.

50. "Memorandum mecanografico, referente al escrito que dirige A.T. Moreaux, al presidente de la republica, considerando ser el momento propicio para aumentar el turismo en Cuba, y solicitandole una entrevista a fin de exponerle su proyecto de fomento turistico. Adjunto dicho escrito," Havana, 19 de agosto de 1925, box 85, Secretaria de Presidencia, ANC.

51. Chapin, "Across Boundary Lines," 26–27, 48. For more on the Miami-Cuba tourism connection, see Rose, "Tourism and the Hispanicization of Race in Jim Crow Miami," 735–56, and Louis A. Pérez Jr., *On Becoming Cuban: Identity, Nationality, and Culture* (Chapel Hill: University of North Carolina Press, 1999).

52. Consulado de Panamá en Miami, box 1, correspondence, 1931–42, ANP.

53. In Panama, Patricia Pizzurno Gelós surveys many of these tourism laws, decrees, and contracts in her article "El turismo y el patrimonio en el Panamá republicano," *Revista Canto Rodado*, no. 2 (2007): 1–22.

54. *Memoria que el secretario de estado.*

55. "New York Men Offer to Build Panama Hotel," *Panama American*, January 1, 1929.

56. "Panama All-Year Resort Is Aim of Association," *Panama American*, January 1, 1929.

57. T. J. English, *Havana Nocturne: How the Mob Owned Cuba and Then Lost It to the Revolution* (New York: William Morrow, 2008), 1–29.

58. For more on the Mafia's influence in Cuba, see Enrique Cirules, *The Empire of Havana* (Havana: Editorial José Martí, 2003).

59. Luis Machado y Ortega, *Informe*, June 14, 1941, Presidencia de Arnulfo A. Madrid, box 6. ANP.

60. Matt Scalena, "La economía del vicio," *La Prensa*, May 18, 2014.

61. Letters from fiscal agent to President Porras, August 1924, box 663, ABP.

62. On alcohol sales and smuggling from Cuba and the Caribbean, see Lisa Lindquist Dorr, *A Thousand Thirsty Beaches: Smuggling Alcohol from Cuba to the South during Prohibition* (Chapel Hill: University of North Carolina Press, 2018).

63. Quoted in Szok, *La última gaviota*, 47.

64. Mark Kurlansky, *Havana: A Subtropical Delirium* (New York: Bloomsbury, 2017), 96.

65. Demetrio Korsi, "Visión de Panamá," in *Los gringos llegan y la cumbia se va* (Panama City: Imprenta Excelsior, 1953).

66. For US perceptions of Panama, see Frenkel, "Jungle Stories," 327. There is also a large literature on US and European perceptions of the American tropics. See, for instance, Pratt, *Imperial Eyes*, and Frederick B. Pike, *The United States and Latin America: Myths and Stereotypes of Civilization and Nature* (Austin: University of Texas Press, 1992).

67. Parker, "Empire's Angst," 75.

68. Quoted in Stephen Birmingham, *"The Rest of Us:" The Rise of America's Eastern European Jews* (Syracuse, NY: Syracuse University Press, 1999), 152. Birmingham explains that this statement by Meyer Lansky "among his friends . . . quickly became known as 'Lansky's Law,' and it would become the basic precept by which organized crime would live from that point onward, just as legitimate capitalist society lived by, and had been living by it, all along."

69. Kurlansky, *Havana*, 93.

70. Parker, "Empire's Angst."

71. *Panama Times*, February 29, 1926.

72. Dorr, *Thousand Thirsty Beaches*, 19.

73. Andreve, *Cómo atraer el turismo a Panamá*, 23.

74. Andreve, *Cómo atraer el turismo a Panamá*, 23.

75. English, *Havana Nocturne*, 4.

76. On the assassination of President José Remón Cantera, see Larry LaRae Pippins, *The Remón Era: An Analysis of a Decade of Events in Panama, 1947–1957* (Stanford, CA: Stanford University Press, 1964).

77. On more recent history of drug trafficking in Central America and the Caribbean, see Julie Marie Bunck and Michael Ross Fowler, *Bribes, Bullets, and Intimidation: Drug Trafficking and the Law in Central America* (University Park: Pennsylvania State University Press, 2012.)

78. On Panamanian folklore, see Alfredo Figueroa Navarro, ed., *El desarrollo de las ciencias sociales en Panamá* (Panama City: Universidad de Panamá, 1983).

79. Pizzurno, "El turismo y el patrimonio," 21–22.

80. Hal Rothman and William P. Clements, eds. *The Culture of Tourism, the Tourism of Culture: Selling the Past to the Present in the American Southwest* (Albuquerque: University of New Mexico Press, 2003).

81. Putnam, *Radical Moves*, 19.

82. Marixa Lasso, "Race and Ethnicity in the Formation of Panamanian National Identity: Panamanian Discrimination against Chinese and West Indians in the Thirties," *Revista Panameña de Política*, no. 4 (July–December 2007): 63.

83. *Star and Herald*, October 23, 1926.

84. George Westerman, *A Minority Group in Panama: Some Aspects of West Indian Life* (Panama City: National Civic League, 1950), 15.

85. Guridy, *Forging Diaspora*, 157.

86. "RP Discriminates in Entry Laws, Writer Charges," *The Nation*, November 22, 1947.

87. Letter from George Westerman to President Jose Antonio Remon, July 30, 1953, George W. Westerman Papers, box 63, SCRBC.

88. B. Traven, *The Death Ship* (1926; repr., Chicago: Chicago Review Press, 1991), 57.

89. On the ways racism continues to play out in the tourism industry, see L. Kaifa Roland, *Cuban Color in Tourism and La Lucha: An Ethnography of Racial Meanings* (New York: Oxford University Press, 2011.)

3. Changing Routes from Sea to Air

1. "The Air-Way to Havana," Pan American Airways promotional brochure (n.d.), collection 341, box 248, folder 11, PAW.

2. Newspaper and Pan Am public relations clippings from the folder "First Passenger Flight, Key West-Havana, January 16, 1928," collection 341, box 248, folder 11, PAW.

3. See James R. Hansen, "Aviation in the Wider View," *Technology and Culture* 30, no. 3 (July 1989): 643–56. On Pan Am's history, see Eugene Banning, *Airlines of Pan*

American since 1927: Its Airlines, Its People, and Its Aircraft (McLean, VA: Paladwr, 2001); Barnaby Conrad, *Pan Am: An Aviation Legend* (Emeryville, CA: Woodford, 1999); R. E. G. Davies, *Pan Am: An Airline and Its Aircraft* (Twickenham, UK: Hamlyn, 1987); and Matthew Josephson, *Empire of the Air: Juan Trippe and the Struggle for World Airways* (New York: Harcourt, Brace, 1944).

4. Jennifer Van Vleck, *Empire of the Air: Aviation and the American Ascendancy* (Cambridge, MA: Harvard University Press, 2013.)

5. Karl Marx, publishing *Grundrisse* in 1857, first explained his theory of the annihilation of space by time. He wrote, "While capital must on one side strive to tear down every spatial barrier to intercourse, i.e. to exchange, and conquer the whole earth for its market, it strives on the other side to annihilate this space with time, i.e. to reduce to a minimum the time spent in motion from one place to another." Karl Marx, *Grundrisse: Foundations of the Critique of Political Economy*, trans. Martin Nicolaus (New York: Vintage, 1973), 538.

6. Inspired by scholars such as Immanuel Wallerstein, we must "unthink" what we think we know about the modern world. Our present is a complex historical collage of taken-for-granted transformations. See Immanuel Wallerstein, *World-Systems Analysis: An Introduction* (Durham, NC: Duke University Press, 2006).

7. For an excellent history of the first decades of aviation, see Robert Wohl, *The Spectacle of Flight: Aviation and the Western Imagination, 1920–1950* (New Haven, CT: Yale University Press, 2005).

8. On the history of modern technology's relationship to cultural change, see Stephen Kern, *The Culture of Time and Space, 1880–1918* (Cambridge, MA: Harvard University Press, 2003); David Harvey, *The Condition of Postmodernity: An Enquiry into the Origins of Cultural Change* (Cambridge, MA: Blackwell, 1990); and John Agnew, "The New Global Economy: Time-Space Compression, Geopolitics, and Global Uneven Development," *Journal of World-Systems Research* 7, no. 2 (Fall 2001): 133–54.

9. Christian Beyer, "Edmund Husserl," Stanford Encyclopedia of Philosophy, November 18, 2020, https://plato.stanford.edu/entries/husserl/. For classic texts on phenomenology, see Edmund Husserl, *Ideas: A General Introduction to Pure Phenomenology* (1931; repr., New York: Collier Books, 1963); Martin Heidegger, *The Basic Problems of Phenomenology*, trans. Alfred Hofstader (1975; repr., Bloomington: Indiana University Press, 1982); and Jean Paul Sartre, *Being and Nothingness*, trans. Hazel Barnes (1943; repr., New York: Washington Square, 1956).

10. Stephen Crane, *The Open Boat and Other Tales of Adventure* (New York: Doubleday & McClure, 1898), 3.

11. On the literary importance of Crane's depiction of sea travel, see Bert Bender, "The Nature and Significance of 'Experience' in 'The Open Boat,'" *Journal of Narrative Technique* 9, no. 2 (Spring 1979): 70–80.

12. Ernest Hemingway, "On the Blue Water: A Gulf Stream Letter," *Esquire*, April 1936.

13. On the cultural significance of ships and the sea, see Blumenberg, *Shipwreck with Spectator*.

14. Herman Melville, *Moby-Dick; or, The White Whale* (1851; repr., Boston: C. H. Simonds, 1892), 7.

15. Zuelow, *History of Modern Tourism*, 58.

16. Paul Sutter, "The Tropics: A Brief History of an Environmental Imaginary," in *Oxford Handbook of Environmental History*, ed. Andrew Isenberg (New York: Oxford University Press), 178–204.

17. "Underwater Cultural Heritage," UNESCO, accessed August 1, 2018, http://www.unesco.org/new/en/culture/themes/underwater-cultural-heritage/underwater-cultural-heritage/wrecks/.

18. On Columbus's journey and the ancient ideologies of geography and navigation guiding him, see Nicolás Wey Gómez, *The Tropics of Empire: Why Columbus Sailed South to the Indies* (Cambridge, MA: MIT Press, 2008). On hurricanes in the Caribbean, see Stuart Schwartz, *Sea of Storms: A History of Hurricanes in the Greater Caribbean from Columbus to Katrina* (Princeton, NJ: Princeton University Press, 2015).

19. Bernard Bailyn, *Atlantic History: Concepts and Contours* (Cambridge, MA: Harvard University Press, 2005).

20. Derek Howse, *Greenwich Time and the Discovery of Longitude* (London: Philip Wilson, 1997); P. Kenneth Seidelmann and Catherine Y. Hohenkerk, eds., *The History of Celestial Navigation: Rise of the Royal Observatory and Nautical Almanacs* (New York: Springer, 2020).

21. Alex Roland, W. Jeffrey Bolster, and Alexander Keyssar, *The Way of the Ship: America's Maritime History Reenvisioned, 1600–2000* (Hoboken, NJ: John Wiley, 2008).

22. Mahan, "The United States Looking Outward," 816–24.

23. Roland, Bolster, and Keyssar, *Way of the Ship*, 255–63.

24. Joseph Conrad, *The Mirror of the Sea* (New York: Doubleday, 1926), 72.

25. "Havana Newspaper Man Describes Plane Trip from That City Here," *Key West Citizen*, January 21, 1928, collection 341, box 248, folder 11, PAW.

26. Charles A. Lindbergh, *Autobiography of Values* (New York: Harcourt Brace Jovanovich, 1977), 63–64.

27. "The Logic of the Air," *Fortune* 27, April 1943, 72–74, quoted in Van Vleck, *Empire of the Air*, 3–4.

28. For an overview of cultural impacts of aviation in the United States, see Dominick Pisano, ed., *The Airplane in American Culture* (Ann Arbor: University of Michigan Press, 2003).

29. Arjun Appadurai, *Modernity at Large: Cultural Dimensions of Globalization* (Minneapolis: University of Minnesota Press, 1996), 37–39.

30. On modern flight's alienating effects, see Walter Kirn, *Up in the Air: A Novel* (New York: Doubleday, 2001.)

31. In the midst of imperial competition, Pan Am was slow to expand its services to French-controlled islands in the Caribbean. "The French," as one Smithsonian scientist observed, "were saving the franchise for some French company." Letter from Waldo Schmitt to Alexander Wetmore, March 6, 1937, RU 7231, box 91, SIA.

32. Alex Roland, *Model Research: The National Advisory Committee for Aeronautics, 1915–1958* (Washington, DC: NASA, 1985.) See Pub. L. 271, 63rd Cong., 3rd sess., passed March 3, 1915 (38 Stat. 930), accessed, December 1, 2018, https://history.nasa.gov/SP-4103/app-a.htm#1.

33. Van Vleck, *Empire of the Air*, 28.

34. On US federal funding of scientific and technological development, see Hunter A. Dupree, *Science in the Federal Government: A History of Policies and Activities to 1940* (New York: Harper & Row, 1964).

35. Rosalie Schwartz, *Flying down to Rio: Hollywood, Tourists, and Yankee Clippers* (College Station: Texas A&M Press, 2004), 221–58.

36. Marilyn Bender and Selig Altschul, *The Chosen Instrument: Pan Am, Juan Trippe, the Rise and Fall of an American Entrepreneur* (New York: Simon & Schuster, 1982).

37. "First Passenger Flight, Key West-Havana, January 16, 1928," collection 341, box 248, folder 11, PAW.

38. Quoted in James Brown Scott, "The Sixth Pan American Conference," *American Journal of International Law* 22, no. 2 (April 1928): 351–62.

39. "Panama's Distinctive Stability," *Panama Times*, January 23, 1926.

40. "First Airmail Miami-Cristobal-Miami, 1929," collection 341, box 250, folder 6, PAW.

41. Banning, *Airlines of Pan Am since 1927*. Today the old Pan Am air terminal is Miami's city hall.

42. For a visual history of clipper ships, see Richard Woodman, *The History of the Ship: The Comprehensive Story of Seafaring form the Earliest Times to the Present Day* (London: Conway Maritime, 2005).

43. Van Vleck, *Empire of the Air*, 1–17.

44. Roger Connor, "Amelia Earhart and the Profession of Air Navigation," Smithsonian National Air and Space Museum, February 12, 2013, https://airand-space.si.edu/stories/editorial/amelia-earhart-and-profession-air-navigation.

45. "Profits from Passengers," undated article, collection 341, box 248, folder 11, PAW.

46. Alain Pelletier, *Boeing: The Complete Story* (Sparkford, UK: Haynes, 2010).

47. Quoted in Anne Jacobsen, *Operation Paperclip: The Secret Intelligence Program That Brought Nazi Scientists to America* (New York: Little, Brown, 2014), 52.

48. Van Vleck, *Empire of the Air*, 241–47. See Peter Dunn, "Why Hasn't Commercial Air Travel Gotten Any Faster since the 1960s?," MIT School of Engineering, February 19, 2009, https://engineering.mit.edu/engage/ask-an-engineer/why-hasnt-commercial-air-travel-gotten-any-faster-since-the-1960s/. From Dunn's article: "Specified cruising speeds for commercial airliners today range between about 480 and 510 knots, compared to 525 knots for the Boeing 707, a mainstay of 1960s jet travel. Why?" In short, the main concern is fuel efficiency. Going faster consumes more fuel.

49. "Pan Am Introduction to Jet Service," Pan American Airways commercial, 1958, https://www.youtube.com/watch?v=bKqQgNZylLw.

50. Michael Lombardi, "Seventh Heaven: 50 Years ago, Boeing and Pan Am Revolutionized Travel with the 707," *Boeing Frontiers*, July 2008, 8–9.

51. "Faith, Progress Mark 30 Years of Pan American Pioneering," Pan American Airways, promotional brochure, 1957, collection 341, box 1, folder 8, PAW.

52. On the fall and rise of cruise ships, see Honey, *Cruise Tourism in the Caribbean*; Jean-Paul Rodrigue and Theo Notteboom, *The Geography of Transport Systems* (New York: Routledge, 2017), 249–50.

53. On the airplane as symbol of modernity, see Wohl, *Spectacle of Flight*, and Pisano, *Airplane in American Culture*.

54. Quoted in Massey, "Global Sense of Place," 154.

55. On the history of container shipping, see Marc Levinson, *The Box: How the Shipping Container Made the World Smaller and the World Economy Bigger* (Princeton, NJ: Princeton University Press, 2006).

56. Gabe Bullard, "The Surprising Origin of the Phrase 'Flyover Country,' " *National Geographic*, March 14, 2016.

57. Walter Benjamin, *One-Way Street and Other Writings*, trans. J. A. Underwood (New York: Penguin Classics, 2009), 52.

58. On the history of automobile travel, see Sutter, *Driven Wild*. On train travel, see Wolfgang Schivelbusch, *The Railway Journey: The Industrialization of Time and Space in the Nineteenth Century* (Oakland: University of California Press, 2014).

59. Walcott, *The Antilles*.

60. See Barbara Ireland, ed., *The New York Times 36 Hours World* (Cologne: Taschen, 2015).

4. The Nature of Tourism

1. Mark V. Barrow Jr., *A Passion for Birds: American Ornithology after Audubon* (Princeton, NJ: Princeton University Press, 1998), 9–10.

2. Theodore Roosevelt Rotunda, American Museum of Natural History, accessed March 3, 2015, http://www.amnh.org/theodore-roosevelt-quotes.

3. Letter from Theodore Roosevelt to Bonnie Roosevelt, August 6, 1876, Oyster Bay, NY, Theodore Roosevelt Center, Dickinson State University, http://www.theodorerooseveltcenter.org.

4. On Roosevelt's experiences as a naturalist, see Michael R. Canfield, *Theodore Roosevelt in the Field* (Chicago: University of Chicago Press, 2015).

5. On the relationship between tourism, exploration, and adventure, see Robert J. Gordon and Luis Antonio Vivanco, eds., *Tarzan Was an Eco-tourist: And Other Tales in the Anthropology of Adventure* (New York: Berghahn Books, 2006).

6. On the Cuba military campaign, see Theodore Roosevelt, *The Rough Riders* (New York: Charles Scribner's Sons, 1899).

7. On Roosevelt's overseas travels, see Kelly Enright, *The Maximum of Wilderness: The Jungle in the American Imagination* (Charlottesville: University of Virginia Press, 2012), 9–34.

8. On the Roosevelt expedition to Brazil, see Candice Millard, *The River of Doubt: Theodore Roosevelt's Darkest Journey* (New York: Broadway Books, 2005).

9. William Cronon, "The Trouble with Wilderness; or, Getting Back to the Wrong Nature," in Cronon, *Uncommon Ground*, 78.

10. Patrick Hemingway, foreword to Ernest Hemingway, *Hemingway on Hunting* (New York: Scribner, 2003), xxvi.

11. On the cultural influence of the National Geographic Society, Catherine A. Lutz and Jane L. Collins, *Reading National Geographic* (Chicago: Chicago University Press, 1993).

12. Albert Camus, *The Myth of Sisyphus, and Other Essays*, ed. Gustavo Aguilera (New York: Vintage Books, 1991), 11. Explaining phenomenology, Camus adds, "Phenomenology declines to explain the world, it wants to be merely a description of actual experience. . . . It resembles the projector that suddenly focuses on an image."

13. Robert E. Kohler, *All Creatures: Naturalists, Collectors, and Biodiversity, 1850–1950* (Princeton, NJ: Princeton University Press, 2006), 88.

14. Donna Haraway, "Teddy Bear Patriarchy: Taxidermy in the Garden of Eden, New York City, 1908–36," *Social Text*, no. 11 (Winter 1984/85): 21.

15. Theodore Roosevelt, "A Zoological Trip through Africa," lecture, March 21, 1911, Science Series of the Throop Extension Courses, *Bulletin of Throop Polytechnic Institute* 10, no. 51, Theodore Roosevelt Center, https://www.theodorerooseveltcen ter.org/Research/Digital-Library/Record?libID=o279320.

16. Theodore Roosevelt, *An Autobiography* (New York: Charles Scribner's Sons, 1920), 19.

17. *Annual Report of the Board of Regents of the Smithsonian Institution, Showing the Operations, Expenditures, and Condition of the Institution for the Year Ending June 30 1912* (Washington: GPO, 1913), 3, SIA.

18. Twain, *Innocents Abroad*, 23.

19. Elizabeth Blair, "Smithsonian, Congress Share a Turbulent History," National Public Radio, May 20, 2007, http://www.npr.org/templates/story/story. php?storyId=10283521.

20. On the role of museums shaping Western cultural beliefs about the rest of the world and particularly the tropics, see James Clifford, *The Predicament of Culture: Twentieth-Century Ethnography, Literature, and Art* (Cambridge, MA: Harvard University Press, 1988); Barbara Kirshenblatt-Gimblett, *Destination Culture: Tourism, Museums, and Heritage* (Berkeley: University of California Press, 1998); and Karsten Schubert, *The Curator's Egg: The Evolution of the Museum Concept from the French Revolution to the Present Day* (London: Ridinghouse, 2009).

21. Heather Ewing, *The Lost World of James Smithson: Science, Revolution, and the Birth of the Smithsonian* (London: Bloomsbury, 2007).

22. Letter from Alexander Wetmore to Frank Chapman, June 23, 1943, RU 7006, box 4, Alexander Wetmore Papers, SIA. The history of Western science and technology, Bruno Latour summarized "is in large part the history of the mobilization of anything that can be made to move and shipped back home." Bruno Latour, *Science in Action: How to Follow Scientists and Engineers through Society* (Philadelphia: Open University Press, 1987), 225.

23. *Annual Report of Board of Regents, Year Ending June 30 1912*, 25, SIA. Following the canal's construction (see chapter 1), islands and communities on the maritime route from the US mainland to the canal, which were previously seen as inaccessible— or worse, deadly—became reimagined as vacation destinations.

24. William L. Stern, oral history interview, July 2, 1997, History of Tropical Biology, RU 9606, SIA.

25. Grove, *Green Imperialism*, 8.

26. Phillip J. Pauly, "The World and All That Is in It: The National Geographic Society, 1888–1918," *American Quarterly* 31, no. 4 (1979): 517.

27. David Arnold, *The Problem of Nature: Environment, Culture, and European Expansion* (Cambridge, MA: Blackwell, 1996), 2.

28. Warder C. Allee and Marjorie Hill Allee, *Jungle Island* (Rand McNally: Chicago, 1925), 10.

29. Quoted in Haraway, "Teddy Bear Patriarchy," 55.

30. On the historical production of scientific knowledge, see Hugh Raffles, *In Amazonia: A Natural History* (Princeton, NJ: Princeton University Press, 2002).

31. Alexander Wetmore Papers, RU 7006, SIA.

32. S. Dillon Ripley and James A. Steed, "Alexander Wetmore, June 18, 1886–December 7, 1978," National Academy of Sciences, *Biographical Memoirs* 56 (1987): 597–626.

33. For biographical information on Wetmore, see Paul H. Oehser, "In Memoriam: Alexander Wetmore," *The Auk,* no. 97 (July 1980): 608–15, and John Sherwood, "His Field Notebook Was Started in 1894: It Is Not Yet Complete," *Washington Star,* January 13, 1977. For a discussion of his contributions to paleornithology, see Storrs L. Olson, "Alexander Wetmore and the Study of Fossil Birds," in *Collected Papers in Avian Paleontology Honoring the 90th Birthday of Alexander Wetmore,* ed. Storrs L. Olson, Smithsonian Contributions to Paleobiology (Washington, DC: Smithsonian Institution Press, 1976): xi–xvi.

34. Letter from Alexander Wetmore to Thomas Barbour, October 28, 1944, RU 7006, box 4, SIA.

35. Alexander Wetmore, "Something about Museums," speech for the opening of the new wing of the Science Museum of the St. Paul Institute, November 29, 1938, RU 7006, box 233, SIA.

36. Alexander Wetmore, "The Value of Travel," Future Farmers of America national radio program, August 7, 1939, RU 7006, box 233, SIA.

37. Alexander Wetmore, oral history interview, RU 9504, SIA.

38. James Dietz, *Economic History of Puerto Rico: Institutional Change and Capitalist Development* (Princeton, NJ: Princeton University Press, 1986). Similar types of capitalist development occurred in Cuba and Panama in the wake of US military occupation. See Marifeli Pérez-Stable, *The Cuban Revolution: Origins, Course, and Legacy* (New York: Oxford University Press, 2012), and Michael L. Conniff, *Panama and the United States: The End of an Alliance* (Athens: University of Georgia Press, 2012).

39. On the historical and cultural roots of US science into the Caribbean, see Megan Raby, *American Tropics: The Caribbean Roots of Biodiversity Science* (Chapel Hill: University of North Carolina Press, 2017.)

40. Letter from Alexander Wetmore to Maj. Gen. Willis Hale, May 6, 1948, RU 7006, box 153, SIA.

41. Letter from Alexander Wetmore to Gen. Hubert R. Harmon, June 12, 1947, RU 7006, box 153, SIA.

42. Letter from Alexander Wetmore to Brig. Gen. E. F. Bullene, November 30, 1943, RU 7006, box 153, SIA.

43. Alexander Wetmore, memorandum, October 23, 1944, RU 7006, box 153, SIA. To learn more about the chemical warfare testing on San José Island, see John Lindsay-Poland, *Emperors in the Jungle: The Hidden History of the U.S. in Panama* (Durham, NC: Duke University Press, 2003), 44–73.

44. Robert Fitzroy, *Narrative of the Surveying Voyages of His Majesty's Ships Adventure and Beagle between the years 1826 and 1836, Volume II* (1839; repr., New York: AMS, 1966), 43.

45. Franz Boas, "Scientists as Spies," *The Nation,* December 20, 1919.

46. Boas, "Scientists as Spies."

47. David H. Price, *Anthropological Intelligence: The Deployment and Neglect of American Anthropology in the Second World War* (Durham, NC: Duke University Press, 2008), 7–14.

48. James Bond, *Birds of the West Indies* (1936; repr., Boston: Houghton Mifflin, 1961).

49. Jim Wright, *The Real James Bond: A True Story of Identity Theft, Avian Intrigue, and Ian Fleming* (Atglen, PA: Schiffler, 2020).

50. Letter from James Bond to Alexander Wetmore, August 25, 1941, RU 7006, box 6, SIA.

51. Letter from James Bond to Smithsonian, June 5, 1973, RU 7006, box 6, SIA.

52. Geoffrey T. Hellman, "Curator Getting Around," *New Yorker*, August 26, 1950.

53. Quoted in Michael Lewis, "Scientists or Spies? Ecology in a Climate of Cold War Suspicion," *Economic and Political Weekly* 37, no. 24 (June 15, 2002): 2323–32.

54. Lewis, "Scientists or Spies?," 2324.

55. Waldo L. Schmitt Papers, 1907–1978, RU 7231, SIA.

56. Fenner A. Chace Jr., oral history interview, October 6 and 11, 1977, RU 9516, SIA.

57. Huntington Hartford, "Gone without the Wind," *Esquire*, October 1938.

58. Dave Kansas, "A&P Heading to the Checkout Counter?," *Wall Street Journal*, December 10, 2010.

59. Quoted in Suzanna Andrews, "Hostage to Fortune," *Vanity Fair*, June 12, 2010.

60. Letter from Waldo Schmitt to Alexander Wetmore, March 6, 1937, RU 7231, box 91, SIA.

61. Hartford, "Gone without the Wind."

62. Waldo Schmitt Diary, March 3–May 12, 1937, Smithsonian-Hartford West Indies Expedition, RU 7231, box 91, SIA.

63. Letter from Waldo Schmitt to Alexander Wetmore, March 6, 1937, RU 7231, box 91, SIA.

64. Hartford, "Gone without the Wind"; Schmitt Diary, March 3–May 12, 1937.

65. Schmitt Diary, March 3–May 12, 1937.

66. Andrews, "Hostage to Fortune."

67. Chace, oral history interview, October 6 and 11, 1977.

68. Richard E. Blackwelder, oral history interview, January 17, 1973, RU 9517, SIA.

69. Letter from Waldo Schmitt to Helen and George Allan Hancock, March 16, 1943, RU 7231, box 14, SIA.

70. Gordon and Vivanco, *Tarzan Was an Eco-tourist*, 1.

71. On ecotourism, see Héctor Ceballos-Lascuráin, *Tourism, Ecotourism, and Protected Areas: The State of Nature-Based Tourism around the World and Guidelines for Its Development* (Gland, Switzerland: International Union for Conservation of Nature and Natural Resources, 1996); Sterling Evans, *The Green Republic: A Conservation History of Costa Rica* (Austin: University of Texas Press, 1999); Martha Honey, *Ecotourism and Sustainable Development: Who Owns Paradise?* (Washington DC: Island, 1999); Deborah McLaren, *Rethinking Tourism and Ecotravel: The Paving of Paradise and What You Can Do to Stop It* (West Hartford, CT: Kumarian, 1998); and Paige West and James G. Carrier, "Ecotourism and Authenticity: Getting Away from It All?," *Current Anthropology* 45, no. 4 (2004): 483–98.

72. George Simmel, "The Adventurer," in *George Simmel on Individuality and Social Forms*, ed. Donald N. Levine, 187–98 (Chicago: University of Chicago Press).

73. Waldo Schmitt, "Knowledge and the Zest of Life," RU 7231, box 73, SIA.

74. Haraway, "Teddy Bear Patriarchy," 168.

75. Nils Lindahl Elliot, "A Memory of Nature: Ecotourism on Panama's Barro Colorado Island," *Journal of Latin American Cultural Studies* 19, no. 3 (December 2010): 237–59.

76. Quoted in Pamela Henson, "Invading Arcadia: Women Scientists in the Field in Latin America, 1900–1950," *The Americas* 58, no. 4 (April 2002): 577.

77. Candace Slater, "Amazonia as Edenic Narrative." in Cronon, *Uncommon Ground*, 114.

78. Fausto Bocanegra, oral history interview, August 15, 1988, RU 9561, SIA.

79. James Clifford, *Routes: Travel and Translation in the Late Twentieth Century* (Cambridge, MA: Harvard University Press, 1997), 33.

80. Valerie Boyd, *Wrapped in Rainbows: The Life of Zora Neale Hurston* (New York: Scribner, 2003), 81.

81. Alexis Pauline Grumbs, *Undrowned: Black Feminist Lessons from Marine Mammals* (Chico, CA: AK, 2020), 95.

82. Clifford, *Predicament of Culture*, 220.

5. Traveling Writers

1. "Editor's Box," *Esquire*, inaugural issue, autumn 1933.

2. Arnold Gingrich, "Publisher's Page," *Esquire*, October 1961.

3. On Gingrich's relationship with Hemingway, see Arnold Gingrich, *Nothing but People: The Early Days at Esquire* (New York: Crown, 1971).

4. Kevin Maier, "'A Trick Men Learn in Paris': Hemingway, *Esquire*, and Mass Tourism," *Hemingway Review* 31, no. 2 (Spring 2012): 68.

5. Ernest Hemingway, "Marlin off the Morro: A Cuban Letter," *Esquire*, Autumn 1933.

6. Russ Pottle, "Travel," in *Ernest Hemingway in Context*, ed. Debra A. Moddelmog and Suzanne del Gizzo, 367–78 (New York: Cambridge University Press, 2013).

7. James Salter, "The Finest Life You Ever Saw," *New York Times Review of Books*, October 2011.

8. *Michael Palin's Hemingway Adventure*, directed by David F. Turnbull (London: BBC, 1999), DVD.

9. "Running with the Bulls," *Snap Judgment*, National Public Radio, December 19, 2014.

10. Ernest Hemingway, *Death in the Afternoon* (New York: Charles Scribner's Sons, 1932), 2.

11. Paul Fussell, *Abroad: British Literary Traveling between the Wars* (New York: Oxford University Press, 1980), 11.

12. Ford Madox Ford, *The English Novel: From the Earliest Days to the Death of Joseph Conrad* (London: Constable, 1930), 9.

13. Emily Rosenberg, ed. *A World Connecting, 1870–1945* (Cambridge, MA: Harvard University Press, 2012), 3.

14. Said, *Orientalism*, 27.

15. Toni Morrison, *Playing in the Dark: Whiteness and the Literary Imagination* (New York: Vintage Books, 1993), 12.

16. Pratt, *Imperial Eyes*, 4.

17. Pratt, *Imperial Eyes*, 221.

18. Helen Carr, "Modernism and Travel, 1880–1940," in *Cambridge Companion to Travel Writing*, ed. Peter Hulme and Tim Youngs, 70–86 (Cambridge: Cambridge University Press, 2002).

19. Fussell, *Abroad*, 38.

20. Morrison, *Playing in the Dark*, 90.

21. David Foster Wallace, "E Unibus Pluram: Television and U.S. Fiction," in *A Supposedly Fun Thing I'll Never Do Again* (New York: Little, Brown, 1997), 51.

22. Hulme and Young, *Cambridge Companion to Travel Writing*, 2.

23. For a complete list of Hemingway's magazine work, see Carlos Baker, *Hemingway: The Writer as Artist* (Princeton, NJ: Princeton University Press, 1980), 409–39.

24. The line "wide lawns and narrow minds" is often attributed to Hemingway, but there is no record of him ever saying or writing it. See Robert K. Elder, "The 'Wide Lawns' Myth: Ernest Hemingway in Oak Park," *Chicago Tribune*, July 17, 2014.

25. Hemingway, "The Great Blue River," *Holiday Magazine*, July 1949.

26. Morrison, *Playing in the Dark*, 70.

27. Arnold Samuelson, *With Hemingway: A Year in Key West and Cuba* (New York: Random House, 1984), 3.

28. Samuelson, *With Hemingway*, 3.

29. Paul Hendrickson, *Hemingway's Boat: Everything He Loved in Life, and Lost* (New York: Vintage Books, 2012), 66.

30. Hemingway, "Monologue to the Maestro: A High Seas Letter," *Esquire*, October 1935.

31. Samuelson, *With Hemingway*, 162.

32. Samuelson, *With Hemingway*, 84.

33. On transnational history as historical method, see Briggs, McCormick, and Way, "Transnationalism"; Mae M. Ngai, "Promises and Perils of Transnational History," *Perspectives on History: The Newsmagazine of the American Historical Association*, December 2012; and Louis A. Pérez Jr., "We Are the World: Internationalizing the National, Nationalizing the International," *Journal of American History* 89, no. 2 (September 2002): 558–66.

34. John Steinbeck, *Cup of Gold: A Life of Sir Henry Morgan, Buccaneer, with Occasional Reference to History* (New York: McBride, 1929).

35. Steinbeck, *Cup of Gold*, 41.

36. John Steinbeck, *The Pearl* (New York: Viking, 1947).

37. John Steinbeck, *Log from the Sea of Cortez* (1951; repr., New York: Penguin Classics, 1995), 21.

38. Richard Halliburton, *The Royal Road to Romance* (Indianapolis, IN: Bobbs-Merrill, 1925), 4.

39. Clare Boothe, "We Nominate for Oblivion," *Vanity Fair*, June 1930.

40. On Halliburton's legacy, see R. Scott Williams, *The Forgotten Adventures of Richard Halliburton: A High-Flying Life from Tennessee to Timbuktu* (Charleston, SC: History Press, 2014).

41. Quoted in Greg Daugherty, "The Last Adventure of Richard Halliburton, the Forgotten Hero of 1930s America," *Smithsonian Magazine*, March 25, 2014.

42. Robert Colls, *George Orwell: English Rebel* (Oxford: Oxford University Press, 2013), 18. On Orwell and his relationship to British colonialism, Colls writes, "For the British, every hill station was somewhere to escape from. . . . [Orwell's] great-great grandfather had been a slave-owner in Jamaica. His father-in-law had been a teak dealer in Burma. His father had been an official in the opium trade. These family heirlooms gave him a personal stake in what he witnessed."

43. Aldous Huxley, "Wordsworth in the Tropics," in *Do What You Will* (London: Chatto & Windus, 1929), 128–29.

44. Greene regularly returned to Latin America and the Caribbean as settings for his storytelling. In Mexico, *The Lawless Roads* (1939) and *The Power and the Glory* (originally *The Labyrinthine Ways*) (1940); in Cuba, *Our Man in Havana* (1958); and in Panama, *Getting to Know the General: The Story of an Involvement* (1984).

45. Quoted in Guridy, *Forging Diaspora*, 124.

46. Langston Hughes, *I Wonder as I Wander* (New York: Hill & Wang, 1956), 25.

47. Claude McKay, *A Long Way from Home* (New York: Arno, 1937), 9.

48. Hulme, *Colonial Encounters*; Sheller, *Consuming the Caribbean*.

49. Harry L. Foster, *The Adventures of a Tropical Tramp* (New York: A. L. Burt, 1922), 2.

50. In 1910 the average number of years of schooling for students in the United States was roughly 8.1 years. By 1940 that number had only increased to 8.6 years. See Thomas Snyder, *120 Years of American Education: A Statistical Portrait; National Center for Education Statistics* (Washington, DC: Department of Education, 1993).

51. Foster, *Adventures of a Tropical Tramp*, 1–8; "Harry L. Foster, Writer, Dies at 37," *New York Times*, March 16, 1932.

52. Foster, *Tropical Tramp with the Tourists*. Foster's ability to pick a destination at whim and head in that direction signified a highly privileged travel identity. For travelers of color or less welcomed nationalities, travel was tightly restricted. On travel restrictions and the role of state authority, see John Torpey, *The Invention of the Passport: Surveillance, Citizenship and the State* (Cambridge: Cambridge University Press, 1999).

53. Harry L. Foster's publications include *If You Go to South America* (1937), *The Caribbean Cruise* (1935), *A Vagabond in the Barbary* (1930), *Combing the Caribbees* (1929), *A Vagabond in Fiji* (1927), *A Tropical Tramp with the Tourists* (1925), *A Gringo in Manana-Land* (1924), *A Beachcomber in the Orient* (1923), and *The Adventures of a Tropical Tramp* (1922).

54. Foster, *Tropical Tramp with the Tourists*, 2.

55. Michael Adas, *Machines as the Measure of Men: Science, Technology, and Ideologies of Western Dominance* (Ithaca, NY: Cornell University Press, 1989), 348.

56. Missal, *Seaway to the Future*.

57. Benjamin, *One-Way Street*, 114.

58. Kern, *Culture of Time and Space*, 130.

59. *Panama Star and Herald*, September 24, 1923.

60. Traven, *Death Ship*, 41.

61. On the history of Prohibition in the United States, see Daniel Okrent, *Last Call: The Rise and Fall of Prohibition* (New York: Simon & Schuster, 2010).

62. Malcolm Cowley, *A Second Flowering: Works and Days of the Lost Generation* (New York: Viking, 1973), 14.

63. Ernest Hemingway, *A Moveable Feast* (New York: Bantam Books, 1965).

64. Jeffrey Schwartz, " 'The Saloon Must Go, and I Will Take It with Me': American Prohibition, Nationalism, and Expatriation in *The Sun Also Rises*," *Studies in the Novel* 33, no. 2 (2001): 196.

65. Carlos Baker, *Ernest Hemingway: A Life Story* (New York: Charles Scribner's Sons, 1969), 180.

66. F. Scott Fitzgerald, *This Side of Paradise* (New York: Scribner, 1920), 256.

67. Fitzgerald, *This Side of Paradise*, 281.

68. Allie Baker, "Hemingway, the Fitzgeralds, and the Lost Generation: An Interview with Kirk Curnutt," The Hemingway Project, August 14, 2018, http://www.thehemingwayproject.com/hemingway-the-fitzgeralds-and-the-lost-generation-an-interview-with-kirk-curnutt/.

69. Harry Franck, *Roaming through the West Indies* (Cornwall, NY: Cornwall, 1920), 484. On Franck's literary career and travels, see Steven L. Driever, "Geographic Narratives in the South American Travelogues of Harry A. Franck: 1917–1943," *Journal of Latin American Geography* 10, no. 1 (2010): 53–69, and "From Travel to Tourism: Harry Franck's Writing on Mexico (1916–1940)," *Journal of Latin American Geography* 12, no. 2 (2013): 7–33.

70. Foster, *Adventures of a Tropical Tramp*, 358.

71. Cowley, *Second Flowering*, 26.

72. Wallace, "E Unibus Pluram," 57.

73. Max Horkeimer and Theodor W. Adorno, *The Dialectic of Enlightenment: Cultural Memory in the Present*, trans. Steven Rendall (1944; repr., New York: Verso 1997), 167.

74. "A Banker's Holiday in Hemingway's Cuba," *Wednesday Journal of Oak Park and River Forest*, April 24, 2012, https://www.oakpark.com/2012/04/24/a-bankers-holiday-in-hemingways-cuba/.

75. Ricardo Salvatore, "The Enterprise of Knowledge: Representational Machines of Informal Empire," in *Close Encounters of Empire: Writing the Cultural History of U.S.-Latin American Relations*, ed. Gilbert Joseph, Catherine LeGrand, and Ricardo Salvatore, 69–104 (Durham, NC: Duke University Press, 1998).

76. Quoted in Cowley, *Second Flowering*, 226.

77. "The Old Man and the City: Hemingway's Love Affair with Pamplona," *The Independent*, February 12, 2015.

78. Ernest Hemingway, *To Have and Have Not* (New York: Charles Scribner's Sons, 1937).

79. Morrison, *Playing in the Dark*, 70.

80. Morrison, *Playing in the Dark*, 82.

81. Samuelson, *With Hemingway*, 20.

82. Hemingway, *To Have and Have Not*, 96.

83. Letters from Hemingway to John Dos Passos, from Havana, May 15, 1933, and from Key West, April 12, 1932, in *Ernest Hemingway: Selected Letters, 1917–1961*, ed. Carlos Baker (New York: Charles Scribner's Sons, 1981), 357, 389.

84. See Robin Moore, *Nationalizing Blackness: Afrocubanismo and Artistic Revolution in Havana; 1920–1940* (Pittsburgh: University of Pittsburgh Press, 1997); Putnam, *Radical Moves*.

85. Sheller, *Consuming the Caribbean*, 186.

86. Gilroy, *Black Atlantic*, 19.

87. Zora Neale Hurston, *Dust Tracks on a Road* (New York: Arno, 1969), 243.

88. Hurston, *Dust Tracks on a Road*, 188.

89. Zora Neale Hurston, *Tell My Horse: Voodoo and Life in Haiti and Jamaica* (1938; repr., New York: Perennial Library, 1990), 249.

90. Ifeoma Kiddoe Nwankwo, "Insider and Outsider, Black and American: Zora Neale Hurston's Caribbean Ethnography," *Radical History Review*, no. 87 (Fall 2003): 63.

91. Hurston, *Tell My Horse*, 249.

92. Nwankwo, "Insider and Outsider," 49–77; Annette Trefzer, "Possessing the Self: Caribbean Identities in Zora Neale Hurston's Tell My Horse," *African American Review* 34, no. 2 (Summer 2000): 299–312.

93. Correspondence between Zora Neale Hurston and Alan Lomax, 1936, Association for Cultural Equity, http://www.culturalequity.org/alan-lomax/friends/hurston.

94. Hurston, *Dust Tracks on a Road*, 141.

95. Herbert Aptheker, ed., *The Correspondence of W. E. B. Du Bois: Volume I, Selections, 1877–1934* (Amherst: University of Massachusetts Press, 1997), 374.

96. J. A. Rogers, "Book Review," *Pittsburgh Courier*, March 5, 1927.

97. On Hemingway's relationship with *Esquire*, see Arnold Gingrich, "Scott, Ernest, Whoever," *Esquire*, December 1966.

98. Amy Kaplan, *The Anarchy of Empire in the Making of U.S. Culture* (Cambridge, MA: Harvard University Press, 2002), 53.

99. On Kerouac's time in Mexico and its influence on his literary creativity, see Jorge Garcia-Robles, *At the End of the Road: Jack Kerouac in Mexico* (Minneapolis: University of Minnesota Press, 2014).

100. Jack Kerouac, *Lonesome Traveler* (New York: Grove, 1960), 22.

6. Burning Privilege

1. "Iban a incendiar el Hotel Tívoli," *La Critica*, January 14, 1964. After the attack, Chan and Allonca planned to "return immediately to Panamanian territory to avoid being shot down by the U.S. military."

2. "Avioneta robada tripulada por dos panameños cae en la bahía," *La Estrella*, January 12, 1964.

3. Daniel Levinson Wilk, "Review of *Hotel: An American History* by A. K. Sandoval-Strausz, *Class Acts: Service and Inequality in Luxury Hotels* by Rachel Sherman, and *Hotel Theory* by Wayne Koestenbaum," *Enterprise and Society* 9, no. 4 (December 2008): 873–77.

4. On historical studies linking US foreign relations and tourism, see Christopher Endy, *Cold War Holidays: American Tourism in France* (Chapel Hill: University of North Carolina Press, 2004), and Merrill, *Negotiating Paradise*. On hotel historiography, see Kevin James, *Histories, Meanings, and Representations of the Modern Hotel* (Bristol, UK: Channel View, 2018).

5. Lisa Smirl, *Spaces of Aid: How Cars, Compounds, and Hotels Shape Humanitarianism* (Chicago: University of Chicago Press, 2015); Kenneth Morrison, *Sarajevo's Holiday Inn on the Frontline of Politics and War* (Basingstoke, UK: Palgrave Macmillan, 2016).

6. Sarah Fregonese and Adam Ramadan, "Hotel Geopolitics: A Research Agenda," *Geopolitics* 20, no. 4 (2015): 793–813.

7. Michael E. Donoghue, *Borderland on the Isthmus: Race, Culture, and the Struggle for the Canal Zone* (Durham, NC: Duke University Press, 2004), 245–55.

8. "Canal Zone Milestone," *New York Times*, January 21, 1951.

9. "Balboa," *Saturday Evening Post*, December 24, 1949.

10. The anticolonial struggles that occurred respectively in Egypt, Cuba, and Panama in the 1950s and 1960s have clear cultural and historical differences. Collectively, though, they highlight local and nationalist resistance to the intersection between imperial control and tourism development. In all three of these movements, tourism and the luxuries of foreign visitors became key targets in the struggle.

11. Robin D. G. Kelley, introduction to *Discourse on Colonialism,* by Aimé Césaire (New York: Monthly Review Press, 2000), 8.

12. On contact zones, see Pratt, *Imperial Eyes*.

13. Hunter S. Thompson, "Why Anti-Gringo Winds Often Blow South of the Border," *National Observer*, August 19, 1963.

14. Claude Lévi-Strauss, *Tristes Tropiques*, trans. Doreen Weightman and John Weightman (1955; repr., New York: Penguin Books, 1974), 126.

15. John Urry, *Consuming Places* (New York: Routledge, 1995), 131.

16. Maurizio Peleggi, "The Social and Material Life of Colonial Hotels: Comfort Zones and Contact Zones in British Colombo and Singapore, ca. 1870–1930," *Journal of Social History* 46, no 1 (2012): 124–53.

17. Clifford, *Routes*, 2.

18. "Panama Eyewitnesses Stress Army Restraint," *Youngstown (OH) Vindicator*, January 28, 1964, in George W. Westerman Papers, US-Panama Relations, box 78, SCRBC. See the Westerman collection for an assortment of firsthand accounts of the 1964 riots.

19. On the 1964 protests and riots in Panama, see Donoghue, *Borderland on the Isthmus*; LaFeber, *Panama Canal*; and Alan L. McPherson, *Yankee No! Anti-Americanism in U.S.-Latin American Relations* (Cambridge, MA: Harvard University Press, 2003), 77–116.

20. "What Really Happened," *Spillway: Publication of the Panama Canal*, January 20, 1964. PCUF.

21. Quoted in Gregorio Selser, "La explosion del 9 de enero de 1964," *Tareas*, no. 97 (September–December 1997): 76.

22. "Chronology of Events Involving the Acting Governor of the Canal Zone, January 9–10, 1964," RG 185, Records of the Panama Canal, Internal Security Office, Declassified General Correspondence, box 4, NARA. The governor of the US Canal Zone (1962–67), Robert John Fleming, was back in the United States when the protests erupted. Parker was lieutenant governor at the time, although he would later serve as the full-time governor (1971–75).

23. "Panama Eyewitnesses Stress Army Restraint."

24. "Tivoli Buffet Interrupted," *Spillway: Publication of the Panama Canal*, January 20, 1964, PCUF.

25. LaFeber, *Panama Canal*, 109. Today on the former site of the Hotel Tivoli is the Smithsonian Tropical Research Institute's main office and library.

26. Donald R. Flynn, "The Battle: An Eyewitness," in Westerman Papers, US-Panama Relations, box 78, SCRBC.

27. Flynn, "Battle."

28. George P. Hunt, "Covering the Riot-Ridden Canal," *Life*, January 24, 1964.

29. Tom Flaherty, "Bullets Fly in Panama over the Right to Fly the Flag: Inside an Ugly Fight," *Life*, January 24, 1964.

30. "Statement," Chiriqui Land Company, unpublished report, January 13, 1964, Westerman Papers, box 78, SCRBC.

31. Robert Richardson, "'Burn, Baby, Burn' Slogan Used as Firebugs Put Area to Torch," *Los Angeles Times*, August 15, 1965.

32. "What Really Happened."

33. Martha Smith, "The Crisis in Panama: 1964," *Tropical Collegian* 29 (Spring 1964), PCUF.

34. Eugene H. Methvin, "Anatomy of a Riot: Panama 1964," *Orbis*, no. 14 (Summer 1970): 463–89; International Commission of Jurists, *Report on the Events in Panama, January 9–12, 1964* (Geneva: International Commission of Jurists, 1964).

35. "Panama's Economy Is Shaken by Crisis," *New York Times*, January 16, 1964.

36. "Desvían itinerario: 9 barcos turísticos cancelan viajes anunciados a Panamá," *La Hora*, January 29, 1964.

37. "Tourist Desert Country: Panama Economy Stricken as Dollar Flow Dries Up," *Miami Herald*, January 30, 1964, Westerman Papers, box 78, SCRBC.

38. Quoted in George Westerman, "Let's Clean up Panama City," *Panama American*, June 27, 1964, Westerman Papers, box 78, SCRBC.

39. McCullough, *Path between the Seas*.

40. *Canal Record*, March 18, 1908.

41. *Canal Record*, August 13, 1913. Tourists wanted to see with their own eyes the construction of the Panama Canal. In 1911, 15,790 tourists visited Panama; in 1912, over 20,000; and in the first six months of 1913, 18,972.

42. "Panama's Distinctive Stability," *Panama Times*, January 23, 1926.

43. Foster, *Tropical Tramp with the Tourists*, 94.

44. Conniff, *Black Labor on a White Canal*.

45. On prostitution in Panama, see Parker, "Empire's Angst."

46. Foster, *Tropical Tramp with the Tourists*, 97.

47. Abbot, *Panama and the Canal*, 224.

48. Merrill, *Negotiating Paradise*, 77.

49. Joaquín C. Beleño, *Gamboa Road Gang* (Panama City: Ministerio de Educación, Departamento de Bellas Artes y Publicaciones, 1960), 180.

50. Patricia Pizzurno, "Zona de contacto y espacio intervenido en Panamá, 1904–1955," *Tareas*, no. 138 (May–August 2011): 85.

51. George Westerman, introduction to Linda Samuels, *An Exhibit on the Races of Mankind* (Panama City: Isthmian Negro Youth Congress, 1946), Westerman Papers, SCRBC.

52. Conniff, *Black Labor on a White Canal*.

53. Pizzurno, "Zona de contacto," 86.

54. "Balboa."

55. Panamanian officials, in this sense, were not so much interested in cutting off the flow of American tourists and their economic capital but rather wanted to

control and profit from it. Capitalist-nationalist tourist alliances were not uncommon in the slow of process of decolonization. Gamal Abdel Nasser, the nationalist leader in the Egyptian revolution of 1952, also made an agreement with Hilton in the 1950s to replace the colonial Shepheard's Hotel.

56. Quoted in "Bullets Fly in Panama."

57. Letter from Mrs. Fairchild to Mrs. Wetmore, February 5, 1964, Alexander Wetmore Papers, RU 7006, box 155, SIA.

58. Edward P. Morgan, "It's a Specious Kind of Patriotism Which Defiles That of Our Allies," *Panama Star and Herald*, January 27, 1964, Westerman Papers, box 78, SCRBC.

59. Joseph Curran, "NMU Can Point the Way to a Just Panama Policy," *NMU Pilot*, January 23, 1964, Westerman Papers, box 78, SCRBC. To better understand British colonial policies in India, see Stephen Legg, *Spaces of Colonialism: Delhi's Urban Governmentalities* (Oxford, UK: John Wiley & Sons, 2008).

60. On the history of enclaves and US cultural influence in Latin America, see Joseph, LeGrand, and Salvatore, *Close Encounters of Empire*.

61. William J. Lederer and Eugene Burdick, *The Ugly American* (New York: Norton, 1958), 108.

62. Quoted in Donoghue, *Borderland on the Isthmus*, 77.

63. Donoghue, *Borderland on the Isthmus*, 58.

64. Greg Grandin, *Empire's Workshop: Latin America, the United States, and the Rise of the New Imperialism* (New York: Metropolitan Books, 2006), 56.

65. A. P. Boxley, "Our Readers Speak: Panama Crisis Could Hurt Coal Exports," *Post Herald* (Beckley, WV), January 23, 1964, Westerman Papers, box 78, SCRBC.

66. Quoted in *La Estrella*, January 12, 1964.

67. William J. Fulbright, "Old Myths and New Realities," United States of America Congressional Record Proceedings and Debates of the 88th Congress, Second Session 110, March 25, 1964, http://scipio.uark.edu/cdm/ref/collection/Fulbright/id/312.

68. Quoted in Robin D. G. Kelley, *Freedom Dreams: The Black Radical Imagination* (Boston: Beacon, 2002), 56.

69. George Westerman, "The Passing Review: Jamaica-Trinidad Independence Triumph of Human Liberty," *Panama Tribune*, July 21, 1962, Westerman Papers, box 78, SCRBC.

70. Martin Travis and James Watkins, "Time Bomb in Panama," *The Nation*, April 30, 1960.

71. On the relationship between British imperialism, economic power, and decolonization in Egypt, see Robert L. Tignor, *Capitalism and Nationalism at the End of Empire: State and Business in Decolonizing Egypt, Nigeria, and Kenya, 1945–1963* (Princeton, NJ: Princeton University Press, 2015).

72. Yasser Elsheshtway, "Urban Transformations: The Great Cairo Fire and the Founding of a Modern Capital, 1952–1970," *Built Environment* 40, no. 3 (Autumn 2014): 408–25.

73. Garrido, *Cuba y el turismo*, 116. For more on Cuba's tourism history, see Schwartz, *Pleasure Island*, and Christine Skwiot, *The Purposes of Paradise: U.S. Tourism and Empire in Cuba and Hawai'i* (Philadelphia: University of Pennsylvania Press, 2010).

74. Merrill, *Negotiating Paradise*, 4.

75. Quoted in Skwiot, *Purposes of Paradise*, 157.

76. Although the Cuban revolutionary government has, since the 1990s, promoted tourism as development, it is important to remember that the original revolution was very much at odds with the type of international tourism dominating the Caribbean in the mid-twentieth century. On racism and tourism in revolutionary Cuba, see Devyn Spence Benson, *Antiracism in Cuba: The Unfinished Revolution* (Chapel Hill: University of North Carolina Press, 2016).

77. Peter Abrahams, "Commentaries: Ambivalence about Tourism," December 14, 1963, Statutory Bodies, record code 3/9/1/671, JARD.

78. "Political Broadcast by Abe Issa," Statutory Bodies, record code 3/9/4/88, JARD.

79. The Supreme Court case *Plessy v. Ferguson* in 1896, which was one of the first and most important challenges to segregation in the South, was in fact about access to tourism. African American Homer Plessy attempted to board a sightseeing train in New Orleans in 1892 but was refused access to the "whites only" car. On tourism and civil rights, see Rose, *Struggle for Black Freedom in Miami*, and Guridy, *Forging Diaspora*.

80. Quoted in John Herbers, "Martin Luther King and 17 Others Jailed Trying to Integrate St. Augustine Restaurant," *New York Times*, June 12, 1964.

81. Stetson Kennedy (as Snow James), "'Seeing St. Aug.' Proves Exciting," *Pittsburgh Courier*, June 6, 1964. On tourism and civil rights in St. Augustine, see Reiko Hillyer, "Cold War Conquistadors: The St. Augustine Quadricentennial, Pan Americanism, and the Civil Rights Movement in the Ancient City," *Journal of Southern History* 81, no. 1 (February 2015): 117–56.

82. Martin Luther King Jr., *I Have a Dream* (New York: Schwartz & Wade, 2012).

83. Letter from Arthur B. Spingarn, president of NAACP, to president of the United States, September 16, 1941, Westerman Papers, box 63, SCRBC.

84. George W. Westerman, "American-Panamanian Relations," *The Crisis* 60, no. 3 (March 1953): 147–53, Westerman Papers, box 94, SCRBC.

85. Ricaurte Soler, "La concentración del poder económico en Panamá," in Gandásegui, *Las clases sociales en Panamá*, 97–98.

86. George W. Westerman "African Freedom Vital Development of the Sixties," *Panama Tribune*, July 7, 1962, Westerman Papers, box 78, SCRBC.

87. E. P. Thompson, *The Making of the English Working Class* (New York: Vintage Books, 1963), 27.

88. Quetzil E. Castañeda, "The Neo-Liberal Imperative of Tourism: Rights and Legitimization in the UNWTO Global Code of Ethics for Tourism," *Practicing Anthropology* 34, no. 3 (Summer 2012): 47–51.

89. Wolfgang Sachs, preface to *The Development Dictionary: A Guide to Knowledge as Power* (New York: Zed Books, 2010), vii.

90. Michael L. Conniff, "George Westerman: A Barbadian Descendant in Panama," in *The Human Tradition in Latin America*, ed. William H. Beezley and Judith Ewell, 141–50 (Lanham, MD: Rowman & Littlefield, 1998).

91. Letter from Hope R. Stevens to George Westerman, June 23, 1964, Westerman Papers, box 14, SCRBC.

92. Letter from S. P. B Magee to George Westerman, September 2, 1974, Westerman Papers, box 14, SCRBC.

93. Letter from George Westerman to Rex Williams, June 21, 1964, Westerman Papers, box 14, SCRBC.

94. Letter from Westerman to Rex Williams, June 21, 1964.

95. Greene, *Getting to Know the General*, 29.

Conclusion

1. David Foster Wallace, "Shipping Out: On the (Nearly Lethal) Comforts of a Luxury Cruise," *Harper's Magazine*, January 1996, 33.

2. "Five Days with David Foster Wallace: Colin Marshall Talks to Author and Journalist David Lipsky," 3 Quarks Daily, July 19, 2010, http://www.3quarksdaily.com/3quarksdaily/2010/07/five-days-with-david-foster-wallace-colin-marshall-talks-to-author-and-journalist-david-lipsky.html.

3. Wallace, "Shipping Out," 34–35.

4. Contrary to popular belief but in line with a long philosophical tradition, ignorance is not bliss. The unexamined life is still not worth living.

5. Wallace, "Shipping Out," 36.

6. Plato, *Republic*, ed. Chris Emlyn-Jones and William Preddy (Cambridge, MA: Harvard University Press, 2013).

7. Wallace, "Shipping Out," 34.

8. Wallace, "Shipping Out," 56.

9. Jamaica Kincaid, *A Small Place* (New York: Farrar, Strauss, Giroux, 2000), 19.

10. On service work and emotional labor, see Amy S. Wharton, "The Sociology of Emotional Labor," *Annual Review of Sociology* 35, no. 1 (August 2009): 147–65.

11. Paul Gootenberg, *Andean Cocaine: The Making of a Global Drug* (Chapel Hill: University of North Carolina Press, 2008), 4.

12. Spalding, "Lifestyle Migration to Bocas del Toro," 67–86; Carla María Guerrón Montero "'Can't Beat Me Own Drum in Me Own Native Land': Calypso Music and Tourism in the Panamanian Atlantic Coast," *Anthropological Quarterly* 79, no. 4 (2006): 633–63.

13. Quoted in "New Tourism Law, Incentives to Promote Industry Growth," *The Visitor / El Visitante*, November 2012.

14. Quoted in Ramachandra Guha, *How Much Should a Person Consume?: Environmentalism in India and the United States* (Berkeley: University of California Press, 2006), 231.

15. United Nations Environment Programme and World Travel and Tourism Council, *Rethinking Single-Use Plastic Products in Travel and Tourism: Impacts, Management Practices and Recommendations* (Nairobi: United Nations Environment Programme, June 2021), https://wedocs.unep.org/bitstream/handle/20.500.11822/36324/RSUP.pdf.

16. Wallace, "Shipping Out," 50.

17. Honey, *Cruise Tourism in the Caribbean*.

18. The worker-to-tourist ratio on luxury cruise ships puts the US public education system to shame with an average 16-to-1 student-to-teacher dynamic. What

would public education look like if there were a teacher for every three to four students?

19. Jim Walker, "Royal Caribbean: The Rich Get Richer, the Poor Get Poorer," Jim Walker's Cruise Law News, February 26, 2014, http://www.cruiselawnews.com/2014/02/articles/crew-member-rights-1/royal-caribbean-the-rich-get-richer-the-poor-get-poorer/.

20. Personal records of ice cream consumption are likely broken while vacationing on a Caribbean cruise. Someone—in fact multiple people—always seem to have a cone in hand, whether in formal dress or bathing suit. No matter morning, afternoon, or night, the ice cream is flowing. It is a similar pattern with beer and a variety of soft drinks.

21. Kelley, introduction to Césaire, *Discourse on Colonialism*, 27.

22. Formal colonial relations still exist in various parts of the Caribbean including in US-controlled territories such as Puerto Rico and the US Virgin Islands. See Immerwahr, *How to Hide an Empire*.

23. James Baldwin, "The White Man's Guilt," *Ebony*, August 1965.

24. What I document is not the experience of all travelers to the Caribbean. There is a spectrum of experience. What I describe is *a history* of tourism shaping the present. There are many histories and social practices involved. Nevertheless, a significant number—a dominant majority—have acted and continue to engage in at least some of these hegemonic traits, which have become part of the Caribbean's tourist culture.

25. Sheller, *Consuming the Caribbean*, 121.

26. Joseph Conrad, *The Heart of Darkness* (1899; repr., Boston: Bedford / St. Martin's, 2011). On Conrad and his relationship to European colonialism, see Edward Said, *Joseph Conrad and the Fiction of Autobiography* (New York: Columbia University Press, 2008), and Maya Jasanoff, *The Dawn Watch: Joseph Conrad in a Global World* (New York: Penguin, 2017).

27. On Western fantasies of the colonial world, see Said, *Orientalism*, and Ann Laura Stoler, *Race and the Education of Desire: Foucault's History of Sexuality and the Colonial Order of Things* (Durham, NC: Duke University Press, 1995).

28. Will Durant and Ariel Durant, *The Lessons of History* (New York: Simon & Schuster, 1968), 12.

29. F. Scott Fitzgerald, "An Interview with F. Scott Fitzgerald," *New York Tribune*, May 7, 1920.

30. Césaire, *Discourse on Colonialism*, 33.

BIBLIOGRAPHY

Archives and Libraries

Archivo Belisario Porras, Panama City
Archivo del Ministerio de Relaciones Exteriores, Panama City
Archivo Nacional de la República de Cuba, Havana
Archivo Nacional de Panamá, Panama City
Archivo y la Biblioteca Ricardo J. Alfaro, Panama City
Benson Latin American Collection, University of Texas at Austin
Biblioteca Interamericana Simón Bolívar, Panama City
Biblioteca Nacional de Cuba, José Marti, Havana
Biblioteca Nacional de Panamá, Ernesto J. Castillero R., Panama City
George A. Smathers Libraries, University of Florida, Gainesville
Jamaica Archives and Records Department, Spanish Town, Jamaica
Manuscript Division, Library of Congress, Washington, DC
Pan American World Airways Records, University of Miami
Schomburg Center for Research in Black Culture, New York
Smithsonian Institution Archives, Washington, DC
US National Archives and Records Administration, College Park, MD

Published Sources

Abbot, Willis J. *Panama and the Canal in Picture and Prose*. New York: Syndicate Publishing, 1913.
Adams, Brooks. *The New Empire*. New York: Macmillan, 1902.
——. "The Spanish War and the Equilibrium of the World." *The Forum* 25, no. 6 (March–August 1898): 641–52.
Adams, Frederick Upham. *Conquest of the Tropics: The Story of the Creative Enterprises Conducted by the United Fruit Company*. New York: Arno, 1914.
Adas, Michael. *Dominance by Design: Technological Imperatives and America's Civilizing Mission*. Cambridge, MA: Belknap Press of Harvard University Press, 2006.
——. *Machines as the Measure of Men: Science, Technology, and Ideologies of Western Dominance*. Ithaca, NY: Cornell University Press, 1989.
Adorno, Theodor W. *The Culture Industry: Selected Essays on Mass Culture*. Edited by J. M. Bernstein. New York: Routledge, 2001.
Aguirre, Robert D. *Mobility and Modernity: Panama in the Nineteenth-Century Anglo-American Imagination*. Columbus: Ohio State University Press, 2017.

Agnew, John. "The New Global Economy: Time-Space Compression, Geopolitics, and Global Uneven Development." *Journal of World-Systems Research* 7, no. 2 (Fall 2001): 133–54.

Akin, Edward N. *Flagler: Rockefeller Partner and Florida Baron*. Gainesville: University Press of Florida, 1991.

Allee, Warder C., and Marjorie Hill Allee. *Jungle Island*. Chicago: Rand McNally, 1925.

Allen, Emory Adams. *Our Canal in Panama: The Greatest Achievement in the World's History*. Cincinnati: United States Publishing, 1913.

Anand, Ascem. *Advance Dictionary of Tourism*. New Delhi: Sarup & Sons, 1997.

Anderson, Malcolm. *Frontier: Territory and State Formation in the Modern World*. Cambridge, UK: Polity Press, 1997.

Andreve, Guillermo. *Cómo atraer el turismo a Panamá*. Panama City: Edición Oficial, 1929.

——. "Escritos de Andreve." *Revista Lotería*, nos. 282–84 (August–October 1979).

Andrews, Suzanna. "Hostage to Fortune." *Vanity Fair*, June 12, 2010.

Andrews, Thomas. "'Made by Toile': Tourism, Labor, and the Construction of the Colorado Landscape, 1858–1917." *Journal of American History* 92, no. 3 (December 2005): 837–63.

Appadurai, Arjun. *Modernity At Large: Cultural Dimensions of Globalization*. Minneapolis: University of Minnesota Press, 1996.

——. *The Social Life of Things: Commodities in Cultural Perspective*. Cambridge: Cambridge University Press, 1988.

Aptheker, Herbert, ed. *The Correspondence of W. E. B. Du Bois: Volume I, Selections, 1877–1934*. Amherst: University of Massachusetts Press, 1997.

Arnold, David. *The Problem of Nature: Environment, Culture, and European Expansion*. Cambridge, MA: Blackwell, 1996.

——, ed. *Warm Climates and Western Medicine: The Emergence of Tropical Medicine, 1500–1900*. Amsterdam: Rodopi, 1996.

Aron, Cindy. *Working at Play: A History of Vacations in the United States*. New York: Oxford University Press, 1999.

Avery, Ralph Emmett. *America's Triumph at Panama*. Chicago: L. W. Walter, 1913.

Bailyn, Bernard. *Atlantic History: Concepts and Contours*. Cambridge, MA: Harvard University Press, 2005.

Bailyn, Bernard, and Patricia L. Denault, eds. *Soundings in Atlantic History: Latent Structures and Intellectual Currents, 1500–1830*. Cambridge, MA: Harvard University Press, 2011.

Bair, Jennifer, ed. *Frontiers of Commodity Chain Research*. Stanford, CA: Stanford University Press, 2009.

Baker, Carlos. *Ernest Hemingway: A Life Story*. New York: Charles Scribner's Sons, 1969.

——, ed. *Ernest Hemingway: Selected Letters, 1917–1961*. New York: Charles Scribner's Sons, 1981.

——. *Hemingway: The Writer as Artist*. Princeton, NJ: Princeton University Press, 1980.

Baldwin, James. *The Price of the Ticket: Collected Nonfiction, 1948–1985*. New York: St. Martin's, 1985.

——. "The White Man's Guilt." *Ebony*, August 1965.

Banning, Eugene. *Airlines of Pan American since 1927: Its Airlines, Its People, and Its Aircraft.* McLean, VA: Paladwr Press, 2001.

Barbour, Thomas. *Naturalist at Large.* Boston: Little, Brown, 1943.

Barrow, Mark V. *Nature's Ghosts: Confronting Extinction from the Age of Jefferson to the Age of Ecology.* Chicago: University of Chicago Press, 2009.

———. *A Passion for Birds: American Ornithology after Audubon.* Princeton, NJ: Princeton University Press, 1998.

Beleño, Joaquín C. *Gamboa Road Gang.* Panama City: Ministerio de Educación, Departamento de Bellas Artes y Publicaciones, 1960.

Belnap, Jeffrey, and Raúl Fernández, eds. *José Martí's "Our America": From National to Hemispheric Cultural Studies.* Durham, NC: Duke University Press, 1998.

Bender, Bert. "The Nature and Significance of 'Experience' in 'The Open Boat.'" *Journal of Narrative Technique* 9, no. 2 (Spring 1979): 70–80.

Bender, Marilyn, and Selig Altschul. *The Chosen Instrument: Pan Am, Juan Trippe; The Rise and Fall of an American Entrepreneur.* New York: Simon & Schuster, 1982.

Benjamin, Walter. "Doctrine of the Similar." *New German Critique* 17, Special Walter Benjamin Issue (1979): 65–69.

———. *Illuminations: Essays and Reflections.* Edited by Hannah Arendt. Translated by Henry Zohn. New York: Schocken Books, 1968.

———. *One-Way Street and Other Writings.* Translated by J. A. Underwood. New York: Verso Books, 1997.

Benson, Devyn Spence. *Antiracism in Cuba: The Unfinished Revolution.* Chapel Hill: University of North Carolina Press, 2016.

Berger, Dina, and Andrew Grant Wood, eds. *Holiday in Mexico: Critical Reflections on Tourism and Tourist Encounters.* Durham, NC: Duke University Press, 2009.

Beyer, Christian. "Edmund Husserl." Stanford Encyclopedia of Philosophy, November 18, 2020. https://plato.stanford.edu/entries/husserl/.

Bhabha, Homi, and Lisa Appignansesi, eds. *Identity: The Real Me.* London: Institute of Contemporary Arts, 1987.

Birmingham, Stephen. *"The Rest of Us": The Rise of America's Eastern European Jews.* Syracuse, NY: Syracuse University Press, 1999.

Bishop, Farnham. *Panama, Past and Present.* New York: Century, 1916.

Bishop, Joseph Bucklin. *Theodore Roosevelt and His Time.* New York: Charles Scribner's Sons, 1920.

Blumenberg, Hans. *Shipwreck with Spectator: Paradigm of a Metaphor for Existence.* Translated by Steven Rendal. Cambridge, MA: MIT Press, 1997.

Boas, Franz. "Scientists as Spies." *The Nation,* December 20, 1919.

Bolland, O. Nigel, ed. *The Birth of Caribbean Civilization: A Century of Ideas about Culture and Identity, Nation and Society.* Kingston, Jamaica: Ian Randle, 2004.

Bolton, Herbert E. *The Spanish Borderlands: A Chronicle of Old Florida and the Southwest.* New Haven, CT: Yale University Press, 1921.

Bond, James. *Birds of the West Indies.* Boston: Houghton Mifflin, 1961. Originally published in 1936 by the Academy of Natural Sciences.

Boothe, Clare. "We Nominate for Oblivion." *Vanity Fair,* June 1930.

Borges, Jorge Luis. *Labyrinths: Selected Stories and Other Writings.* Edited by Donald A. Yates and James E. Irby. New York: New Directions, 1964.

Boyd, Valerie. *Wrapped in Rainbows: The Life of Zora Neale Hurston*. New York: Scribner, 2003.

Briggs, Laura, Gladys McCormick, and J. T. Way. "Transnationalism: A Category of Analysis." *American Quarterly* 60, no. 3 (September 2008): 625–48.

Brown, Dona. *Inventing New England: Regional Tourism in the Nineteenth Century*. Washington, DC: Smithsonian Institution Press, 1995.

Browne, Jefferson B. *Key West: The Old and the New*. St. Augustine, FL: Record, 1912.

Bucheli, Marcelo. *Bananas and Business: The United Fruit Company in Colombia, 1899–2000*. New York: New York University Press, 2005.

Bullard, Arthur. *Panama: The Canal, the Country, and the People*. New York: Macmillan, 1914.

Bullard, Gabe. "The Surprising Origin of the Phrase 'Flyover Country.'" *National Geographic*, March 14, 2016.

Bunck, Julie Marie, and Michael Ross Fowler. *Bribes, Bullets, and Intimidation: Drug Trafficking and the Law in Central America*. University Park: Pennsylvania State University Press, 2012.

Burns, E. Braford. *The Poverty of Progress: Latin America in the Nineteenth Century*. Berkeley: University of California Press, 1983.

Calvo, Alfredo Castillero, ed. *Historia general de Panamá*. Panama City: Comisión Nacional del Centenario, 2004.

———. "Transitismo y dependencia: El caso del istmo de Panamá." *Nueva Sociedad*, no. 5 (1973): 35–50.

Camus, Albert. *The Myth of Sisyphus, and Other Essays*. Edited by Gustavo Aguilera. New York: Vintage Books, 1991.

Canfield, Michael R. *Theodore Roosevelt in the Field*. Chicago: University of Chicago Press, 2015.

Capó, Julio. *Welcome to Fairyland: Queer Miami before 1940*. Chapel Hill: University of North Carolina Press, 2017.

Cardoso, Fernando Henrique, and Enzo Faletto. *Dependency and Development in Latin America*. Translated by Marjory Mattingly Urquidi. Berkeley: University of California Press, 1979.

Carey, Mark. "Inventing Caribbean Climates: How Science, Medicine, and Tourism Changed Tropical Weather from Deadly to Healthy." *Osiris* 26, no. 1 (2011): 129–41.

Carse, Ashley. *Beyond the Big Ditch: Politics, Ecology, and Infrastructure at the Panama Canal*. Cambridge, MA: MIT Press, 2014.

Carse, Ashley, Christine Keiner, Pamela M. Henson, Marixa Lasso, Paul S. Sutter, Megan Raby, and Blake Scott. "Panama Canal Forum: From the Conquest of Nature to the Construction of New Ecologies." *Environmental History* 21, no. 2 (2016): 206–87.

Carson, Clayborne, David J. Garrow, Bill Kovach, and Carol Polsgrove, eds. *Reporting on Civil Rights: Part Two, American Journalism, 1963–1973*. New York: Library of America, 2003.

Castañeda, Quetzil E. "The Neo-Liberal Imperative of Tourism: Rights and Legitimization in the UNWTO Global Code of Ethics for Tourism." *Practicing Anthropology* 34, no. 3 (Summer 2012): 47–51.

Castillero Reyes, Ernesto J. *La causa inmediata de la emancipación de Panamá: Historia de los orígenes, la formación y el rechazo por el senado colombiano, del tratado Herrán-Hay*. Panama City: Imprenta Nacional, 1933.

Castro, Guillermo Herrera. *El agua entre los mares*. Panama City: Editorial Ciudad del Saber, 2007.

Castronovo, Russ. "'On Imperialism, See. . .': Ghosts of the Present in Cultures of United States Imperialism." *American Literary History* 20, no. 3 (2008): 427–38.

Ceballos-Lascuráin, Héctor. *Tourism, Ecotourism, and Protected Areas: The State of Nature-Based Tourism around the World and Guidelines for Its Development*. Cambridge, UK: International Union for Conservation of Nature and Natural Resources, 1996.

Césaire, Aimé. *Discourse on Colonialism*. Translated by Joan Pinkham. New York: Monthly Review Press, 2000.

Chandler, David Leon. *Henry Flagler*. New York: Macmillan, 1986.

Chapin, Ora E. "Across Boundary Lines: Rotarians of Cuba and Florida Adopt Rotary's Good-Will Formula." *The Rotarian*, no. 36 (January 1930).

Chiriboga, Vilma. *Relatos de viajeros: Visión extranjera de la Ciudad de Panamá en la segunda mitad del siglo XIX*. Panama City: Cultural Portobelo, 2007.

Chomsky, Aviva. "'Barbados or Canada?'" Race, Immigration, and Nation in Early-Twentieth-Century Cuba." *Hispanic American Historical Review* 80, no. 3 (August 2000): 415–62.

——. *West Indian Workers and the United Fruit Company in Costa Rica, 1870–1940*. Baton Rouge: Louisiana State University Press, 1996.

Cirules, Enrique. *The Empire of Havana*. Translated by Douglas Edward. Havana: Editorial José Martí, 2003.

Clifford, James. *The Predicament of Culture: Twentieth-Century Ethnography, Literature, and Art*. Cambridge, MA: Harvard University Press, 1988.

——. *Routes: Travel and Translation in the Late Twentieth Century*. Cambridge, MA: Harvard University Press, 1997.

Cocks, Catherine. *Tropical Whites: The Rise of the Tourist South in the Americas*. Philadelphia: University of Pennsylvania Press, 2013.

Colantonio, Andrea, and Robert B. Potter. *Urban Tourism and Development in the Socialist State: Havana during the "Special Period."* Burlington, VT: Ashgate, 2006.

Collins, John O. "The Panama Canal and Its Jonah." *Pan-American Magazine* 22, no. 2 (November 1915).

——. *The Panama Guide*. Mount Hope, Canal Zone: I.C.C. Press, 1912.

——. *Recreation in Panama*. Culebra, Canal Zone: self-published, 1914.

Colls, Robert. *George Orwell: English Rebel*. Oxford: Oxford University Press, 2013.

Conn, Steven. *Museums and American Intellectual Life, 1876–1926*. Chicago: University of Chicago Press, 1998.

Conniff, Michael L. *Black Labor on a White Canal: Panama, 1904–1981*. Pittsburgh: University of Pittsburgh Press, 1985.

——. "George Westerman: A Barbadian Descendant in Panama." In *The Human Tradition in Latin America*, edited by William H. Beezley and Judith Ewell, 141–50. Lanham, MD: Rowman & Littlefield, 1998.

——. *Panama and the United States: The End of an Alliance*. Athens: University of Georgia Press, 2012.

Conrad, Barnaby. *Pan Am: An Aviation Legend*. Emeryville, CA: Woodford Press, 1999.

Conrad, Joseph. *The Heart of Darkness*. Boston: Bedford / St. Martin's, 2011.

——. *The Mirror of the Sea*. New York: Doubleday, 1926.

Cooper, Frederick. *Colonialism in Question: Theory, Knowledge, History*. Berkeley: University of California Press, 2005.

Cooper, Frederick, and Jane Burbank. *Empires in World History: Power and the Politics of Difference*. Princeton, NJ: Princeton University Press, 2010.

Core, Sue. *Maid in Panama*. New York: Clermont Press, 1938.

Coronil, Fernando. *The Magical State: Nature, Money, and Modernity in Venezuela*. Chicago: University of Chicago Press, 1997.

Covert, Lisa Pinley. *San Miguel de Allende: Mexicans, Foreigners, and the Making of a World Heritage Site*. Lincoln: University of Nebraska Press, 2017.

Cowley, Malcolm. *A Second Flowering: Works and Days of the Lost Generation*. New York: Viking, 1973.

Craft, Renée Alexander. "¡Los gringos vienen!' ('The Gringos Are Coming!'): Female Respectability and the Politics of Congo Tourist Presentations in Portobelo, Panama." *Transforming Anthropology: Journal of the Association of Black Anthropologists* 16, no. 1 (2008): 20–31.

Crane, Stephen. *The Open Boat and Other Tales of Adventure*. New York: Doubleday & McClure, 1898.

Crenshaw, Kimberlé. "Mapping the Margins: Intersectionality, Identity Politics, and Violence against Women of Color." *Stanford Law Review* 43, no. 6 (July 1991): 1241–99.

Cronon, William, ed. *Uncommon Ground: Rethinking the Human Place in Nature*. New York: W. W. Norton, 1995.

Cullen, Deborah and Elvis Fuentes, eds. *Caribbean: Art at the Crossroads of the World*. New Haven, CT: Yale University Press, 2012.

Culver, Lawrence. *The Frontier of Leisure: Southern California and the Shaping of Modern America*. Oxford: Oxford University Press, 2010.

Curtin, Philip D. *Death by Migration: Europe's Encounter with the Tropical World in the Nineteenth Century*. New York: Cambridge University Press, 1989.

——. "'The White Man's Grave': Image and Reality, 1780–1850." *Journal of British Studies* 1, no. 1 (November 1961): 94–110.

Daugherty, Greg. "The Last Adventure of Richard Halliburton, the Forgotten Hero of 1930s America." *Smithsonian Magazine*, March 25, 2014.

Davies, R. E. G. *Pan Am: An Airline and Its Aircraft*. Twickenham, UK: Hamlyn, 1987.

Davis, Richard Harding. *Three Gringos in Venezuela and Central America*. New York: Harper & Brothers, 1896.

Dayton, Richard. *Nature's Government: Science, Imperial Britain, and the "Improvement" of the World*. New Haven, CT: Yale University Press, 2000.

De la Fuente, Alejandro. *Havana and the Atlantic in the Sixteenth Century*. Chapel Hill: University of North Carolina Press, 2008.

Denning, Andrew. "From Sublime Landscapes to 'White Gold:' How Skiing Transformed the Alps after 1930." *Environmental History* 19, no. 1 (2014): 78–108.

Dietz, James. *Economic History of Puerto Rico: Institutional Change and Capitalist Development*. Princeton, NJ: Princeton University Press, 1986.

Donoghue, Michael E. *Borderland on the Isthmus: Race, Culture, and the Struggle for the Canal Zone*. Durham, NC: Duke University Press, 2014.

Dorr, Lisa Lindquist. *A Thousand Thirsty Beaches: Smuggling Alcohol from Cuba to the South during Prohibition*. Chapel Hill: University of North Carolina Press, 2018.

Driever, Steven L. "From Travel to Tourism: Harry Franck's Writing on Mexico (1916–1940)." *Journal of Latin American Geography* 12, no. 2 (2013): 7–33.

——. "Geographic Narratives in the South American Travelogues of Harry A. Franck: 1917–1943." *Journal of Latin American Geography* 10, no. 1 (2010): 53–69.

Du Bois, W. E. Burghardt. *The Souls of Black Folk: Essays and Sketches*. Chicago: A. C. McClurg, 1907.

Dunn, Peter. "Why Hasn't Commercial Air Travel Gotten Any Faster since the 1960s?" MIT School of Engineering, February 19, 2009. https://engineering. mit.edu/engage/ask-an-engineer/why-hasnt-commercial-air-travel-gotten-any-faster-since-the-1960s/.

Dupree, Hunter A. *Science in the Federal Government: A History of Policies and Activities to 1940*. New York: Harper & Row, 1964.

Durant, Will, and Ariel Durant. *The Lessons of History*. New York: Simon & Schuster, 1968.

Elliot, J. H. *Empires of the Atlantic World: Britain and Spain in America*. New Haven, CT: Yale University Press, 2006.

Elliot, Nils Lindahl. "A Memory of Nature: Ecotourism on Panama's Barro Colorado Island." *Journal of Latin American Cultural Studies* 19, no. 3 (December 2010): 237–59.

Elsheshtway, Yasser. "Urban Transformations: The Great Cairo Fire and the Founding of a Modern Capital, 1952–1970." *Built Environment* 40, no. 3 (Autumn 2014): 408–25.

Emerson, Ralph Waldo. *Essays: First and Second Series*. New York: Vintage Books, 1990.

Endy, Christopher. *Cold War Holidays: American Tourism in France*. Chapel Hill: University of North Carolina Press, 2004.

English, T. J. *Havana Nocturne: How the Mob Owned Cuba and Then Lost It to the Revolution*. New York: William Morrow, 2008.

Enright, Kelly. *The Maximum of Wilderness: The Jungle in the American Imagination*. Charlottesville: University of Virginia Press, 2012.

Escobar, Arturo. *Encountering Development: The Making and Unmaking of the Third World*. Princeton, NJ: Princeton University Press, 2001.

Espino, Ovidio Diaz. *How Wall Street Created a Nation: J. P. Morgan, Teddy Roosevelt, and the Panama Canal*. New York: Basic Books, 2003.

Espinosa, Mariola. *Epidemic Invasions: Yellow Fever and the Limits of Cuban Independence, 1878–1930*. Chicago: University of Chicago Press, 2009.

——. "The Question of Racial Immunity to Yellow Fever in History and Historiography." *Social Science History* 38, nos. 3–4 (Fall/Winter 2014): 437–53.

Evans, Sterling. *The Green Republic: A Conservation History of Costa Rica*. Austin: University of Texas Press, 1999.

Ewing, Heather. *The Lost World of James Smithson: Science, Revolution, and the Birth of the Smithsonian*. London: Bloomsbury, 2007.

Feifer, Maxine. *Tourism in History: From Imperial Rome to the Present*. New York: Stein & Day, 1986.

Fenstermaker, John. "Ernest Hemingway in *Esquire.*" In *Literature and Journalism: Inspirations, Intersections, and Inventions from Ben Franklin to Stephen Colbert*. Edited by Mark Canada, 187–207. New York: Palgrave Macmillan, 2013.

Ferrer, Ada. *Insurgent Cuba: Race, Nation, and Revolution, 1868–1898*. Chapel Hill: University of North Carolina Press, 1999.

Figueroa, Alfredo Navarro, ed. *El desarrollo de las ciencias sociales en Panamá*. Panama City: Universidad de Panamá, 1983.

Fitzgerald, F. Scott. *This Side of Paradise*. New York: Scribner, 1920.

Fitzroy, Robert. *Narrative of the Surveying Voyages of His Majesty's Ships Adventure and Beagle between the Years 1826 and 1836, Volume II*. New York: AMS, 1966. Originally published in 1839 by Henry Colburn.

Flaherty, Tom. "Bullets Fly in Panama over the Right to Fly the Flag: Inside an Ugly Fight." *Life*, January 24, 1964.

Fletcher, Robert. *Romancing the Wild: Cultural Dimensions of Ecotourism*. Durham, NC: Duke University Press, 2014.

Foglesong, Richard E. *Married to the Mouse: Walt Disney and Orlando*. New Haven, CT: Yale University Press, 2001.

Ford, Ford Madox. *The English Novel: From the Earliest Days to the Death of Joseph Conrad*. London: Constable, 1930.

Foster, Harry L. *The Adventures of a Tropical Tramp*. New York: A. L. Burt, 1922.

———. *A Tropical Tramp with the Tourists*. New York: Dodd, Mead, 1925.

Foucault, Michel. *Language, Counter-Memory, Practice: Selected Essays and Interviews*. Edited by Donald F. Bouchard, Ithaca, NY: Cornell University Press, 1977.

Foust, Clifford. *John Frank Stevens: Civil Engineer*. Bloomington: Indiana University Press, 2013.

Franck, Harry A. *Roaming through the West Indies*. Cornwall, NY: Cornwall Press, 1920.

———. *Zone Policeman 88: A Close Range Study of the Panama Canal and Its Workers*. New York: Century, 1913.

Frank, Andre Gunder. *Capitalism and Underdevelopment in Latin America: Historical Studies of Chile and Brazil*. New York: Monthly Review Press, 1967.

Frederick, Rhonda. *Colón Man a Come: Mythographies of Panama Canal Migration*. Lanham, MD: Lexington Books, 2005.

Fregonese, Sarah, and Adam Ramadan. "Hotel Geopolitics: A Research Agenda." *Geopolitics* 20, no. 4 (2015): 793–813.

Frenkel, Stephen. "Jungle Stories: North American Representations of Tropical Panama." *Geographical Review* 86, no. 3 (July 1996): 317–33.

———. "Old Theories in New Places: On Environmental Determinism and Bioregionalism." *Professional Geographer* 46, no. 3 (1994): 289–95.

Fussell, Paul. *Abroad: British Literary Traveling between the Wars*. New York: Oxford University Press, 1980.

Galeano, Eduardo. *Open Veins of Latin America: Five Centuries of the Pillage of a Continent*. Translated by Cedric Belfrage. New York: Monthly Review Press, 1997.

Galton, Francis. *The Art of Travel; or, Shifts and Contrivances Available in Wild Countries*. London: John Murray, 1872.

Gandásegui, Marco A., ed. *Las clases sociales en Panamá: Grupos humanos, clases medias, elites y oligarquía*. Panama City: Centro de Estudio Latinoamericanos, 2008.

Garcia-Robles, Jorge. *At the End of the Road: Jack Kerouac in Mexico*. Minneapolis: University of Minnesota Press, 2014.

Garrido, Evaristo Villalba. *Cuba y el turismo*. Havana: Editorial de Ciencias Sociales, 1993.

Geertz, Clifford. "The Wet and the Dry: Traditional Irrigation in Bali and Morocco." *Human Ecology* 1, no. 1 (March 1972): 23–29.

Gibson, Carrie. *Empire's Crossroads: A History of the Caribbean from Columbus to the Present Day*. New York: Grove Atlantic, 2015.

Gillis, John R. *Islands of the Mind: How the Human Imagination Created the Atlantic World*. New York: Palgrave Macmillan, 2004.

Gilroy, Paul. *The Black Atlantic: Modernity and Double Consciousness*. Cambridge, MA: Harvard University Press, 1993.

Gingrich, Arnold. *Nothing but People: The Early Days at* Esquire. New York: Crown, 1971.

——. "Scott, Ernest, Whoever." *Esquire*, December 1966.

Ginzburg, Carlo. *The Cheese and the Worms: The Cosmos of a Sixteenth-Century Miller*. Baltimore: Johns Hopkins University Press, 1992.

Glacken, Clarence J. *Traces on the Rhodian Shore: Nature and Culture in Western Thought from Ancient Times to the End of the Eighteenth Century*. Berkeley: University of California Press, 1967.

Gmelch, George. *Behind the Smile: The Working Lives of Caribbean Tourism*. Bloomington: Indiana University Press, 2003.

Gobat, Michel. *Confronting the American Dream: Nicaragua under U.S. Imperial Rule*. Durham, NC: Duke University Press, 2005.

——. *Empire by Invitation: William Walker and Manifest Destiny in Central America*. Cambridge, MA: Harvard University Press, 2018.

Goldberg, Mark H. *"Going Bananas": 100 Years of American Fruit Ships in the Caribbean*. Kings Point, NY: American Merchant Marine Museum, 1993.

Gootenberg, Paul. *Andean Cocaine: The Making of a Global Drug*. Chapel Hill: University of North Carolina Press, 2008.

Gordon, Robert J., and Luis Antonio Vivanco, eds. *Tarzan Was an Eco-tourist: And Other Tales in the Anthropology of Adventure*. New York: Berghahn Books, 2006.

Gorgas, Marie D., and Burton J. Hendrick. *William Crawford Gorgas, His Life and Work*. Garden City, NY: Doubleday, 1924.

Gorgas, William Crawford. "The Conquest of the Tropics for the White Race." President's address at the Sixtieth Annual Session of the American Medical Association, Atlantic City, NJ, June 9, 1909. *Journal of the American Medical Association* 52, no. 25 (1909): 1967–69.

——. *Sanitation in Panama*. New York: D. Appleton, 1915.

Graham, Stephen. *In Quest of El Dorado*. London: Macmillan, 1924.

Grandin, Greg. *Empire's Workshop: Latin America, the United States, and the Rise of the New Imperialism*. New York: Metropolitan Books, 2006.

——. *The End of the Myth: From the Frontier to the Border Wall in the Mind of America*. New York: Metropolitan Books, 2019.

Greene, Graham. *Getting to Know the General: The Story of an Involvement.* London: Bodley Head, 1984.

———. *The Labyrinthine Ways.* New York: Viking, 1940.

———. *The Lawless Roads.* London: Longmans, 1939.

———. *Our Man in Havana.* London: Heinemann, 1958.

Greene, Julie. *The Canal Builders: Making America's Empire at the Panama Canal.* New York: Penguin, 2009.

Grove, Richard. *Green Imperialism: Colonial Expansion, Tropical Island Edens, and the Origins of Environmentalism, 1600–1800.* New York: Cambridge University Press, 1996.

Grumbs, Alexis Pauline. *Undrowned: Black Feminist Lessons from Marine Mammals.* Chico, CA: AK Press, 2020.

Gubernick, Lisa Rebecca. *Squandered Fortune: The Life and Times of Huntington Hartford.* New York: Putnam, 1991.

Guerrón Montero, Carla. "Can't Beat Me Own Drum in Me Own Native Land: Calypso Music and Tourism in the Panamanian Atlantic Coast." *Anthropological Quarterly* 79, no. 4 (2006): 633–63.

———. *From Temporary Migrants to Permanent Attractions: Tourism, Cultural Heritage, and Afro-Antillean Identities in Panama.* Tuscaloosa: University of Alabama Press, 2020.

Guha, Ramachandra. *How Much Should a Person Consume?: Environmentalism in India and the United States.* Berkeley: University of California Press, 2006.

Guridy, Frank A. *Forging Diaspora: Afro-Cubans and African Americans in a World of Empire and Jim Crow.* Chapel Hill: University of North Carolina Press, 2010.

Halliburton, Richard. *The Royal Road to Romance.* Indianapolis: Bobbs-Merrill, 1925.

Hansen, James R. "Aviation in the Wider View." *Technology and Culture* 30, no. 3 (July 1989): 643–56.

Haraway, Donna. "Teddy Bear Patriarchy: Taxidermy in the Garden of Eden, New York City, 1908–36." *Social Text*, no. 11 (Winter 1984/85): 19–64.

Hartford, Huntington. "Gone without the Wind." *Esquire*, October 1938.

Harvey, David. *The Condition of Postmodernity: An Enquiry into the Origins of Cultural Change.* Cambridge, MA: Blackwell, 1990.

Haskins, Frederick. *The Panama Canal.* Garden City, NY: Doubleday, 1914.

Healy, David. *Drive to Hegemony: The United States in the Caribbean, 1898–1917.* Madison: University of Wisconsin Press, 1988.

Heckadon Moreno, Stanley, ed. *Panamá en sus usos y costumbres.* Panama City: Editorial Universitaria, 1994.

Heidegger, Martin. *The Basic Problems of Phenomenology.* Translated by Alfred Hostader. Bloomington: Indiana University Press, 1982.

Hellman, Geoffrey T. "Curator Getting Around." *New Yorker*, August 26, 1950.

Hemingway, Ernest. *Death in the Afternoon.* New York: Charles Scribner's Sons, 1932.

———. "The Great Blue River." *Holiday Magazine*, July 1949.

———. *Hemingway on Hunting.* New York: Scribner, 2003.

———. "Marlin off the Morro: A Cuban Letter." *Esquire*, Autumn 1933.

———. "Monologue to the Maestro: A High Seas Letter." *Esquire*, October 1935.

———. *A Moveable Feast.* New York: Bantam Books, 1965.

——. "On the Blue Water: A Gulf Stream Letter." *Esquire*, April 1936.

——. *To Have and Have Not*. New York: Charles Scribner's Sons, 1937.

Hendrickson, Paul. *Hemingway's Boat: Everything He Loved in Life, and Lost*. New York: Vintage Books, 2012.

Henson, Pamela. "Invading Arcadia: Women Scientists in the Field in Latin America, 1900–1950." *The Americas* 58, no. 4 (April 2002): 577–600.

Hill, Robert A., and Barbara Bair, eds. *Marcus Garvey: Life and Lessons*. Berkeley: University of California Press, 1987.

Hills, Alfred Kimball, ed. "Hygiene at Panama." *Medical Times*, no. 36 (April 1908): 114–15.

Hillyer, Reiko. "Cold War Conquistadors: The St. Augustine Quadricentennial, Pan Americanism, and the Civil Rights Movement in the Ancient City." *Journal of Southern History* 81, no. 1 (February 2015): 117–56.

——. *Designing Dixie: Tourism, Memory, and Urban Space in the New South*. Charlottesville: University of Virginia Press, 2014.

Hobsbawm, Eric, and Terence Ranger, eds. *The Invention of Tradition*. New York: Cambridge University Press, 1992.

Hogue, John S. "Cheeseburger in Paradise: Tourism and Empire at the Edges of Vacationland." *American Quarterly* 63, no. 1 (March 2011): 203–14.

Holland, Robert. *The Warm South: How the Mediterranean Shaped the British Imagination*. New Haven, CT: Yale University Press, 2018.

Honey, Martha. *Ecotourism and Sustainable Development: Who Owns Paradise?* Washington, DC: Island Press, 1999.

——, ed. *Cruise Tourism in the Caribbean: Selling Sunshine*. London: Routledge, 2019.

Horkeimer, Max, and Theodor W. Adorno. *The Dialectic of Enlightenment: Cultural Memory in the Present*. Translated by Steven Rendall. New York: Verso, 1997.

Howe, James. *A People Who Would Not Kneel: Panama, the United States, and the San Blas Kuna*. Washington, DC: Smithsonian Institution Press, 1998.

Howse, Derek. *Greenwich Time and the Discovery of Longitude*. London: Philip Wilson, 1997.

Hughes, Langston. *I Wonder as I Wander*. New York: Hill & Wang, 1956.

Hulme, Peter. *Colonial Encounters: Europe and the Native Caribbean, 1492–1797*. London: Methuen, 1986.

Hulme, Peter, and Tim Youngs, eds. *Cambridge Companion to Travel Writing*. Cambridge: Cambridge University Press, 2002.

Humphreys, Margaret. *Yellow Fever and the South*. New Brunswick, NJ: Rutgers University Press, 1992.

Hunt, George P. "Covering the Riot-Ridden Canal." *Life*, January 24, 1964.

Hurston, Zora Neale. *Dust Tracks on a Road*. New York: Arno, 1969.

——. *Tell My Horse: Voodoo and Life in Haiti and Jamaica*. New York: Perennial Library, 1990.

Husserl, Edmund. *Ideas: A General Introduction to Pure Phenomenology*. New York: Collier Books, 1963.

Huxley, Aldous. *Along the Road: Notes and Essays of a Tourist*. London: Chatto & Windus, 1925.

——. *Do What You Will*. London: Chatto & Windus, 1929.

Hyde, Anne Farrar. *An American Vision: Far Western Landscape and National Culture, 1820–1920*. New York: New York University Press, 1990.

Immerwahr, Daniel. *How to Hide an Empire: A History of the Greater United States*. New York: Farrar, Straus & Giroux, 2019.

International Commission of Jurists. *Report on the Events in Panama, January 9–12, 1964*. Geneva: International Commission of Jurists, 1964.

Ireland, Barbara, ed. *The New York Times 36 Hours World*. Cologne: Taschen, 2015.

Jacobsen, Anne. *Operation Paperclip: The Secret Intelligence Program That Brought Nazi Scientists to America*. New York: Little, Brown, 2014.

Jacobson, Matthew Frye. *Barbarian Virtues: The United States Encounters Foreign Peoples at Home and Abroad, 1876–1917*. New York: Hill & Wang, 2000.

James, C. L. R. *Beyond a Boundary*. Durham, NC: Duke University Press, 1993.

James, Kevin. *Histories, Meanings, and Representations of the Modern Hotel*. Bristol, UK: Channel View, 2018.

James, Winifred. *The Mulberry Tree*. London: Chapman & Hall, 1913.

Jasanoff, Maya. *The Dawn Watch: Joseph Conrad in a Global World*. New York: Penguin, 2017.

Joseph, Gilbert M., Catherine C. LeGrand, and Ricardo D. Salvatore, eds. *Close Encounters of Empire: Writing the Cultural History of U.S.-Latin American Relations*. Durham, NC: Duke University Press, 1998.

Josephson, Matthew. *Empire of the Air: Juan Trippe and the Struggle for World Airways*. New York: Harcourt, Brace, 1944.

Kagan, Robert. *Dangerous Nation: America's Foreign Policy from Its Earliest Days to the Dawn of the Twentieth Century*. New York: Vintage Books, 2007.

Kaplan, Amy. *The Anarchy of Empire in the Making of U.S. Culture*. Cambridge, MA: Harvard University Press, 2005.

Kaplan, Amy, and Donald E. Pease, eds. *Cultures of United States Imperialism*. Durham, NC: Duke University Press, 1993.

Karsten, Peter. "The Nature of 'Influence': Roosevelt, Mahan and the Concept of Sea Power." *American Quarterly* 23, no. 4 (October 1971): 585–600.

Kelley, Robin D. G. *Freedom Dreams: The Black Radical Imagination*. Boston: Beacon, 2002.

Kern, Stephen. *The Culture of Time and Space, 1880–1918*. Cambridge, MA: Harvard University Press, 2003.

Kerouac, Jack. *Lonesome Traveler*. New York: Grove, 1960.

Kidd, Benjamin. *Social Evolution*. New York: Macmillan, 1894.

Kincaid, Jamaica. *A Small Place*. New York: Farrar, Strauss & Giroux, 2000.

King, Martin Luther, Jr. *I Have a Dream*. New York: Schwartz & Wade, 2012.

Kirn, Walter. *Up in the Air: A Novel*. New York: Doubleday, 2001.

Kirshenblatt-Gimblett, Barbara. *Destination Culture: Tourism, Museums, and Heritage*. Berkeley: University of California Press, 1998.

Klein, Kerwin L. "Frontier Products: Tourism, Consumerism, and the Southwestern Public Land, 1890–1990." *Pacific Historical Review* 62, no. 1 (1993): 39–71.

——. *Frontiers of Historical Imagination: Narrating the European Conquest of Native America, 1890–1990*. Berkeley: University of California Press, 1997.

Knowlton, Christopher. *Bubble in the Sun: The Florida Boom of the 1920s and How It Brought on the Great Depression*. New York: Simon & Schuster, 2020.

Kohler, Robert E. *All Creatures: Naturalists, Collectors, and Biodiversity, 1850–1950.* Princeton, NJ: Princeton University Press, 2006.

Korsi, Demetrio. *Los gringos llegan y la cumbia se va.* Panama City: Imprenta Excelsior, 1953.

Kurlansky, Mark. *Havana: A Subtropical Delirium.* New York: Bloomsbury, 2017.

LaFeber, Walter. *The New Empire: An Interpretation of American Expansionism, 1860–1898.* Ithaca, NY: Cornell University Press, 1963.

——. *The Panama Canal: The Crisis in Historical Perspective.* New York: Oxford University Press, 1978.

LaFollette, Marcel Chotkowski. *Science on the Air: Popularizers and Personalities on Radio and Early Television.* Chicago: University of Chicago Press, 2008.

Langley, Wright, and Joan Langley. *Key West and the Spanish American War.* Key West, FL: Langley Press, 1998.

Larkin, Emma. *Finding George Orwell in Burma.* New York: Penguin Books, 2006.

Larson, Brooke. *Trials of Nation-Making: Liberalism, Race, and Ethnicity in the Andes, 1810–1910.* Cambridge: Cambridge University Press, 2004.

Lasso, Marixa. *Erased: The Untold Story of the Panama Canal.* Cambridge, MA: Harvard University Press, 2019.

——. "Nationalism and Immigrant Labor in a Tropical Enclave: The West Indians of Colón, 1850–1936." *Citizenship Studies* 17, no. 5 (2013): 551–56.

——. "Race and Ethnicity in the Formation of Panamanian National Identity: Panamanian Discrimination against Chinese and West Indians in the Thirties." *Revista Panameña de Política*, no. 4 (July–December 2007): 61–92.

Latour, Bruno. *Science in Action: How to Follow Scientists and Engineers through Society.* Philadelphia: Open University Press, 1987.

Lawrence, Mark Atwood. "Exception to the Rule? The Johnson Administration and the Panama Canal." In *Looking Back at LBJ: White House Politics in a New Light.* Edited by Mitchell B. Lerner, 20–52. Lawrence: University Press of Kansas, 2005.

Lears, T. J. Jackson. *No Place of Grace: Antimodernism and the Transformation of American Culture, 1880–1920.* Chicago: University of Chicago Press, 1994.

Lederer, William J., and Eugene Burdick. *The Ugly American.* New York: Norton, 1958.

Legg, Stephen. *Spaces of Colonialism: Delhi's Urban Governmentalities.* Oxford, UK: John Wiley & Sons, 2008.

Leiper, Neil. "An Etymology of 'Tourism.'" *Annals of Tourism Research* 10, no. 2 (1983): 277–81.

Lepore, Jill. "Historians Who Love Too Much: Reflections on Microhistory and Biography." *Journal of American History* 88, no. 1 (June 2001): 129–44.

Levenstein, Harvey. *The Seductive Journey: American Tourists in France from Jefferson to the Jazz Age.* Chicago: University of Chicago Press, 2000.

Levinson, Marc. *The Box: How the Shipping Container Made the World Smaller and the World Economy Bigger.* Princeton, NJ: Princeton University Press, 2006.

Lévi-Strauss, Claude. *The Savage Mind.* Chicago: University of Chicago Press, 1966.

——. *Tristes Tropiques.* Translated by Doreen Weightman and John Weightman. New York: Penguin Books, 1974.

Lewis, Michael. *Inventing Global Ecology: Tracking the Biodiversity Ideal in India, 1947–1997.* Athens: Ohio University Press, 2004.

——. "Scientists or Spies? Ecology in a Climate of Cold War Suspicion." *Economic and Political Weekly* 37, no. 24 (June 2002): 2323–32.

Lindbergh, Charles A. *Autobiography of Values*. New York: Harcourt Brace Jovanovich, 1977.

Lindsay-Polland, John. *Emperors in the Jungle: The Hidden History of the U.S. in Panama*. Durham, NC: Duke University Press, 2003.

Lipsky, David. *Although of Course You End Up Becoming Yourself: A Road Trip with David Foster Wallace*. New York: Broadway Books, 2010.

Lombardi, Michael. "Seventh Heaven: 50 Years Ago, Boeing and Pan Am Revolutionized Travel with the 707." *Boeing Frontiers*, July 2008.

Lutz, Catherine A., and Jane L. Collins. *Reading* National Geographic. Chicago: Chicago University Press, 1993.

Luxemburg, Rosa. "The Idea of May Day on the March." In *Selected Political Writings of Rosa Luxemburg*. Edited by Dick Howard. New York: Monthly Review Press, 1971.

MacCannell, Dean. *The Tourist: A New Theory of the Leisure Class*. New York: Schocken Books, 1976.

Magnússon, Sigurður Gylfi, and István M. Szíjártó. *What Is Microhistory? Theory and Practice*. Milton Park, UK: Routledge, 2013.

Mahan, Alfred T. *The Interest of America in Sea Power, Present and Future*. London: Sampson Low, Marston, 1897.

——. "The United States Looking Outward." *Atlantic Monthly*, December 1890, 816–24.

Maier, Kevin. "'A Trick Men Learn in Paris': Hemingway, *Esquire*, and Mass Tourism." *Hemingway Review* 31, no. 2 (Spring 2012): 65–83.

Maribona, Armando. *Turismo y ciudadania*. Havana: Grafica Moderna, 1943.

Marx, Karl. *Grundrisse: Foundations of the Critique of Political Economy*. Translated by Martin Nicolaus. New York: Vintage, 1973.

Martin, Tony. *Race First: The Ideological and Organizational Struggles of Marcus Garvey*. Dover, MA: Majority, 1986.

Massey, Doreen. *Space, Place, and Gender*. Minneapolis: University of Minnesota Press, 1994.

Maurer, Noel, and Carlos Yu. *The Big Ditch: How America Took, Built, and Ultimately Gave Away the Panama Canal*. Princeton, NJ: Princeton University Press, 2011.

May, Stacy, and Galo Plaza. *The United Fruit Company and Latin America*. New York: National Planning Association, 1958.

McCain, William D. *The United States and the Republic of Panama*. New York: Russell & Russell, 1937.

McCoy, Alfred W., and Francisco A. Scarano, eds. *Colonial Crucible: Empire in the Making of the Modern American State*. Madison: University of Wisconsin Press, 2009.

McCullough, David G. *The Greater Journey: Americans in Paris*. New York: Simon & Schuster, 2011.

——. *The Path between the Seas: The Creation of the Panama Canal. 1870–1914*. New York: Simon & Schuster, 1977.

McGuinness, Aims. *Path of Empire: Panama and the California Gold Rush*. Ithaca, NY: Cornell University Press, 2008.

McKay, Claude. *A Long Way from Home*. New York: Arno, 1937.

McKenna, Rebecca. *American Imperial Pastoral: The Architecture of US Colonialism in the Philippines*. Chicago: University of Chicago Press, 2017.

McLaren, Deborah. *Rethinking Tourism and Ecotravel: The Paving of Paradise and What You Can Do to Stop It*. West Hartford, CT: Kumarian, 1998.

McNeill, John R. *Atlantic Empires of France and Spain: Louisbourg and Havana, 1700–1763*. Chapel Hill: University of North Carolina Press, 1985.

——. *Mosquito Empires: Ecology and War in the Greater Caribbean*. New York: Cambridge University Press, 2010.

McPherson, Alan L. *Yankee No! Anti-Americanism in U.S.-Latin American Relations*. Cambridge, MA: Harvard University Press, 2003.

Melville, Herman. *Moby-Dick; or, The White Whale*. Boston: C. H. Simonds, 1892. Originally published in 1851 by Harper & Brothers.

Merrill, Dennis. *Negotiating Paradise: U.S. Tourism and Empire in Twentieth-Century Latin America*. Chapel Hill: University of North Carolina Press, 2009.

Methvin, Eugene H. "Anatomy of a Riot: Panama 1964." *Orbis*, no. 14 (Summer 1970): 463–89.

Mignolo, Walter. *Local Histories / Global Designs: Coloniality, Subaltern Knowledges, and Border Thinking*. Princeton, NJ: Princeton University Press, 2000.

Milanich, Jerald T. *Florida's Indians from Ancient Times to the Present*. Gainesville: University Press of Florida, 1998.

Millard, Candice. *The River of Doubt: Theodore Roosevelt's Darkest Journey*. New York: Broadway Books, 2005.

Miller, George A. *Prowling about Panama*. New York: Abingdon, 1919.

Miller, Tom. *The Panama Hat Trail: A Journey from South America*. New York: Morrow, 1986.

Minca, Claudio, and Tim Oakes. *Travels in Paradox: Remapping Tourism*. Lanham, MS: Rowman & Littlefield, 2006.

Mintz, Sidney. *Sweetness and Power: The Place of Sugar in Modern History*. New York: Viking, 1985.

——. *Three Ancient Colonies: Caribbean Themes and Variations*. Cambridge, MA: Harvard University Press, 2010.

Miró, Rodrigo. "Don Guillermo Andreve y su labor literaria." *Epocas*, July 2000.

Missal, Alexander. *Seaway to the Future: American Social Visions and the Construction of the Panama Canal*. Madison: University of Wisconsin Press, 2008.

Moddelmog, Debra A., and Suzanne del Gizzo. *Ernest Hemingway in Context*. New York: Cambridge University Press, 2013.

Monk, Craig. *Writing the Lost Generation: Expatriate Autobiography and American Modernism*. Iowa City: University of Iowa Press, 2008.

Monzote, Reinaldo Funes. *From Rainforest to Cane Field in Cuba: An Environmental History since 1492*. Translated by Alex Martin. Chapel Hill: University of North Carolina Press, 2008.

Moore, Robin. *Nationalizing Blackness: Afrocubanismo and Artistic Revolution in Havana, 1920–1940*. Pittsburgh: University of Pittsburgh Press, 1997.

Mormino, Gary R. *Land of Sunshine, State of Dreams: A Social History of Modern Florida*. Gainesville: University Press of Florida, 2008.

Morris, Edmund. *The Rise of Theodore Roosevelt*. New York: Coward, McCann & Geoghegan, 1979.

Morrison, Kenneth. *Sarajevo's Holiday Inn on the Frontline of Politics and War*. Basinstoke, UK: Palgrave Macmillan, 2016.

Morrison, Toni, *Playing in the Dark: Whiteness and the Literary Imagination*. New York: Vintage Books, 1993.

Ngai, Mae M. "Promises and Perils of Transnational History." *Perspectives on History: The Newsmagazine of the American Historical Association*, December 1, 2012.

Nixon, Angelique V. *Resisting Paradise: Tourism, Diaspora, and Sexuality in Caribbean Culture*. Jackson: University of Mississippi Press, 2015.

Nwankwo, Ifeoma Kiddoe. "Insider and Outsider, Black and American: Zora Neale Hurston's Caribbean Ethnography." *Radical History Review*, no. 87 (Fall 2003): 49–77.

Oehser, Paul H. "In Memoriam: Alexander Wetmore." *The Auk,* no. 97 (July 1980): 608–15.

Okrent, Daniel. *Last Call: The Rise and Fall of Prohibition*. New York: Simon & Schuster, 2010.

Olson, Storrs L., ed. *Collected Papers in Avian Paleontology Honoring the 90th Birthday of Alexander Wetmore*. Washington, DC: Smithsonian Institution Press, 1976.

Ortiz, Fernando. "La inmigración desde el punto de vista criminológico." *Derecho y Sociología* 1, no. 5 (May 1906): 54–64.

O'Toole, Patricia. *When Trumpets Call: Theodore Roosevelt after the White House*. New York: Simon & Schuster, 2005.

Paige, Jeffery M. *Coffee and Power: Revolution and the Rise of Democracy in Central America*. Cambridge, MA: Harvard University Press, 1997.

Palmié, Stephan, and Francisco A. Scarano, eds. *The Caribbean: A History of the Region and Its Peoples*. Chicago: University of Chicago Press, 2011.

Parker, Jeffrey Wayne. "Empire's Angst: The Politics of Race, Migration, and Sex Work in Panama, 1903–1945." PhD diss., University of Texas at Austin, 2013.

Parker, Matthew. *Panama Fever: The Epic Story of One of the Greatest Achievements of All Time—the Building of the Panama Canal*. New York: Doubleday, 2007.

Parks, Pat. *The Railroad That Died at Sea: The Florida East Coast's Key West Extension*. Key West, FL: Langley, 1968.

Patterson, Gordon. *The Mosquito Crusades: A History of the American Anti-Mosquito Movement from the Reed Commission to the First Earth Day*. New Brunswick, NJ: Rutgers University Press, 2009.

Pattullo, Polly. *Last Resorts: The Cost of Tourism in the Caribbean*. Kingston, Jamaica: Ian Randle, 1996.

Pauly, Phillip J. "The World and All That Is in It: The National Geographic Society, 1888–1918." *American Quarterly* 31, no. 4 (1979): 517–32.

Peleggi, Maurizio. "The Social and Material Life of Colonial Hotels: Comfort Zones and Contact Zones in British Colombo and Singapore, ca. 1870–1930." *Journal of Social History* 46, no. 1 (2012): 124–53.

Pelletier, Alain. *Boeing: The Complete Story*. Sparkford, UK: Haynes, 2010.

Pemble, John. *The Mediterranean Passion: Victorians and Edwardians in the South*. Oxford: Oxford University Press 1987.

Pennell, Joseph. *Pictures of the Panama Canal*. Philadelphia: J. B. Lippincott, 1912.

Pérez, Louis A. *Cuba: Between Reform and Revolution*. Oxford: Oxford University Press, 2010.

——. *Cuba under the Platt Amendment, 1902–1934*. Pittsburgh: University of Pennsylvania Press, 1986.

——. *On Becoming Cuban: Identity, Nationality, and Culture*. Chapel Hill: University of North Carolina Press, 1999.

——. *The War of 1898: The United States and Cuba in History and Historiography*. Chapel Hill: University of North Carolina Press, 1998.

——. "We Are the World: Internationalizing the National, Nationalizing the International." *Journal of American History* 89, no. 2 (September 2002): 558–66.

Pérez-Stable, Marifeli. *The Cuban Revolution: Origins, Course, and Legacy*. New York: Oxford University Press, 2012.

Pike, Frederick B. *The United States and Latin America: Myths and Stereotypes of Civilization and Nature*. Austin: University of Texas Press, 1992.

Pippins, Larry LaRae. *The Remón Era: An Analysis of a Decade of Events in Panama, 1947–1957*. Stanford, CA: Stanford University Press, 1964.

Pisano, Dominick, ed. *The Airplane in American Culture*. Ann Arbor: University of Michigan Press, 2003.

Pizzurno Gelós, Patricia. "El turismo y el patrimonio en el Panamá republicano." *Revista Canto Rodado*, no. 2 (2007): 1–22.

——. "Zona de contacto y espacio intervenido en Panamá." *Tareas*, no. 138 (2011): 83–112.

Pizzurno Gelós, Patricia, and Celestino Andrés Araúz. *Estudios sobre el Panamá Republicano, 1903–1999*. Cali, Colombia: Manfer, 1996.

——. *La modernización del estado panameño bajo las administraciones de Belisario Porras y Arnulfo Arias Madrid*. Panama City: Editorial Mariano Arosemena del Instituto Nacional de Cultura, 1992.

Plato, *Republic*. Edited by Chris Emlyn-Jones and William Preddy. Cambridge, MA: Harvard University Press, 2013.

Pons, Frank Moya. *History of the Caribbean: Plantations, Trade, and War in the Atlantic World*. Princeton, NJ: Markus Wiener, 2007.

Porras, Belisario. *La venta del istmo: Manifesto a la nación*. Panama City: Editorial Portobelo, 1996.

——. *Trozos de la vida*. San José, Costa Rica: Imprenta Alsina, Sauter, Arias, 1931.

Porras, Hernán F. *Papel histórico de los grupos humanos en Panamá*. Panama City: Editorial Portobelo, 1998.

Porter, Charlotte M. *The Eagle's Nest: Natural History and American Ideas, 1812–1842*. Tuscaloosa: University of Alabama Press: 1986.

Pratt, Mary Louise. *Imperial Eyes: Travel Writing and Transculturation*. London: Routledge, 1992.

Price, David H. *Anthropological Intelligence: The Deployment and Neglect of American Anthropology in the Second World War*. Durham, NC: Duke University Press, 2008.

Putnam, Lara. *The Company They Kept: Migrants and the Politics of Gender in Caribbean Costa Rica, 1870–1960*. Chapel Hill: University of North Carolina Press, 2002.

———. *Radical Moves: Caribbean Migrants and the Politics of Race in the Jazz Age*. Chapel Hill: University of North Carolina Press, 2013.

———. "To Study the Fragments/Whole: Microhistory and the Atlantic World." *Journal of Social History* 39, no. 3 (2006): 615–30.

Raby, Megan. *American Tropics: The Caribbean Roots of Biodiversity Science*. Chapel Hill: University of North Carolina Press, 2017.

Raffles, Hugh. *In Amazonia: A Natural History*. Princeton, NJ: Princeton University Press, 2002.

Redfield, Peter. *Space in the Tropics: From Convicts to Rockets in French Guiana*. Berkeley: University of California Press, 2000.

Renda, Mary A. *Taking Haiti: Military Occupation and the Culture of U.S. Imperialism, 1915–1940*. Chapel Hill: University of North Carolina Press, 2001.

Revels, Tracy. *Sunshine Paradise: A History of Florida Tourism*. Gainesville: University Press of Florida, 2011.

Rice, Mark. *Making Machu Picchu: The Politics of Tourism in Twentieth-Century Peru*. Chapel Hill: University of North Carolina Press, 2018.

Rodrigue, Jean-Paul, and Theo Notteboom, *The Geography of Transport Systems*. New York: Routledge, 2017.

Roland, Alex. *Model Research: The National Advisory Committee for Aeronautics, 1915–1958*. Washington, DC: National Aeronautics and Space Administration, 1985.

Roland, Alex, W. Jeffrey Bolster, and Alexander Keyssar. *The Way of the Ship: America's Maritime History Reenvisioned, 1600–2000*. Hoboken, NJ: John Wiley & Sons, 2008.

Roland, L. Kaifa. *Cuban Color in Tourism and La Lucha: An Ethnography of Racial Meanings*. New York: Oxford University Press, 2011.

Roosevelt, Theodore. *An Autobiography*. New York: Charles Scribner's Sons, 1920.

———. *The Rough Riders*. New York: Charles Scribner's Sons, 1902.

Rose, Chanelle Nyree. *The Struggle for Black Freedom in Miami: Civil Rights and America's Tourist Paradise, 1896–1968*. Baton Rouge: Louisiana State University Press, 2015.

———. "Tourism and the Hispanicization of Race in Jim Crow Miami, 1945–1965." *Journal of Social History* 45, no. 3 (Spring 2012): 735–56.

Rosenberg, Emily, ed. *Financial Missionaries to the World: The Politics and Culture of Dollar Diplomacy, 1900–1930*. Cambridge, MA: Harvard University Press, 1999.

———. *A World Connecting, 1870–1945*. Cambridge, MA: Harvard University Press, 2012.

Ross, Ronald. *Mosquito Brigades and How to Organize Them*. London: George Philip, 1902.

Rothman, Hal K. *Devil's Bargains: Tourism in the Twentieth-Century American West*. Lawrence: University Press of Kansas, 1998.

Rothman, Hal K., and William P. Clements, eds. *The Culture of Tourism, the Tourism of Culture: Selling the Past to the Present in the American Southwest*. Albuquerque: University of New Mexico Press, 2003.

Rydell, Robert W. *All the World's Fair: Visions of Empire at American International Expositions, 1876–1916*. Chicago: University of Chicago Press, 1987.

Sachs, Wolfgang, ed. *The Development Dictionary: A Guide to Knowledge as Power*. New York: Zed Books, 2010.

Said, Edward. *Culture and Imperialism*. New York: Vintage Books, 1994.

——. *Joseph Conrad and the Fiction of Autobiography*. New York: Columbia University Press, 2008.

——. *Orientalism*. New York: Vintage Books, 1979.

Salter, James. "The Finest Life You Ever Saw." *New York Times Review of Books*, October 2011.

Samuelson, Arnold. *With Hemingway: A Year in Key West and Cuba*. New York: Random House, 1984.

Sartre, Jean Paul. *Being and Nothingness*. Translated by Hazel Barnes. New York: Washington Square, 1956. Originally published in 1943 by Gallimard.

Scalena, Matthew. "Illicit Nation: State, Empire, and Illegality on the Isthmus of Panama." PhD diss., Stony Brook University, 2013.

Schivelbusch, Wolfgang. *The Railway Journey: The Industrialization of Time and Space in the Nineteenth Century*. Oakland: University of California Press, 2014.

Schubert, Karsten. *The Curator's Egg: The Evolution of the Museum Concept from the French Revolution to the Present Day*. London: Ridinghouse, 2009.

Schwartz, Jeffrey. " 'The Saloon Must Go, and I Will Take It with Me': American Prohibition, Nationalism, and Expatriation in *The Sun Also Rises*." *Studies in the Novel* 33, no. 2 (2001): 180–201.

Schwartz, Rosalie. *Flying down to Rio: Hollywood, Tourists, and Yankee Clippers*. College Station: Texas A&M Press, 2004.

——. *Pleasure Island: Tourism and Temptation in Cuba*. Lincoln: University of Nebraska Press, 1997.

Schwartz, Stuart. *Sea of Storms: A History of Hurricanes in the Greater Caribbean from Columbus to Katrina*. Princeton, NJ: Princeton University Press, 2015.

Scott, Erastus Howard. *Panama, Yosemite, Yellowstone*. Chicago: Scott, Foresman, 1925.

Scott, James Brown. "The Sixth Pan American Conference." *American Journal of International Law* 22, no. 2 (April 1928): 351–62.

Scranton, Philip, and Janet F. Davidson, eds. *The Business of Tourism: Place, Faith, and History*. Philadelphia: University of Pennsylvania Press, 2021.

Sears, John F. *Sacred Places: American Tourist Attractions in the Nineteenth Century*. Amherst: University of Massachusetts Press, 1998.

Seidelmann, P. Kenneth, and Catherine Y. Hohenkerk, eds. *The History of Celestial Navigation: Rise of the Royal Observatory and Nautical Almanacs*. New York: Springer, 2020.

Seigel, Micol. *Uneven Encounters: Making Race and Nation in Brazil and the United States*. Durham, NC: Duke University Press, 2009.

Selser, Gregorio. "La explosion del 9 de enero de 1964." *Tareas*, no. 97 (September–December 1997): 71–88.

Sheller, Mimi. *Consuming the Caribbean: From Arawaks to Zombies*. London: Routledge, 2003.

——. *Mobility Justice: The Politics of Movement in an Age of Extremes*. New York: Verso, 2018.

Simmel, George. "The Adventurer." In *George Simmel on Individuality and Social Forms*. Edited by Donald N. Levine, 187–98. Chicago: University of Chicago Press, 1971.

Skwiot, Christine. *The Purposes of Paradise: U.S. Tourism and Empire in Cuba and Hawai'i.* Philadelphia: University of Pennsylvania Press, 2010.

Smirl, Lisa. *Spaces of Aid: How Cars, Compounds, and Hotels Shape Humanitarianism.* Chicago: University of Chicago Press, 2015.

Smith, Peter. *Talons of the Eagle: Dynamics of U.S.-Latin American Relations.* New York: Oxford University Press, 2008.

Snyder, Thomas. *120 Years of American Education: A Statistical Portrait; National Center for Education Statistics.* Washington, DC: Department of Education, 1993.

Soler, Ricaurte. *Formas ideologicas de la nación panameña.* Panama City: Ediciones de la Revista Tareas, 1963.

Soluri, John. *Banana Cultures: Agriculture, Consumption, and Environmental Change in Honduras and the United States.* Austin: University of Texas Press, 2005.

——. "Empire's Footprint: The Ecological Dimensions of a Consumers' Republic." *OAH Magazine of History* 25, no. 4 (2011): 15–20.

Sontag, Susan. *On Photography.* New York: Farrar, Straus & Giroux, 1977.

Spalding, Ana K. "Lifestyle Migration to Bocas del Toro, Panama: Exploring Migration Strategies and Introducing Local Implications of the Search for Paradise." *International Review of Social Research* 3, no. 1 (February 2013): 67–86.

Standiford, Les. *Last Train to Paradise: Henry Flagler and the Spectacular Rise and Fall of the Railroad That Crossed an Ocean.* New York: Crown, 2002.

Steinbeck, John. *Cup of Gold: A Life of Sir Henry Morgan, Buccaneer, with Occasional Reference to History.* New York: McBride, 1929.

——. *Log from the Sea of Cortez.* New York: Penguin Classics, 1995. Originally published in 1951 by Viking.

——. *The Pearl.* New York: Viking, 1947.

Stepan, Nancy Leys. *The Hour of Eugenics: Race, Gender, and Nation in Latin America.* Ithaca, NY: Cornell University Press, 1991.

——. *Picturing Tropical Nature.* London: Reaktion Books, 2001.

Stoler, Ann Laura. *Race and the Education of Desire: Foucault's History of Sexuality and the Colonial Order of Things.* Durham, NC: Duke University Press, 1995.

Strachan, Ian G. *Paradise and Plantation: Tourism and Culture in the Anglophone Caribbean.* Charlottesville: University of Virginia Press, 2002.

Stronza, Amanda. "Anthropology of Tourism: Forging New Ground for Ecotourism and Other Alternatives." *Annual Review of Anthropology* 30 (2001): 261–83.

Sutter, Paul S. *Driven Wild: How the Fight against Automobiles Launched the Modern Wilderness Movement.* Seattle: University of Washington Press, 2002.

——. "Nature's Agents or Agents of Empire? Entomological Workers and Environmental Change during the Construction of the Panama Canal." *Isis* 98, no. 4 (December 2007): 724–54.

——. "The Tropics: A Brief History of an Environmental Imaginary." In *Oxford Handbook of Environmental History.* Edited by Andrew Isenberg. New York: Oxford University Press, 178–204.

Szok, Peter A. *La última gaviota: Liberalism and Nostalgia in Early Twentieth-Century Panama.* Westport, CT: Greenwood, 2001.

Taussig, Michael. *Mimesis and Alterity: A Particular History of the Senses.* New York: Routledge, Chapman and Hall, 1993.

Taylor, Frank Fonda. *To Hell with Paradise: A History of the Jamaican Tourist Industry.* Pittsburgh: University of Pittsburgh Press, 1993.

Theodossopoulos, Dimitrios. "Emberá Indigenous Tourism and the Trap of Authenticity: Beyond Inauthenticity and Invention." *Anthropological Quarterly* 86, no. 2 (Spring 2013): 397–425.

Thompson, E. P. *The Making of the English Working Class.* New York: Vintage Books, 1963.

Thompson, Hunter S. *The Great Shark Hunt: Strange Tales from a Strange Time.* New York: Simon & Schuster, 2003.

——. "Why Anti-Gringo Winds Often Blow South of the Border." *National Observer,* August 19, 1963.

Thompson, Krista. *An Eye for the Tropics: Tourism, Photography, and Framing the Caribbean Picturesque.* Durham, NC: Duke University Press, 2007.

Tignor, Robert L. *Capitalism and Nationalism at the End of Empire: State and Business in Decolonizing Egypt, Nigeria, and Kenya, 1945–1963.* Princeton, NJ: Princeton University Press, 2015.

Topik, Stephen, Carlos Marichal, and Zephyr Frank, eds. *From Silver to Cocaine: Latin American Commodity Chains and the Building of the World Economy, 1500–2000.* Durham, NC: Duke University Press, 2006.

Torpey, John. *The Invention of the Passport: Surveillance, Citizenship and the State.* Cambridge: Cambridge University Press, 1999.

Traven, B. *The Death Ship.* Chicago: Chicago Review Press, 1991.

Trefzer, Annette. "Possessing the Self: Caribbean Identities in Zora Neale Hurston's Tell My Horse." *African American Review* 34, no. 2 (Summer 2000): 299–312.

Trouillot, Michel-Rolph. *Silencing the Past: Power and the Production of History.* Boston: Beacon, 1995.

Tucker, Richard P. *Insatiable Appetite: The United States and the Ecological Degradation of the Tropical World.* Berkeley: University of California Press, 2000.

Twain, Mark. *The Innocents Abroad, or The New Pilgrims' Progress.* Hartford, CT: American Publishing, 1869.

United Nations Environment Programme and World Travel and Tourism Council, *Rethinking Single-Use Plastic Products in Travel and Tourism: Impacts, Management Practices and Recommendations.* Nairobi: United Nations Environment Programme, June 2021.

Urraca, Beatriz. "A Textbook of Americanism: Richard Harding Davis's Soldiers of Fortune." In *Tropicalizations: Transcultural Representations of Latinidad.* Edited by Frances R. Aparicio and Susana Chávez-Silverman, 21–50. Hanover, NH: University Press of New England, 1997.

Urry, John. *Consuming Places.* New York: Routledge, 1995.

Urry, John, and Jonas Larsen, *The Tourist Gaze 3.0.* London: SAGE, 2011.

Valencius, Conevery Bolton. *The Health of the Country: How American Settlers Understood Themselves and Their Land.* New York: Basic Books, 2002.

Van Vleck, Jennifer. *Empire of the Air: Aviation and the American Ascendancy.* Cambridge, MA: Harvard University Press, 2013.

Verrill, A. Hyatt. *Panama, Past and Present.* New York: Dodd, Mead, 1921.

——. *Panama of Today.* New York: Dodd, Mead, 1935.

Vierba, Ezer. *The Singer's Needle: An Undisciplined History of Panamá*. Chicago: University of Chicago Press, 2020.

Vuic, Jason. *The Swamp Peddlers: How Lot Sellers, Land Scammers, and Retirees Built Modern Florida and Transformed the American Dream*. Chapel Hill: University of North Carolina Press, 2021.

Wade, Peter. *Blackness and Race Mixture: The Dynamics of Racial Identity in Colombia*. Baltimore: Johns Hopkins University Press, 1993.

Walcott, Derek, *The Antilles: Fragments of Epic Memory; The Nobel Lecture*. New York: Farrar, Straus & Giroux, 1993.

Wallace, David Foster. "Shipping Out: On the (Nearly Lethal) Comforts of a Luxury Cruise." *Harper's Magazine*, January 1996.

Wallace, Mike. *Mickey Mouse History and Other Essays on American Memory*. Philadelphia: Temple University Press, 1996.

Wallerstein, Immanuel. *World-Systems Analysis: An Introduction*. Durham, NC: Duke University Press, 2006.

Walsh, Kevin. *The Representation of the Past: Museums and Heritage in the Post-Modern World*. New York: Routledge, 1992.

Walrond, Eric. *Tropic Death*. New York: Collier Books, 1972.

Walters, Glenda A. *Panama City*. Charleston, SC: Arcadia, 2008.

Ward, Christopher. *Imperial Panama: Commerce and Conflict in Isthmian America, 1550–1800*. Albuquerque: University of New Mexico Press, 1993.

Ward, Evan R. *Packaged Vacations: Tourism Development in the Spanish Caribbean*. Gainesville: University Press of Florida, 2008.

Warren, Louis S. *Buffalo Bill's America: William Cody and the Wild West Show*. New York: Alfred A. Knopf, 2005.

Weinberg, Albert. *Manifest Destiny: A Study of Nationalist Expansionism in American History*. Baltimore: Johns Hopkins University Press, 1935.

Welch, Margaret. *The Book of Nature: Natural History in the United States 1825–1875*. Boston: Northeastern University Press, 1998.

West, Paige, and James G. Carrier. "Ecotourism and Authenticity: Getting Away from it All?" *Current Anthropology* 45, no. 4 (2004): 483–98.

Westerman, George. *A Minority Group in Panama: Some Aspects of West Indian Life*. Panama City: National Civic League, 1950.

Wey Gómez, Nicolás. *The Tropics of Empire: Why Columbus Sailed South to the Indies*. Cambridge, MA: MIT Press, 2008.

Wharton, Amy S. "The Sociology of Emotional Labor." *Annual Review of Sociology* 35, no. 1 (August 2009): 147–65.

Wilk, Daniel Levinson. "Review of *Hotel: An American History* by A. K. Sandoval-Strausz, *Class Acts: Service and Inequality in Luxury Hotels* by Rachel Sherman, and *Hotel Theory* by Wayne Koestenbaum," *Enterprise and Society* 9, no. 4 (December 2008): 873–77.

Williams, R. Scott. *The Forgotten Adventures of Richard Halliburton: A High-Flying Life from Tennessee to Timbuktu*. Charleston, SC: History Press, 2014.

Williams, William Appleman. *Empire as a Way of Life: An Essay on the Causes and Character of America's Present Predicament, along with a Few Thoughts about an Alternative*. New York: Oxford University Press, 1980.

——. "The Frontier Thesis and American Foreign Policy." *Pacific Historical Review* 24, no. 4 (November 1955): 379–95.

——. *The Shaping of American Diplomacy: Readings and Documents in American Foreign Relations, 1750–1955*. Chicago: Rand McNally, 1956.

Winegard, Timonthy C. *The Mosquito: A Human History of Our Deadliest Predator*. Melbourne, Australia: Text Publishing, 2019.

Wohl, Robert. *The Spectacle of Flight: Aviation and the Western Imagination, 1920–1950*. New Haven, CT: Yale University Press, 2005.

Wood, Andrew, ed. *The Business of Leisure: Tourism History in Latin America and the Caribbean*. Lincoln: University of Nebraska Press, 2021.

Woodman, Richard. *The History of the Ship: The Comprehensive Story of Seafaring form the Earliest Times to the Present Day*. London: Conway Maritime, 2005.

Wright, Jim. *The Real James Bond: A True Story of Identity Theft, Avian Intrigue, and Ian Fleming*. Atglen, PA: Schiffler, 2020.

Wrobel, David, and Patrick Long, eds. *Seeing and Being Seen: Tourism in the American West*. Lawrence: University Press of Kansas, 2001.

Zuelow, Eric G. E., ed. *A History of Modern Tourism*. New York: Palgrave, 2016.

——. *Touring beyond the Nation: A Transnational Approach to European Tourism History*. New York: Routledge, 2011.

INDEX

Page numbers in italics refer to figures.